Realism in International Relations and International Political Economy

The Continuing Story of a Death Foretold

'This is an excellent book on political realism. I think that Guzzini's is really an outstanding work of original analysis and criticism.'

Robert Gilpin *Princeton University*

'I can think of no single volume that provides such a succinct and useful overview of the last 60 years of theorizing about international relations. I would gladly recommend this book to my students and colleagues.'

David Baldwin *Columbia University*

Stefano Guzzini's study offers an understanding of the evolution of the realist tradition within International Relations and International Political Economy. It sees the realist tradition not as a school of thought with a static set of fixed principles, but as a repeatedly failed attempt to turn the rules of European diplomacy into the laws of a US social science.

Realism in International Relations and International Political Economy concentrates on the evolution of a leading school of thought, its critiques and its institutional environment. As such it will provide an invaluable basis to anyone studying International Relations theory.

Stefano Guzzini is Assistant Professor at the Central European University, Budapest College.

D0061217

The New International Relations
Edited by Barry Buzan,
University of Westminster, and
Gerald Segal
International Institute for Strategic Studies, London

The field of International Relations has changed dramatically in recent years. This new series will cover the major issues that have emerged and reflect the latest academic thinking in this particularly dynamic area.

International Law, Rights and Politics
Developments in Eastern Europe and the CIS
Rein Mullerson

The Logic of Internationalism
Coercion and accommodation
Kjell Goldmann

Russia and the Idea of Europe
A Study in Identity and International Relations
Iver B. Neumann

The Future of International Relations
Masters in the Making?
Edited by Iver B. Neumann and Ole Wæver

Realism in International Relations and International Political Economy

The continuing story of a death foretold

Stefano Guzzini

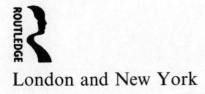

London and New York

First published 1998 by Routledge
11 New Fetter Lane, London EC4P 4EE

Simultaneously published in the USA and Canada
by Routledge
29 West 35th Street, New York, NY 10001

Typeset in Times by BC Typesetting, Bristol
Printed and bound in Great Britain by Clays Ltd, St Ives PLC

British Library Cataloguing in Publication Data
A catalogue record for this book is available from the British Library

Library of Congress Cataloging in Publication Data
Guzzini, Stefano.
    Realism in international relations and international political
economy: the continuing story of a death foretold/Stefano
Guzzini.
        p.   cm – (The new international relations)
    Includes bibliographical reference and index.
    ISBN 0–415–14249–0 (hbk: alk. paper). – ISBN 0–415–14402–7 (pbk)
    1. International relations.   2. Realism.   I. Title.   II. Series.
JZ1307.G89   1998   97-43910
327–dc21   CIP

ISBN 0–415–14249–0 (hbk)
ISBN 0–415–14402–7 (pbk)

Contents

List of illustrations

FIGURES

TABLES

Preface

A reflection on realism in International Relations might be well-advised to follow the strategy of the Turin school of philosophy in adding to the question 'which socialism?' (Bobbio 1976), 'which realism?' For realism shares with more famous political theories (or ideologies) an impressive internal variety. There are nearly as many realist theories as realist theoreticians.

This awareness of internal diversity is a relatively recent development. In the post-war period, the discipline assumed a common realist language. Theoretical treaties were used as introductions at a higher level, which could, without further theoretical discussion, concentrate on the study of particular topics or concepts, for example, the study of power politics (Morgenthau 1947), war (Waltz 1957, Aron 1962) or order in world politics (Bull 1977). With realism negatively defined against idealism, more was not needed.

Today, such a self-evident approach both to realism and the discipline of International Relations is no longer possible. The 1980s and 1990s saw a self-reflective moment in the discipline. Here, realism appears as only one of several contending theories of International Relations. Such typologies of theories in International Relations offer clear-cut boxes, but realism still seems to evade easy categorization. Realism, we are told, has something to do with the central role of the state in International Relations, an assumption hardly unique. Hence, some would contend that realism concentrate on states as the sole international actors. But this is incorrect, as not only realist theories in International Political Economy bear witness. The same can be said for other core concepts of realism, such as power, which, too, is central to other approaches, as for instance dependency theories. Also realism's normative inclination to scepticism does not set it apart: on this terrain it finds itself recently outdone by post-structuralism.

The closest we can get to an assumption which would demarcate realism is the idea of anarchy. Anarchy refers to the basic idea that there is no international government comparable to national ones. This distinction is said to have a decisive influence on state behaviour. But again, traditional defenders of collective security, usually assembled under the category of idealism, have the same theoretical starting point. Rather than setting realism apart from other international theories, the assumption of anarchy sets International Relations apart from other disciplines. So, last but not least, one might argue that realism corresponds to a particular mix of categories and assumptions. But unfortunately not all realists subscribe to the same set. Indeed, conceived in this way, realism appears as a variety of 'pick-and-choose' theories.

The present study shares with this reflective moment in International Relations the conviction that there can be no self-evident definition of realism. Yet it is written against the kind of typologies usually offered to the young scholar, which, almost magically, always present three main menus for choice. Indeed, in the Interlude, I will argue that such typologies should rather be understood as the historical self-reflections of a discipline in crisis. Similarly, I will argue that International Political Economy is a reaction, partly within, partly against, the more systemic and restrictive mode of realism inspired by Kenneth Waltz. This offers an explanation for the emergence of this new field of research which is sometimes subsumed under, or offered as a replacement for, traditional International Relations, and sometimes treated as an entirely different discipline.

Instead of defining realism through static typologies, this study conceives realism as a historical tradition or a cluster of debates. One can show how realist thinkers follow-up the ideas of their predecessors, either to develop or to bury them. If realism can be understood as a tradition, it is necessary to concentrate on individual thinkers within the historical evolution of the discipline, as has been undertaken convincingly by Michael Smith (1986). The framework of the following discussion, however, goes further. It is based on the assumption that an understanding of the multiplicity of the contemporary debates and the growth of knowledge in International Relations requires not only a historical but also a sociological analysis of the relationship between international practice and reflection. It is on the basis of this assumption, that realism must be differently defined.

What became paradigmatic about realist International Relations was the drive felt by scholars, such as Morgenthau, to instill the US as the new and only Western superpower, with the rules of the international society as it developed and expanded from Europe. Initially, realism was thus an attempt to make US foreign policy-makers acquainted with what these scholars saw as the inevitable intricacies of world politics and the sometimes unpleasant responsibilities of a superpower. Whereas European foreign offices were used to and abused by, and also trained and retrained in this diplomatic culture, the unprepared US supposedly needed a crash course which came in the form of a scientific theory. Not socialized into the rules of old-fashioned European great power politics, the political elite in the US required conscious education by those realists, often European emigrants, who became the founding fathers of the new discipline of International Relations.

Hence, in the present study, realism will be understood as the attempt to turn the maxims characteristic for nineteenth-century diplomacy in Europe into a scientific theory, practised mainly in the US. My primary concern is how realism, understood as the set of practical rules shared by the diplomatic culture in the community of states as it developed over the last few centuries, was turned into the scientific backbone of a new social science as it evolved in the particular academic and political context of a new superpower. Such an approach views realist thought as influencing a new social science and a new diplomacy in the US after 1945. It also attempts to apprehend the influence of US foreign policy concerns and the more positivist tradition of US social sciences on the evolution of realist thought. This approach does not imply that the US academic community masterminded theoretical evolutions, or, that international theories would be better today if only the discipline had developed somewhere else. Given the preponderance of research in one country, the study simply refers to the fact that the legitimate political and academic concerns of one academic community had a major impact on the evolution of the discipline and its major school of thought.

In this endeavour, the present study must tie together two stories. There is an internal story about the development of central realist debates. And, closely connected, there is also an external story about the evolution of realism within 'an American social science' (Hoffmann 1977). This external story focuses on the community of researchers responding to their political and scientific environment.

This study aims to show that by examining this series of attempts to turn a set of practical rules into a scientific canon, one can offer an understanding of realism which is both multifaceted and coherent. It claims that whatever important insights thus gathered, these attempts have so far failed. Realist scholars still face the same basic dilemma: either they update the practical knowledge of a diplomatic culture rather than science, and risk losing scientific credibility. Or they cast these maxims into a scientific mould which distorts the realist tradition. The story of realism as a causal explanatory theory is the continuing story of a death foretold.

PURPOSES AND LIMITS

This study claims to give a better understanding of realism than is usually offered in textbooks. The study has been additionally conceived to serve two further purposes. First, it can serve as a supplement to more general introductions to theoretical debates on International Relations and – to a lesser degree – into those of International Political Economy. Second, it aims to show the importance of theoretical studies for International Relations.

The study has a limited focus, and hence can be no more than a supplement to general introductions. For despite the central place of realism in International Relations and International Political Economy, this study is not a general history of international thought. It is a history of a discipline analysed through an unsuccessful attempt to turn the practical knowledge of realism into a scientific theory. It is even less a general theory of International Relations, or a kind of renewed realism. Nor does it try to provide even the basic information necessary for introducing other theories, or sub-disciplines of International Relations. Some fields are barely mentioned (for instance the study of international organizations or peace research). Others (for instance foreign policy analysis), get only a short entry.

This more restricted focus responds to a peculiar mismatch which seems emblematic of International Relations in the last decade or so. In this period, an increasing public and scholarly curiosity meets a discipline which appears less able than ever to provide a coherent picture of itself, and its subject-matter. Usual introductions are either traditional theoretical treaties or comprehensive textbooks. The former stress coherence at the expense of comprehensiveness. Conversely, textbooks cover the vast variety of research and thought at the inevitable price of cohesion. Both strategies have their undoubted value. The present study tries out one way for combining variety with coherence by concentrating on the evolution of the leading school of thought, its critiques and its institutional environment. It has been written for those who feel rather lost after their repeated contacts with International Relations. But this study of realism cannot, and does not want to, replace more general introductions of the usual kind, or indeed, the reading of the original texts. It can only serve as a clarifying supplement.

A further purpose of this analysis of realism is to show the necessity of theoretical studies for International Relations and International Political Economy. This can be elaborated by a paradox. Let us assume that the thesis of this study is correct: many central theoretical debates of the disci-pline have been marked by attempts to turn the rules of international society into a scientific theory. But, according to the thesis, these attempts have all failed. So, the question is then what good is an introduction into the core theory of a discipline if it consists in the historical and conceptual analysis of a major failure?

Scholars are interested in theories for their instrumental value. Theories are tools that provide us with the (often) causal links that should allow us to explain phenomena and, in a practical science like politics, to think of the most appropriate policy options. Having this conception of theorization in mind, the present study does not offer much more than some contestable interpretations of theoretical deadlocks, at least where realism is concerned.

Yet, this book is also written with another theoretical interest in mind. Theory is not only the result of knowledge, whereby empirical findings are generalized; theory is also the very condition of knowledge – we need categories and perceptive schemes to make sense of the world. Data does not speak for itself. In the unending flow of data and events, theories pro-vide selective devices to distinguish the significant from the insignificant. This could be called the constitutive function of theories (Smith 1995: 26–8). Here the cognitive interest is more hermeneutical: by understanding theories from their inner logic it becomes possible to ascertain how they shape empirical perceptions, and consequently, explanations. In other words, we are interested not only in how one can use theories to analyse given events, but how the determination and analysis of these very events is in itself constructed by different theories.

The conceptual schemes of realism are part of the collective memory of the discipline. Though the scientific attempts of realism have proven unsuccessful, their story can indirectly help us in acquiring a sense for the classical and present debates. For those concepts are not only part of explanatory theories, but also of the symbolic heritage of the discipline (as the balance of power, or power, for instance). As Ole Wæver (1989) has already forcefully argued, one cannot just decide to step out of the rules of practical knowledge – they are embedded in the diplomatic culture (which as such exists), and in the collective memory of the discipline.

The aim of this better understanding of realism is to provide the necessary background for critical thought. Some would object that, if the aim is to be critical about realism, to start with the debate of such concepts is to entrap the reader into realist assumptions about international politics. Yet, although categories are necessary for knowledge, it is not impossible to step out of them; we are not their prisoners.

One of the major skills needed to escape the hold of such categories is to be first aware of the way our debates are structured. This enhances the ability to detect implicit methodological and theoretical assumptions. This reflective awareness is all the more significant since the realist language is more often than not used in non-theoretical academic texts or contemporary political debates. Equally important is the second step, namely of acquiring the capacity to translate one theory, however incompletely, into another, and to see one's own assumptions through other lenses. This is the hermeneutical skill which, by providing an understanding of realism both from within and without, this study sets itself the task of fostering. Rather than the professional scientific application of the laws of the international environment, it is this hermeneutical skill which prepares us for, and is an incidental of, practical diplomacy.

STRUCTURE

In keeping with its introductory purpose, the chapters become more specialized, as they proceed. The initial chapters will be elementary for many, though the evolution of realism's main concepts has seldom been traced as explicitly; and of course any, even established, interpretation can be contested. During and after the interlude, each chapter will increasingly explore the state of present research. The concluding chapters analyse the state of the art in the present debates and are pitched at the level of the specialized debate in International Relations.

The structure of the book also reflects the idea that realism can be understood within both a historical and a sociological context. It corresponds to a tradition which developed in close connection with both the requirements of an American social science and the agenda of US foreign policy structure.

These three levels are tied together as follows: Parts I and II cover the evolution of the internal debate and the link to US foreign policy. The first chapters of Parts I and II discuss the evolution of realist thought within the discipline of International Relations. The later chapters in both parts develop the mutual exchange between realist thought and US foreign policy. In Part I, Chapters 5 and 6 relate realism to the origins of the Cold War and the Cuban missile crisis. In Part II, realist theories in International Political Economy are related to US concerns about hegemonic decline and the functioning of the global political economy.

The focus on realism as an academic community and practice shapes the basic structure of the book. Therefore, the internal history of the evolution of realist thought, developed in Parts I and II, is enframed and punctuated with chapters – the introductory section, the interlude and the concluding section – which explicitly show the relationship to the self-understanding and the developing criteria of the academic environment. The introduction presents the general framework and its assumptions. Here realism and the self-reflection of the discipline still form a coherent whole. Some decades later, this is no longer the case. In the interlude, which discusses realism in the crisis of the seventies, realism has lost its paradigmatic status: it is one theory among many. Finally, in the conclusion, two chapters show how, not only the discipline, but also realism itself appears increasingly fragmented. For in many critiques of realism, the strong influence of realism has been a disaster for the development of the discipline. But conversely its proponents also rightly worry now about what the discipline has done to realism.

Acknowledgements

This book started as a series of ten lectures I held at the first *College for New Europe* organized by the International Cultural Centre at the Polonia College of the Jagellonian University, Kraków, in July 1991. In June 1992, a revised and expanded version, entitled *The Continuing Story of a Death Foretold: Realism in International Relations/International Political Economy*, was published as Working Paper SPS 92/20 by the European University Institute in Florence. A first acknowledgement should go to the EUI Department of Political and Social Science, and to the generosity of Andreas Frijdal and Brigitte Schwab who helped me publish a working paper of 290 pages. Indeed, I feel particularly grateful to faculty, staff, and my fellow students at the European University Institute, who provided a unique intellectual and personal environment without which this book would never have been possible. Likewise, I want to thank the Central European University which granted me a much needed sabbatical term to finalize the book.

This book owes many intellectual debts, some of them I incurred several years ago. Hans Wassmund's seminar on Henry Kissinger's foreign policy at the Universität des Saarlandes, Saarbrücken introduced me for the first time systematically into realist thought. At the Institut d'Etudes Politiques de Paris, some earlier ideas on the topics of Chapters 4 and 5 were presented and criticized in Denise Artaud's seminar on US foreign policy, and in Alfred Grosser's seminar on the interaction between domestic and foreign policy. I am particularly grateful to Marisol Touraine for giving an example of how a sharp analytical, and often realist, mind can make sense of contemporary international politics.

In 1988, my MSc thesis at the London School of Economics and Political Science argued that the inter-paradigm debate gave a mistaken picture both of Kuhn's history of science and of the present debates in International Relations and International Political Economy. Although Michael Banks might not share all my views, without his courses and encouragement, and the seminar discussions, I would never have been able to develop them. Different updated versions of my MSc thesis, which are the forerunners of parts of Chapters 1, 8, and 12 of this book, were included in a longer research report on my PhD in 1989 (the June Paper of the EUI), and were circulated since March 1992 as *Borders of the Unknown: The 'International' after the Inter-Paradigm Debate*. For their comments on these or on the published working paper, I am grateful to Robert Cox, Robert Gilpin, Pierre Hassner, Chris Hill, Mark Hoffman, Reinhard Meyers, Gunther Teubner, Roger Tooze, Rob Walker, and two anonymous referees of Routledge. I also want to thank Claire Braithwaite, Kate Hopgood, Victoria Smith and Caroline Wintersgill from the editorial staff of Routledge, who patiently and professionally helped me to turn my manuscript into a book.

Some people's desks have been continously invaded by my writings. I want to thank my MA students at the Central European University, Budapest College, who gave me invaluable feedback. David Rosen's editing of the entire text helped me to clarify expression and thought. Jef Huysmans, Ronen Palan, and Heikki Patomäki had been using the Working Paper with their students and provided me with many comments and advice. The book can only suggest my debt to Susan Strange over the many years in London and Florence. A special thanks goes to Ole Wæver who always encouraged me, and gave me ideas on how to develop my views of the MSc thesis and June Paper. He persuaded me to turn the Kraków lectures into a book, part of which was taking shape in autumn 1991 while we were sharing a flat and ideas in Fiesole. I owe most to my innumerable discussions with my wife Anna Leander. By taking much time from her academic work in order to settle my worries, she made all this possible.

Although this book in many respects no longer resembles the initial lectures in Kraków, it remains attached to that very special experience. In July 1991, after the Soviet attack in Lithuania, just before the coup in Moscow, nobody knew if this was not going to be the last meeting of its kind with people from the still existing USSR. We all felt that we shared an intense and privileged time. I want to dedicate this book to all those who participated at the first *College for New Europe*.

Stefano Guzzini
Budapest, February 1997

1 Assumptions of a historical sociology of realism

This study claims that the evolution of realist thought in International Relations can be fruitfully understood as the attempt, repeated and repeatedly failed, to translate the maxims of nineteenth century's European diplomatic practice into more general laws of an American social science. Therefore, two accounts are needed for understanding the evolution of realism. First, there is an internal story of the debates around central realist concepts and assumptions. Realist theoreticians were influenced by previous research and theories. But they continued to revise them when they found conceptual and logical flaws, and when underlying assumptions and deduced explanations did not fit the empirical evidence. Second, this internal debate took place in a particular political and academic environment. Realist theorizing shaped, and in turn was shaped by, US international policy concerns and the scholarly criteria typical for academic communities in US social sciences.

The proposed understanding of the evolution of realism as the inter-relation between an internal and external story of a discipline is informed by debates in the philosophy of science. In particular, it relies on Thomas Kuhn's concept of paradigm. The double story follows Kuhn in at least three ways (see also Bernstein 1983: 77, 131). Like Kuhn (and others), this study assumes that theories should be understood within their evolution, that is, their history. A second, more specific, borrowing from Kuhn is his emphasis on the nature, function and dynamics of communities of inquirers for the understanding of theories and their evolution. Finally, a qualified use of Kuhn's concept of paradigm is the very starting point for understanding realist theories. Kuhn was himself concerned about using his approach in the social sciences (see Chapter 12). But realism has played a rather unique role in International Relations in that it was conceived initially as over-lapping with the boundaries and the self-conceptions of an entire discipline and its practitioners. Indeed, it is the concept of paradigm which ties the internal and external story of realism together.

The first section of this chapter discusses Kuhn's concept of paradigm and introduces the framework for a historical sociology of realism. The present study concentrates on the exchange between the internal conceptual debates and the external context of realist thought by focusing on the academic community as the binding link between these two stories. Consequently, it is a historical sociology of a fairly limited kind. It is historical, because ideas are understood within the evolution of academic debates. Moreover, these debates interrelate with the historical development of post-war US foreign policy. It is sociological, because its understanding of the evolution of realism does not only include a reference to scholarly debates, as if they happened in a social vacuum, but also to the changing self-conception of the academic community and its individual scholars. It is a limited historical sociology because it does not touch all of the relevant social and political environments of the discipline of International Relations inside and outside the US, nor its material organization – both of which would be necessary for a comprehensive sociology of this knowledge.

Interpreting the evolution of realism through Kuhn's conceptual framework is made possible by the peculiar relationship between realism and the discipline of International Relations. It is probably safe to say that none of the social sciences in the West has known this nearly perfect overlap between one school of thought and a discipline as such. International Relations departments which were established during the first decades after the Second World War more often than not took the realist research agenda for granted. Only when the hold of realism declined did the academic community at large become aware of the extent to which the assumptions of the entire discipline were tacitly derived from realism.

This peculiar confusion of realism and International Relations was possible, as argued here, because realism was understood not just as one theory among others, but as one theory which contributed to legitimately demarcate an independent discipline from other social sciences. As the second part of this chapter shows, International Relations lacks clear-cut boundaries with other social sciences. It has neither an obvious subject-matter of its own, nor a method specific to it. Its identity is permanently contested both from within and without. Yet some realist assumptions, such as the qualitative difference between internal and international politics, could have become fundaments of the discipline at large. On the basis of this latter assumption in particular, realism legitimated research done in different departmental tracks.

In other words, the discipline of International Relations suffers from an endemic identity crisis for which realist assumptions could offer a way out. Initially, realist assumptions were used to defend the legitimate independence of the discipline. Increasingly the institutional defence of the discipline and its academic community, in turn, influenced the internal discussion on realist assumptions. This overlap between discipline and theory had effects in both directions.

REALISM: THE INITIAL PARADIGM OF INTERNATIONAL RELATIONS

Over the last decades, International Relations more openly started to reflect on its own development. This self-reflection has been much influenced by approaches in the philosophy and history of science. In particular, Thomas Kuhn's (1970a) concept of paradigm has become prominent in the discipline. Indeed, by now some scholars cannot help but make slightly mocking remarks on this apparently inevitable commonplace of using Kuhn for understanding the evolution of International Relations (Smouts 1993: 451).

This section shows that Kuhn's approach, duly qualified, is a good starting point for an introduction into realism, although, as argued later (Chapters 8 and 12), I certainly do not share many of the views of those who have used Kuhn in International Relations.

The concept of paradigm

Kuhn's studies of the history of physics were the background upon which he developed the concept of a paradigm. The history of a science used to be presented in terms of progress, that is, of an accumulation of knowledge. Older theories would be replaced by new ones after a rational comparison as to which of the competing theories had a better empirical fit. Kuhn's thesis was that, in fact, the change from one theory to another did not necessarily follow this pattern. Some theoretical breaks, at least, such as the shift to Galilean and then to Einstein's physics, rather than being the effect of piecemeal cumulation more accurately resembled sudden breaks. First, new theories were chosen before one could know whether the new one explained more than the older ones. The choice was rather more influenced by whether the new theory yielded higher expectations for solving some major anomalies and unexplained phenomena. Second, it seems imprecise to say that the shift to a world-view which set the sun in its centre explained more phenomena, or the same ones but better. Rather, phenomena changed their meaning with each new explanation. 'When Aristotle and Galilei looked at swinging stones, the first saw constraint fall, the second a pendulum' (Kuhn 1970a: 121). Kuhn referred to this shift as a gestalt-switch. Hence, for him, major theoretical breakthroughs were like revolutions, i.e. they imply changes of entire world views.

Kuhn's argument raised important questions for the understanding of science and its historical development. It left Kuhn to wonder what everyday, non-revolutionary, scientific work was all about. Also, since there were scientific choices which did not rely entirely on logic and empirical fit, he had to devise a more general framework for the understanding of scientific deliberations, choice and changes.

It is in this context that Kuhn developed his concept of the paradigm. There have been innumerable discussions about what exactly he meant by this. Margaret Mastermann (1970) found seventeen meanings alone in Kuhn's own text. By looking at his own definition, one can, however, distinguish two main meanings. Kuhn defines a paradigm as: 'one or more past scientific achievements', which were (1) 'sufficiently unprecedented to attract an enduring group of adherents away from competing modes of scientific activity'; and (2) 'sufficiently open minded to leave all sorts of problems for the redefined group of practitioners to resolve' (Kuhn 1970a: 11). Broadly speaking, there are two facets of this concept, one which refers to the content of these achievements, the other to the group of practitioners for which the paradigm functions as a legitimating and discipline-defining tool. It defines the academic consensus, the very core of the discipline (see also Gutting 1980: 1–2).

The first facet, the content of the paradigm, reflects the idea of an internal logic, of a world view which guides research, defines the problems to be solved, and suggests the methods to be used. For Kuhn, the existence of a paradigm that guides research is a necessary condition for the establishment of a scientific social subsystem and of individual disciplines. Without a paradigm, there is no deepening research, no criterion for choosing research problems (Kuhn 1970: 37). Once such a paradigm exists, as in Newtonian physics, for instance, science can work normally. Hence, what Kuhn calls 'normal science' is essentially a puzzle-solving activity, filling out the gaps of knowledge as they appear through the lenses of the paradigm. But, at some point, puzzles appear as anomalies. Since paradigms constitute the basic tool of research in normal science, normal science in turn cannot correct the paradigm (Kuhn 1970a: 122). Hence, a new paradigm can only be born by a radical new world-view, that is, by the abandonment of the old paradigm. This is why Kuhn calls it a revolution. (What exactly happens when competing schools debate with each other will be taken up in Chapter 8.) Since their logical contact is incomplete, 'paradigm debates always involve the question: which problem is more significant to have solved?' (Kuhn 1970a: 110).

This leads straight to the second facet of a paradigm, namely its connection with historical contexts and its function for the academic community. Without a paradigm, there can be no scientific community, no firmly established discipline (Kuhn 1970a: 19), and no mature science. To some extent, the analysis of paradigms has to start with the sociological location of the responsible group. In a less quoted passage, Kuhn wrote that: 'A paradigm governs, in the first instance, not a subject matter, but a group of practitioners. Any study of paradigm directed or paradigm shattering research must begin by locating the responsible group or groups' (Kuhn 1970a: 180).

Taking this quote seriously gives a sociological twist to Kuhn's ideas. Indeed, instead of the general attitude which asks how social sciences fit Kuhn's approach, we have first to ask what Kuhn's approach contributes to social sciences (Barnes 1982). Since Kuhn demonstrates that knowledge is to a certain extent conventional, sociologists have to ask which 'critical and regulative ideals' (Bernstein 1983) guide judgements in the scientific community. Likewise, the development of theoretical debates is influenced by the general social setting of the scientific community and by the wider sociopolitical agenda of the societies scientists work in. This study analyses the evolution of the realist paradigm understood in this double meaning.

The realist paradigm in International Relations

The literature in International Relations has used Kuhn's concept of paradigm in mainly two contexts. They are by no means exclusive. But their respective focus is slightly different and for the purpose of easier presentation, this difference will be emphasized.

Common to both approaches is the perception that International Relations has had one single paradigm, namely realism. The first approach focuses on why and how realism developed as a paradigm, whereas the second stresses its crisis and the resulting debate between competing schools of thought. The first discussion will be taken up here. Realism in crisis will be tackled in the Interlude (Chapter 8).

Kuhn's description of the function of a paradigm seems to fit rather well the development of realism and of its discipline, International Relations. Starting from an analysis of the scientific academic community (that is, its activities in university and in public office or debate), the resources available for that activity and the communal goals towards the attainment of which the activity is directed, one can see several similarities in the development of international theory after the First and Second World Wars. There is, for instance, the link between the dominance of certain states in the international system and the study of International Relations in and outside these countries.

Idealism after World War I had thus the same function as realism after World War II: it provided legitimacy for the foreign policy of the dominant states and for the *status quo* of the international system. This is not to make the functional fallacy to assume these to be the only reasons for explaining why these theories knew such a success. Nor should idealism and realism be seen as consciously used tools of legitimation, at least in the aftermath of the wars. Only when peaceful change, advantageous for less powerful states, appeared more and more difficult, did this function become important. In Carr's words:

> The utopian assumption that there is a world interest in peace which is identifiable with the interest of each individual nation helped politicians and political writers everywhere to evade the unpalatable fact of a fundamental divergence of interest between nations desirous of maintaining the *status quo* and nations desirous to change it.

> (Carr 1946: 53)

World War II was seen as signifying the bankruptcy of the idealist position. Anti-appeasement was the new consensus. The dynamics of changing power relations were acknowledged, and peaceful change was discredited. The only way to cope with change was to contain it by power-politics. As Britain before, the US perceived itself as having global responsibilities as a super-power. Thus, for devising a rational foreign policy, the scientific community was encouraged to look at global phenomena. A distinct discipline developed.

Yet the US school differed on one very important point from the British scientific community – the ties to politics (the following relies heavily on Hoffmann 1977; see also Smith 1987 and Grosser 1956). The American aca-demic community was characterized by three things: first a scientific approach to social sciences, inspired by economics; and second, the domi-nance of scholars emigrated from Europe with strong historical backgrounds who 'wanted to find out the meaning and the causes of the catastrophe that had uprooted them, and perhaps the key to a better world' (Hoffmann 1977: 47); and third, the general desire of social scientists to be helpful to the national community, that is, to reflect upon and improve American foreign policy.

Moreover, the ties between university and government (the so-called Kissinger-syndrome) and the network of research foundations laid the ground for the mutual influence of the realist schools and the queries, curios-ities, and given perspectives and interests of US foreign policy.[1] Realism functioned as a paradigm in setting the boundaries of 'legitimate' research. As John Vasquez has convincingly argued, it provided the basic tool of analysis for generations of puzzle-solvers. Or, to use his own words, it 'tells the scholar what is known about the world, what is unknown about it, how we should view the world if we want to know the unknown and finally what is worth knowing' (Vasquez 1983: 5).

Most importantly, realism defined a community by setting the boundaries of the discipline. The community in turn defined the discipline. This aspect is of double importance. First, it explains why, once International Relations became established as an independent discipline in the US, the new depart-ments created outside the US tended to adopt realism as the leading para-digm of International Relations. In the beginning, several European countries imported the discipline with its attached research programme. In a certain sense, the discipline and realism were identical. Perhaps only in the UK did an independent older tradition, the so-called English school of International Relations, survive. But in Germany for instance, where International Relations is still today overwhelmingly part of the political science department, the dominant power-approach linked both. Realism became an up-to-date US formulation of the traditional German 'Real-

---

[1]   Fred Halliday (1987: 227) notes very rightly that US International Relations theory knows a great diversity within and outside the realist paradigm, but that this was denied by main-stream scholars both within and outside the US.

politik', the echo of German emigrants back home. This, at least, is the claim of the Munich school of neorealism (Kindermann 1986).

On the other hand, by one of its assumptions, realism gave the new discipline a much longed for and very suitable demarcation from other sciences. Beside the assumption of the state being the most important actor, and power the most important goal of politics, realism claims that there is a qualitative difference between the laws which govern domestic societies and those governing the nature of the international system. Perhaps most outspoken is Raymond Aron who argued that as long as there was no universal state, there would be an essential difference between domestic and international politics. In their relations, states were, according to Aron, still in a 'state of nature', as opposed to a (domestic) state of law. If they were not, there would be no way to demarcate a particular (political) theory of international relations (Aron 1962: 19). It is this feature, as the next section will argue, which sealed the initial relationship, or confusion, between realism and International Relations.

REALISM AND THE ENDEMIC IDENTITY CRISIS OF INTERNATIONAL RELATIONS

International Relations is a discipline, whose core and borders are even more elusive than those of other social sciences. There are two traditional ways to set a discipline apart. There is, first, the possibility of defining it through an independent subject-matter, as, for instance, economics which, at least in the understanding of some scholars, is about the efficient distribution of value in a world of scarcity. Second, the definition can be made through a methodological distinction. Here, social sciences are not distinguished through their empirical focus, but through the particular way of approaching it.[2] Hence, it makes sense to distinguish, for instance, the historical approach, the economistic, that is, individualist value-maximising, approach, or structuralist approaches, which are sometimes dubbed 'sociological'. This section argues that none of the classical core definitions of a social science provide much succor for International Relations as an independent discipline.

Yet, when the discipline was created anew in the US after 1945, its major theory, realism, offered a conceptual apparatus which held out the possibility of defining a distinctive subject. Realism became inextricably linked to the self-conception of the scientific discipline and its academic community.

---

[2] The very definition of the general category to which International Relations belongs is contested. In this book, the term 'social science' refers, if not otherwise specified, both to social sciences in a more narrow sense, as it is used in particular in Anglo-American countries, and also to a subpart of 'humanities', as, for instance, history and philosophy. It corresponds, hence, to the German *Gesellschafts- und Geisteswissenschaften*.

A discipline with no approach of its own

The increasingly accepted concept underpinning the division of labour amongst different approaches in the social sciences is that while subject-matters may be shared (i.e. the study of society), methods and purposes are different. This can be most easily exemplified by looking at the relationship between the discipline of 'history' and other social sciences. Were it the subject-matter which set disciplines apart, none of the other social sciences should look at the past – when this is the very thing they do most of the time. But social sciences distinguish themselves from history through the purpose of their endeavour. Historical methods are, in general, part of the hermeneutical tradition. Originally, hermeneutics (or, as sometimes used interchangeably, interpretivism) refers to the close reading and interpretation of texts, but increasingly also of any system of signs and meanings. Hermeneutics does not assume the purpose of science to be the formulation of explanations that would eventually build up general laws as in the natural sciences. The reason is that in the human world, the object and subject of our knowledge are inextricably linked. Other social sciences look at history in different ways. Early sociologists, for instance, insisted both on a particular set of methods and a purpose to derive more general insights into human societies (Durkheim 1937). Today, the reference to a sociological approach normally implies a methodology for studying human action in all social and political fields as norm-guided. It often concentrates on structures, institutions and their perpetuation. Similarly, economics set itself apart by a particular approach which explains social and political phenomena through the lense of value-maximization, where the main emphasis is on the rationality of individual choices.

Such a division of social sciences according to different methodologies, which leave the social world a coherent whole is logically compelling. It is indeed difficult to see how one could legitimately demarcate some issues for one social science at the expense of others. Political science, among other things, certainly studies the behaviour of politicians. But, it is far from obvious why politicians could not be studied as value-maximizers, as rent-seekers within an economic approach (Olson 1965). Economists, in turn, study markets. But again, there is no scientific plausible reason to exclude the market, understood as a socially embedded institution, from a sociological analysis (Polanyi 1957; Granowetter 1985).

Yet as helpful as these distinctions might be for other disciplines, they offer little comfort for International Relations. Its practitioners have used a variety of different methods. Traditional International Relations uses approaches which are very close to legal and historical methods, as well as traditional philosophy. The economic approach has been prominent in strategic studies. Nuclear deterrence theories are sometimes even considered closer to the rational choice model than the *homo economicus* of some economic theories (Aron 1967a: 200). Sociological models have intruded into

International Relations mainly during the behaviouralist phase, as with Parson's–Easton's system theory (see Chapter 3). International Relations is often therefore thought of as inherently interdisciplinary, that is, relying on several disciplines at once, or, more ambitiously, as an integrative discipline, combining insights and methods.

But there is yet no internationalist method – this concept does not even exist – which could be demarcated at the methodological level. Yet, International Relations scholars have used two methods of defining such an independent internationalist approach, and both are linked to the realist tradition.

The elusive definition of International Relations by its subject-matter

The more common-sensical strategy to the division of academic labour consisted in dividing the social world into different spheres. The division resulted here in a number of spheres, set apart by their different presumed object of study, rather than by method and purpose. International Relations have been classically defined, and founded, by reference to a unique subject-matter; a definition much helped by some key realist assumptions. But, as argued here, it encounters rather formidable difficulties in this area.

The first chairs in International Relations, as for instance in Aberystwyth, Wales, were put up immediately after the Great War of 1914–18 with the explicit aim of avoiding a similar tragedy. The study of war and peace came to be identified with the study of International Relations. More precisely, International Relations specifically focused on the avoidance of war by drawing on a variety of different disciplines that existed before, especially international law, philosophy, and international history.

Undeniably, peace and war remain central features of today's discipline. But they are not enough to demarcate International Relations from other social sciences. The explanation of war, or the avoidance of conflict, is covered by other disciplines as well, e.g. social psychology, sociology, and philosophy. Inversely, as the remarkably large panoply of treatises on war (for instance, Elshtain 1987) and its causes (Levy 1989; Suganami 1996) show, International Relations itself must rely on several other disciplines for constructing its explanations.

In a second step, International Relations came to be understood as the political and military interplay between states, or, in other words, as the study of the external relations of states. Although still prominent among scholars and practitioners alike, this demarcation, too, is unconvincing. How could it be possible to study the external relations of governments, without including anything about the internal relations into the explanation – and vice versa. For example, in the mid-eighties, the British government had lowered the taxation of managers, a policy which had the neomercantilist aim of making the UK a more attractive location for economic activity. It affected the ongoing decisions of the German government which, at the time, was also negotiating a tax reform. This is just one example of how a specific domestic policy can have immediate international repercussions. These repercussions must not be intended or foreseen as they were in this case. When the Federal Reserve raises interest rates to diminish inflationary pressures in the US, it is a domestic decision taken for a domestic purpose, but its repercussions are felt in every place which is linked to the international financial structure. There are fewer and fewer spheres where domestic politics could be neatly demarcated from the external international sphere of politics.

Not surprisingly, definitions offered in International Relations textbooks have become increasingly loose. John Burton (1986) defines conflict as the subject-matter of International Relations. Marcel Merle (1982: 90), for lack of another defining principle, refers to International Relations as the 'flows that pass or just tend to pass a border'. These definitions might bypass some of the more restrictive definitions just mentioned. But they suffer from the opposite flaw: conflict is one of the underlying themes of all social science, and flows across borders excluding very little indeed.

Faced with the need to include many more causal factors, domestic or transnational, for undertaking the analysis of state behaviour, International Relations was caught in a dilemma. Either it accepted the challenge of the increasing agenda and became the international component of other disciplines in the social sciences. Or it refused to be merged, but then was in dire need of a scientific legitimation. It needed arguments which would show a qualitative difference of international affairs such as to make scientific approaches as they derived from the study of domestic societies not applicable. Realism was used to propose such arguments.

The realist defence of the legitimate independence of International Relations

When realism became the dominant school of International Relations after 1945, it imported several of the assumptions which characterized diplomatic practices and lessons of the nineteenth century. Foreign policy was said to be of a different kind than domestic politics. It required a special expertise and independence from domestic scrutiny. Similarly, foreign policy concerns were said to overrule domestic ones (*Primat der Außenpolitik* so to speak). When the diplomatic practice turned into a scientific theory, these traditional concerns needed explicit justification. These justifications, in turn, provided a welcome demarcation from other sciences. Realism became inextricably linked to the self-conception of the scientific discipline and its academic community.

The chapters of this book witness several attempts to restate the independence of International Relations from other social sciences, indeed, sometimes from 'social sciences' as such. Initially, the founding fathers were mainly interested in keeping law and economics at bay. Morgenthau tried repeatedly to demarcate an independent political sphere, which included inter-state relations (see Chapter 2). Here, International Relations was just a subdiscipline of political science. In later phases of the development of the discipline, when political science turned more scientific, realist writers defended a qualitative difference of International Relations from other social sciences, the latter now including political science. In a famous essay, Martin Wight (1966: 17–34) argued that International Relations does not know laws (of progress), but just of repetition. For the study of these repetitive features, traditional political theory was of as little use as modern scientific theories mainly modelled on domestic politics. Similarly, Raymond Aron (1962) had argued earlier that, for the unavailable equivalent to money in economic theory, international affairs were qualitatively different from economics (see Chapter 3).

Underlying these defences was what became the main distinctive feature for establishing the independence of International Relations: the supposedly qualitative difference between domestic and international politics. This opposition is labelled with different name-tags. Sometimes the international system is likened to a state of nature, different to the state of law where the social contract has created and legitimated a central authority. Sometimes, international anarchy with a multiplicity of equally sovereign states is opposed to the relations within the state where one centre has the legitimate monopoly of violence. Finally, international relations are likened to a society of its own kind which features a particular set of institutions such as diplomacy, great power management, the balance of power, international law, and (limited) war. Whatever the name, the consequence is always the same: theories and arguments which rely on an analogy with domestic politics (or any other social science which developed with reference to domestic societies i.e. all social sciences) are potentially mistaken.

This domestic analogy was already castigated in early realist attacks against Idealism. It was later resurrected against attempts to subsume International Relations under another discipline and its explanatory models. In both cases, realists defended not only the plausibility of their own theory, but the legitimacy of the way research in the discipline was conducted. In other words, for a discipline with an endemic identity problem, realist theorizing initially defined, and then became inextricably linked with, the boundaries of the subject-matter and of the scientific community.

CONCLUSION

Realism is understood here as the attempt to translate the rules of the diplomatic practice in the nineteenth century into scientific rules of social science which developed mainly in the US. The present study of realism is inspired by Kuhn's concept of paradigm. It proposes a limited historical sociology of realism. Paradigms refer to what the scientific community does, i.e. both the internal debates of a science which follow the standards of a discipline, as well as the external relationship of this discipline with its social and political environment. Paradigms govern research by suggesting issues, methods and possible solutions at the expense of others. Through establishing criteria for legitimate research (standards), paradigms also define the competent community of researchers. Focusing on the research community in International Relations after 1945, the evolution of realism has two essential facets: the internal story of conceptual refinements and rebuttals, embedded and responding to the academic and political environment of its research community.

The rather unique features of realism in International Relations make Kuhn's concept of paradigm appealing for the study of realism. A social science with an endemic identity problem, unable to define itself by a different methodology, or a unique subject-matter, International Relations has relied on realist assumptions to set itself apart. For long, the two could be easily conflated. They developed in the US where social sciences are required to respond to certain (scientific) criteria – originally alien to realism.

The evolution of realism is marked by the ongoing attempt to make traditional European diplomatic culture coincide with US foreign policy visions and the scientific requirements of a US social science. It is with this purpose that International Relations was reborn after 1945. This book argues that, although temporarily successful, the rift between these three requirements widened such as to make their combination impossible. But some of the initial purpose still survives, enough to make individual scholars repeat earlier attempts of combining them. This book is the story of their continuously repeated, but ultimately failing, attempts to turn realist maxims into an American social science.

Part I

Realism from containment to détente

2 Classical realism: Carr, Morgenthau and the crisis of collective security

Nous entrons dans l'avenir à reculons.[1]
Paul Valéry

Political thought is influenced by the historical context in which it is formulated. After the Second World War, when International Relations became mainly a US science, realism appeared as the first leading school of thought, the core school which later prompted different criticisms. Yet the origins of the discipline as an independent academic institution are found earlier. The beginning of International Relations is not marked by realism, but by an idealist moment, itself a reaction against the diplomatic practices of nineteenth century diplomacy.

The First World War was seen as the collapse of the European Concert, which was based on balance-of-power politics run by an aristocratic diplomacy. The sheer scope of devastation and human death during the First World War, as well as the first widespread use of mass-destructive weapons (gas), prompted a fundamental rethinking both of the role of diplomacy and warfare, and the general causes of war.

On the political front, this sea-change in thinking was led by US President Woodrow Wilson, leader of the only nation to emerge from the War unscathed, in fact far stronger than it had been in the summer of 1914. At a time when Europe was no longer able to control its destiny, the end of the war marked the beginning, albeit hesitant, of a major international role for the United States. President Wilson became the most fervent advocate of a new diplomacy. The new policy challenged the traditional primacy or independence of foreign policy from domestic politics. It redefined the means and ends of foreign policy, indeed the very conception of foreign relations.

The discipline of International Relations was born with this normative concern for understanding the origins of war and peace. As will be developed in more detail, the idealists found the causes for armed conflicts not in the inherently war-prone international environment, but in the irrational

[1] 'We enter the future walking backwards'.

breakdown of a potential world community of nations. This idealist inter-war period of International Relations later saw the emergence of a realist critique and of the discipline of International Relations as we know it today.

The idealist–realist debate is called the first debate of International Relations. But it is more than that: realism derives its internal logic from the constant counter-position to an often idealized idealism. R.N. Berki (1981) and Martin Griffiths (1992: 159) go as far as to argue that realism consists merely of negative claims. Indeed, philosophically speaking, realism is unthinkable without the background of a prior idealist position deeply committed to the universalism of the Enlightenment and democratic political theory (Walker 1993a: 22, 42, 77, 86).

Therefore, the first debate is part and parcel of realist thought, and hence relevant to much of the further development of the discipline. Starting a book on the evolution of realism with the crisis of idealism is not only a convention, it is a logical imperative if one is to elucidate the realist position from within.

The founding fathers of the new discipline, E.H. Carr and Hans J. Morgenthau, represent the classic expression of this realism derived from anti-idealism. Carr's more mitigated realist position was, in the short run at least, less successful than Morgenthau's *Politics Among Nations* which became the paradigmatic text of the emerging US social science. Apart from being the most widely read textbook, Morgenthau's approach is paradigmatic for two reasons. First, Morgenthau puts particular stress on defining a field of politics independent from other social inquiry. He thus demarcates the competent observer and practitioner. Second, maybe more than any other text, it exemplifies the attempt to revive the practical knowledge of nineteenth century (European) diplomacy, and to turn it into an explanatory theory of International Relations.

THE RISE AND FALL OF IDEALISM AFTER THE FIRST WORLD WAR

What came to be called idealism in the inter-war period was based upon three major tenets (for the following, see also Meyers 1979: 38–51). First, human nature is not reducible to egoistic motivation and material needs. Understanding human behaviour therefore requires the reference to specific aims and the way ideals influence these aims. Second, these ideals, which deeply affect human aims and hence human behaviour, are potentially universal in that they represent the real long-term interests of individuals, as much as of states and the whole world community. In other words, there exists a potential harmony of interests and therefore, conversely, irreconcilable conflicts of interests are not inevitable. Central to this political philosophy are therefore reason and reasoned communication in order to ensure that such harmony of interest be reached.

In short, idealism holds that through reason alone mankind can overcome the state of nature in inter-state relations. With reason, universal principles can be understood and translated into norms, laws, and human and government behaviour. Politics should therefore encourage both the education of people in order to make them understand their own long-term interests, and the democratization of the political sphere. These assumptions gave rise to a conception of international relations and foreign policy. It differed from traditional diplomacy, and later realism, in how it understood what could be called the 'objective' and 'subjective' causes of war.

Objective causes of war usually refer to the immutability of human nature and the nature of politics. With idealism, since mankind is considered potentially good, there must exist at least a possible harmony of interests. Thus, war must be the failure or breakdown of the rational communication that politics should provide in order to translate the more harmonious universal principles into reality. Thus not the system but governments are responsible for the outbreak of wars. They start them – against the interests of their citizens. Non-democratic, or at least illegitimate, governments are one of the primary causes of war. War can be avoided through the democratization of politics, starting from the local to the national and finally to the international level. In the non-democratic international environment of the nineteenth century, egoism turned into nationalism, and inevitably led to war.

As for the idealist's subjective causes, old diplomacy stands out as the primary one. According to the idealist critique, this diplomacy had several major shortcomings. First, diplomats made decisions in many countries over the heads of their people. Instead, foreign policy should become democratized and responsive to the will of the sovereign people. Second, the primacy of foreign policy (*Primat der Außenpolitik*) justified that its activities be kept secret both from the domestic sphere, and from other diplomats. Yet, secret policy avoids the rational debate that is required for making the most reasonable solution eventually prevail. Indeed, secret diplomacy was understood to have triggered the outbreak of the war. Had Russia known about the treaty between the German and the Austro-Hungarian Empires, had all the actors been given the information necessary to anticipate the spiral which eventually escalated the Serbian turmoil into a general war, the war would not in fact have started. Third, the balance of power, far from being the main means of preventing war, was one of the main reasons for its outbreak. Power balancing depends on the very possibility of conflict. One does not look for a system of international conflict control, but clings to the egoistic great powers to limit international violence. Idealism sees old diplomacy as the incarnation of élite arrogance using the international arena as a playground (for a contemporary nonidealist critique of the games diplomats play, see Krippendorff 1985, 1988).

Building on the failure of the traditional diplomacy to guarantee peace, idealism endeavoured to introduce new principles and practices of international politics. In several regards, idealism is the attempt to transpose the principles of domestic liberal–democratic regimes to the international realm. On the one hand, this included most prominently the right of national self-determination as a recognition of the negative role multinational empires had played in the outbreak of the First World War (after all, the war had started in the polyglot Austro-Hungarian Empire). On the international level, power politics, with its changing and eventually destabilizing alliances, was to be replaced by a system of collective security where the international community as a whole would more efficiently deter and oppose any illegitimate use of violence. Not the balance of power, but an international body, the League of Nations, should be the means of international diplomacy. Public deliberation of the best solutions for peace would be decided and implemented by all nations on an equal standing against all nations that failed to comply with decisions made democratically. Peace would become possible through a procedural solution inspired by reason: 'war does not pay'. In short, by taking national rights seriously and removing nationalist causes of international conflict, an international security system could be designed to override those national interests detrimental to the avoidance of war. The precondition for the acceptance of such a system was its publicity which gave reasoned argument time to make policy options adjust.

Yet international politics in the inter-war period did not seem to conform to the world-view of idealism. The world economic crisis (1929–33) put an end to the international monetary system of the time (the gold standard) and led to the breakdown of international economic cooperation. Instead of a free trade regime, the international economic system was characterized by: first, protectionism, that is, a national policy which privileges domestic markets and producers, and second, mercantilism, a policy which subordinates economics to the aims of national foreign policy. Individual attempts to export economic problems through 'beggar-thy-neighbour' policies resulted collectively in an ever worsening international economic crisis. Bringing idealism's world-view into further question, disarmament conferences, such as the one in Geneva 1933–4, failed. When Italy invaded Ethiopia in 1935, the League of Nations proved unable to provide security even for its most long-standing African member. Remilitarization of the Rhineland and of European politics, exemplified by the Spanish Civil War in 1936, was neither deterred, nor met with counter-pressure by the international community.

The system collapsed entirely when Nazi Germany obtained a part of Czechoslovakia, a sovereign country, through military pressure. However, this act was ironically legitimized in terms of idealist self-determination in the Munich Accords (1938) which the European great powers (excluding the USSR) signed in the hope of avoiding a major war. Nazi Germany's propaganda trapped the victorious powers from 1918 in their own logic: the German government claimed to be acting in defence of the Sudeten-German right of self-determination. The ideals of a peaceful order had become part of the Nazi war-machine. The democracies' strategy to prevent another major war with Germany, labelled by critics ever after as appeasement, was a series of concessions which were meant to buy German restraint. But under conditions where resistance was needed, this strategy, meant to avoid war, did nothing more than postpone it – and made it worse when it eventually came. Appeasement became the most important and powerful international political symbol in the post-Second World War world. The lessons learned from its manifest failure composed a major part of the background of thought behind the soon ascendant realist paradigm.

THE REALIST CRITIQUE OF IDEALISM: E.H. CARR'S ATTACK ON THE HARMONY OF INTERESTS

Idealism was inspired by the desire to avoid recreating the conditions that had led to a war that nobody wanted (at least not in the way it actually happened). Realists too were motivated by the will to limit the phenomenon of war, although they maintained that war is a sometimes necessary means of foreign policy. Idealism presupposed the underlying principle of nineteenth century diplomacy, moderation, and tried to apply it to a new context, where war was no longer considered a possible means of politics. It aimed at applying a system of collective security to moderated states. Realism, on the other hand, endeavoured to adjust international politics to the phenomenon of total war which results from the reversal of the Clausewitzian dictum, namely that peace becomes the prolongation of war by other means. For the realist, power politics is no historical accident, but, as Morgenthau called it, a 'human fact' and a 'logical necessity'.

The single most famous critique of the prevailing Idealism of the inter-war period is E.H. Carr's *Twenty Years' Crisis* (1939). At least this is the way the second edition of the book (1946) was received after the war. Since the first edition (1939) did not oppose Chamberlain's appeasement policy, and the second edition failed to unconditionally endorse realism, this rather partial reception is, at best, slightly ironic. Yet the book presented a series of opposing categories which have organized international thought in the first debate and later. The following will show Carr's famous arguments against utopian thought, its limits, and the internal tensions of his own solution.

British realism versus Britain's idealism

The main subject of Carr's critique was the non-existent harmony of interests. Idealism, as he stated it, has three basic flaws: priority is given to reason over interests, to ethics over politics, and to theory over practice.

Carr viewed realism as starting from opposite premises. It is a consequentialist approach; it looks first at the potential consequences of actions and argues backwards. It judges politics not on the basis of a prior theoretical blueprint, but from its actual work and effects. Political analysis and action is informed not by what the world should be, but by what it is. Realism has thus a strong utilitarian and empiricist bias.[2] It does not address the possible changes of actor's interests; it takes them as constant. Politics is designed to adapt to given interests – and not based on the mistaken assumption that they can be changed.

Carr introduced his famous concept of the harmony of interests from liberal economic thought. The concept mainly corresponds to the principle of the invisible hand in market economies. The first flaw of the harmony of interests, so Carr states, lies in the prime place which this assumption assigns to reason:

> In pursuing his own interest, the individual pursues that of the community, and in promoting the interest of the community he promotes his own. This is the famous doctrine of the harmony of interests. It is a necessary corollary of the postulate that moral laws can be established by right reasoning. The admission of any ultimate divergence of interests would be fatal to this postulate; and any apparent clash of interests must therefore be explained as the result of wrong calculation.
>
> (Carr 1946: 42)

Carr further argued that values are derived from power, and ethics from politics. Since the actual world shows no sign of a harmony of interests, it seems of little use as a universal premise of political thought. Since ethics derive from politics and not *vice versa*, the claim to a harmony of interests is nothing other than the result of a specific configuration of power which is mighty enough to implement the dictates of its particular interests and to make those interests appear universal:

> Once industrial capitalism and the class system had become the recognised structure of society, the doctrine of the harmony of interests acquired a new significance, and became . . . the ideology of a dominant group concerned to maintain its predominance by asserting the identity of interests with those of the community as a whole. . . . No country but Great Britain had been commercially powerful enough to believe in the international harmony of economic interests.
>
> (Carr 1946: 44, 46)

To the extent the interests of the less powerful social groups are linked to the interests of their élite, there is also an objective ground on which both sets of interests coincide. However this ground is not the universal nature of these interests, but the sheer power of the privileged which leaves the community no other alternative but to link its interests to theirs (Carr 1946: 80–81). Therefore, Carr saw another, less peaceful, origin of the liberal creed of a harmony of interests. He, not very innocently, called it economic Darwinism,

---

[2] For an outstanding discussion of three different normative strands in realism, namely scepticism, empiricism, and consequentialism, see Klaus-Gerd Giesen (1992: Chapter 3).

namely the idea that for the economy (read: community, national or international), it is best in the long run if only the fittest firms (read: élite or great powers) survive.

Applied to international politics, the harmony of interests in fact corresponds to the powerful's ideology of the *status quo* which 'helped politicians and political writers everywhere to evade the unpalatable fact of a fundamental divergence between nations desirous of maintaining the *status quo* and nations desirous of changing it' (Carr 1946: 53). Carr heavily criticized the behaviour of the victorious powers after the First World War who regarded every change (whether or not they were achieved by peaceful means) as a disturbance of peace. The politics of collective security as used by the winners of 1918 did not amount to the management of conflict that necessarily arises between states, but to the denial that such conflict exists. Yet, if peace meant nothing more that the keeping of the *status quo* of benefits and power, then it was doomed to fail. This order deprived diplomacy of the necessary flexibility to adapt to inevitable changes. For Carr, foreign policy must instead be based on preventive peaceful change, whenever possible, and on military conflict management, whenever necessary.

Carr's sceptical critique of realism

Carr's materialist theory of ideologies is not without flaws. This can be exemplified by the way he treats internationalist ideologies. Following the usual realist (and materialist) approach that social conditions determine rules, principles, and entire ideologies, Carr claimed that all internationalist ideologies were mere rationalizations given by dominating *status quo* powers in order to protect their privileged position. But, as we will immediately see, this claim is inconsistent in its own terms: even if we assume all ideas to derive from particular interests, not all hegemonic interests have been automatically accompanied by an internationalist ideology which rests upon a harmony of interests.

For Carr, the Nazi German government should be understood as just another revisionist force, whose claims for changing international affairs were as good or bad as all claims by rising powers (for the following critique, see also Smith 1986: 77, 96–7). 'Germany, if she became supreme in Europe, would adopt international slogans and establish some kind of international organisation to bolster up her power' (Carr 1946: 86). And indeed, Hitler's Germany desperately tried to mobilize support based on the idea of 'Europeanization'. Yet its racist ideology, which by definition could only include a certain part of Europe, produced an internationalism which never claimed to assume a harmony of interests. Although Carr might have been right in criticizing the complacency of the British and French governments with regard to the Weimar Republic, putting their occasional internationalism on the same footing as Hitler's seems absurd. Even if we assume that all governments in privileged international positions cherish universalist legitimation of their status – which is nothing more than an assumption, and not general historical record – there are qualitative differences between these legitimations. For liberals and those who assume a potential harmony of interests, internationalism means the realization of a universalist philosophy which can and does constrain themselves as well. For nationalists or racists, who pursue an internationalist legitimation, the latter ultimately cannot be checked by a universal appeal: it is nothing more than the international imposition of a particularist ideology.

Neglecting the difference of ideologies and domestic systems, Carr was unable to distinguish between the attempts of Stresemann to revise the Versailles treaties by keeping the principles of the international regime untouched, and those of Hitler, who wanted to change them. Consequently, he commented on Munich as an incident of peaceful change, that is, the preventive attempt to accompany changes deemed necessary for the accomplished shifts in relative national power. What a strange realism indeed which, for its one-sided sarcasm against the self-complacency of *status quo* powers, including Carr's own country, does not investigate the legitimacy of the policies of revisionary powers, and therefore must eventually advocate a form of appeasement. In other words, his scepticism criticized the *status quo* through arguments that could be perfectly reapplied to those who want to change it.

This one-sided critique is a curious example of a truly central insight that Carr himself developed in his book. Realism is a sceptical theory which unmasks the apparent innocence of the truth of the day. But therefore, being a consistent realist, he noted, is ultimately self-contradictory: for realist scepticism must, if consistently pursued, also undermine the realist truth of the day:

> Indeed, realism itself, if we attack it with its own weapons, often turns out in practice to be just as much conditioned as any other mode of thought. In politics, the belief that certain facts are unalterable or certain trends irresistible commonly reflects a lack of desire or a lack of interest to change or resist them. The impossibility of being a consistent and thorough-going realist is one of the most certain and most curious lessons of political science.
>
> (Carr 1946: 89)

It is rather curious that Carr remains celebrated only for his staunch realist critique of idealism. On the one hand, as the preceding discussion suggests, his clear-cut distinction between the Utopian and realist conception of politics might not be the strongest, but the weakest point of his book. Rob Walker's comment that 'any analysis which manages to force, say, Plato and Woodrow Wilson into some undifferentiated category of "idealists" is, at best, perverse' (Walker 1980: 27), applies also to his realist category where Machiavelli meets Marx and Hitler. Realism appears as a residual category regrouping all economic and power materialists.

Similarly, since Carr was aware of the internal problems of realism, his outspoken aim was not to furnish a purely realist theory, but rather to provide a synthesis of Utopianism and realism that tried to avoid the pitfalls of both (for a similar attempt, see Herz 1950). Utopianism suffers from its impracticability, while realism lacks perspective and reduces politics to a blind and pragmatic adjustment to the necessities of international relations. As a historian and also as a person who felt responsibility for political action, Carr refused this deterministic approach to politics. Realism becomes utterly unrealistic when pushed to its extreme, because neither relativism, nor fatalism, nor stasis, actually characterizes the international realm. Political action can make a difference.

Since Carr constructed such opposing types, his own synthesis could hardly be on the conceptual or theoretical level. Instead, he proposed a solution which was coherent with his own vision where the change from realism to idealism and back corresponded to a dialectical movement. His synthesis was not based on particular values, but unfolded in the mere negation of the leading ideology of the day: at times it required a critique of Utopianism, as during the inter-war period, and at others a critique of the stasis of *Realpolitik*, as during the heyday of the Cold War (Carr 1961: 177). Carr might be closer than anybody else to the political realist position as reconstructed by Berki and Griffiths, which consists merely of negative claims.

THE NEW PARADIGM: MORGENTHAU'S *POLITICS AMONG NATIONS*

Carr's stance was too ambiguous and his style too polemic to found a school of thought, to provide an emerging discipline with a paradigmatic example. But he prepared the ground. The model was to come from that country which took over the role of the British Empire. Here, Carr's mitigated realist critique did not persist. The anti-totalitarian struggle that nearly failed against Hitler (and Japan) could not afford another period of appeasement. Idealism was now understood not just as a mistaken approach when taken to its extreme (as was also realism for Carr), but a sign of the final 'decadence of liberalism' which could not conceive of legitimate war even against Fascism (Morgenthau 1946: 68–71). Liberalism was the origin of a disease which has beset Western political thought. 'The political and military catastrophes of the thirties and early forties . . . are but the outward manifestations of an intellectual, moral, and political disease which has its roots in the basic philosophic assumptions of the age' (Morgenthau 1946: 5–6). The world was given another chance to be cured from rationalist liberalism in international relations.

Even though Morgenthau was not the Machiavellian he is at times interpreted to be, his tone and approach definitely differed from Carr. Whereas Carr had little to say about the nature of power, Morgenthau heavily emphasized the brutish and dim, as well as 'inevitable . . . fact of power politics'. Morgenthau more strongly criticized the general move to apply concepts from the domestic to the international sphere, while Carr himself used these domestic analogies as, for instance, when he proposed conciliation between social classes as a model for international conflict management (Carr 1946: 237) or when he compared domestic revolutionary settings with the international community (Carr 1946: 109).

Morgenthau's *Politics Among Nations* was published when the Cold War had just started. This partly explains why the different shades of his thought were lost and only some features gained prominence in the kind of simple-minded anti-communist containment policy which was the despair of more than one realist, Morgenthau included. In other times, his critique of the Hobbesian picture and solution of the state of nature (1948: 397–8) and of Machiavellianism (1948: 169) would not have been so quickly forgotten. Instead, it was and still is his emphasis on the struggle for power that impressed most readers.

But this one-sided reception was also partly due to Morgenthau himself. Since he wanted to influence and advise the foreign policy of the most powerful yet allegedly internationally inexperienced country, he created and stressed a realist set of axioms that inevitably had to be followed. Those 'necessities' should be the basis for any 'truly rational' foreign policy (Morgenthau 1946: 220). In this way, he created the impression of certainty in the study and practice of international politics; a certainty whose impossibility he was so apt at demonstrating in his historical examples. In any event, this certainty proved necessary for the rebirth of the science and discipline of International Relations in its new environment.

The central stage of his book is taken up by power politics, or, better, the necessity for such politics. The concept and reality of power enters at all stages of his argument. It defines the objective background, the possible options, the most significant means, and, in particular circumstances, the ends of foreign policy, where power needs to be balanced. Although it is difficult to imagine how one phenomenon and concept could do all this, Morgenthau tied together a theoretical package which seemed to work and certainly did appeal. The following section will discuss the causal links in Morgenthau's explanatory theory ranging from its anthropological foundations to actual foreign policy (see Fig. 2.1).

The struggle for power: from human nature to national actors

Realists define the political sphere by power and authority relations. Individuals, groups, and nations struggle for power, understood both as the effective control of means of coercion and authority relations based on legitimacy. History follows in eternal cycles, and no catharsis can put an end to these permanent struggles (Bobbio 1981: 217).

Power seemed so self-evident, and power politics so much the rule of international relations, that realist theorists only seldom retrace the origins

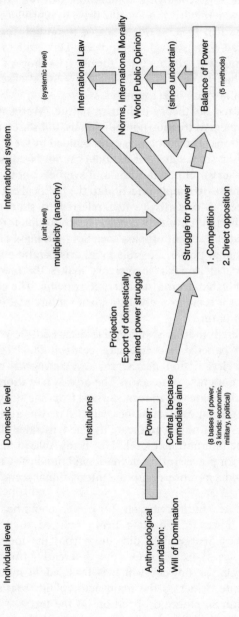

Figure 2.1 A synopsis of the explanatory approach in Hans J. Morgenthau's *Politics Among Nations*

Individual level

Domestic level

International system

Anthropological
foundation:
Will of Domination

Institutions

Power:

Central, because
immediate aim

(8 bases of power,
3 kinds: economic,
military, political)

Projection
Export of domestically
tamed power struggle

Struggle for power

1. Competition
2. Direct opposition

(unit level)
multiplicity (anarchy)

(since uncertain)

Balance of Power

(5 methods)

International Law

Norms, International Morality
World Public Opinion

(systemic level)

of their key-concept. Morgenthau was one of the few writers who rooted and defined the concept of power (Krippendorff 1977: 36–7) and of politics. He gave it a universal psychological foundation. For him, there were three basic drives of all men: the drive to live, the drive to reproduce, and the drive to dominate (1948: 17). In a world of scarce resources, their aggregation must inevitably lead to a struggle for power. This 'will to power' is the nature of politics and war, although the former falls short of using physical violence (Morgenthau 1933: 43, 63). It sets the political observer and practitioner apart from lawyers or economists.

Once having rooted his theory in human nature, Morgenthau faced the classical realist problem of treating not individuals, but states, as the actors in International Relations. The problem is compounded by the often underlying empiricism of realists: since states (or nations) cannot be empirically sensed, they do not 'really' exist, although ideas and symbols about them do.

One solution consists in simply referring to the political élite when talking about states. Indeed, Morgenthau often referred to state representatives rather than to collective entities when he spoke about foreign policy or national power. But the advent of mass societies (and mass armies) expands the calculus of national power. Possible in an aristocratic political context, the increasing place of popular sovereignty makes the mere reference to policy élites as a shorthand for a state less convincing. The conception of a unitary national actor remains a great problem for any realist theory which is based on human nature.

Morgenthau offered another solution. He discussed the phenomenon of nationalism which papered over the gap between the larger population and the state élite. Here nationalism serves as a conceptual bridge between the individual and a unitary state actor. The origins of nationalist solidarity with the foreign policy élite are, in turn, derived from the struggle for power. He argued that on the national level, the central state was able to control the struggle for power – but not to eradicate it. The frustrated drive for power was exported to the international level. 'Not being able to find full satisfaction of their desire for power within the national boundaries, the people project those unsatisfied aspirations onto the international scene' (Morgenthau 1948: 74).

Consequently, states, in their struggle for power, could be treated as individuals, without, however, the state being reduced to a unitary actor (although sometimes Morgenthau did jump from the individual level to the unitary state, see 1948: 327). Or, put differently, Morgenthau could reapply the 'struggle for power', which is founded in human nature, to the level of the state, which is the main actor of international relations. The reference to human nature dropped out of the text.

This approach enabled Morgenthau to tackle also another analytical problem. It could be used to define and emphasize the specificity of the international realm. Here, no overarching authority, comparable to the state at the national level, copes with the struggle for power. The international sphere is characterized by multiplicity, or what was later called anarchy, that is, the lack of a world government. With no arbiter above them, states are caught in a continuous struggle for survival. Although Morgenthau has an essentially uniform definition of politics as a struggle for power, the different environments in which it is fought allow him to distinguish categorically domestic from international politics. After having set politics apart from other fields, Morgenthau's approach defined an independent field of study and its competent actors. It set the paradigmatic boundaries of the discipline.

In the phenomenon of uniting nationalism, Morgenthau offered not only a conceptual bridge between the individual and the political élite, between human nature and the level of the state, but also a possible explanation for the phenomenon of total war in the twentieth century. For him, total war was the result of a particularly virulent form of nationalism, possible with the advent of mass societies. Mass societies, whether totalitarian or democratic, rely on an increasingly broader base of political legitimacy. In times of social disintegration and personal insecurity, an ever greater number of popular aspirations, at home unsatisfied but now legitimate, are projected abroad: Morgenthau argued for a close link between the advent of mass societies, the ferocity of modern nationalistic powers, and uncompromising warfare. For him, this universalization of nationalist drives, or what he calls 'nationalistic universalism', was the greatest danger in twentieth century world politics since it undermined the moderating force of the norms shared by the 'Aristocratic International' (for the two concepts, see Morgenthau 1948: 184ff.).

National power and international mechanisms of order

The international level is characterized by a struggle for power which opposes those who want to keep and those who want to change the current distribution of power.[3] There are two main features of world order, the necessary balance of power and, for the system to work more peacefully, normative mechanisms.

Morgenthau explained at length the articulation of the balance of power: the work of central (and great) powers, buffer states, protectorates, and, what he calls interest-states, that is, states which are important in terms of the great power competition. He gives examples of balance of power methods, such as 'divide and rule', compensation arrangements, arms races, alliances, or the role of the 'balancer'.

In the opening passages of his chapter on the balance of power, Morgenthau attacked idealism by stating that the balance of power was

---

[3] Power itself is understood as a causal concept in which A has the ability to affect B's behaviour. It is grounded on eight different bases: geography, natural resources, industrial capacity, military preparedness, population, national character, national morale, and the quality of diplomacy.

not a question of policy choice, but rather natural and inevitable. Analogous to the price equilibrium in a market, the balance of power was the natural outgrowth of the struggle for power. Its goal is the stability and the preservation of all elements of the system. These passages gave rise to the scientific understanding of realism which will be addressed in the next chapter.

Morgenthau did, however, not believe that the balance of power would inevitably function: for him, the balance of power was unable in itself to guarantee efficient conflict limitation. The reason lies in the nature of power: it cannot be measured. The assessment of the eight bases of power is vitiated by three main fallacies. Power is not an absolute category. It is relative and must be assessed in comparison with other national powers. It is not permanent either, because power bases change. Finally, there is no single factor from which one could derive power, in particular not the military strength.[4] Morgenthau concluded that 'rational calculation of the relative strength of several nations, which is the very lifeblood of the balance of power, becomes a series of guesses the correctness of which can be asserted only in retrospect' (Morgenthau 1948: 152). Therefore, Morgenthau considered arguments for the working of the balance of power for preserving peace as non-existent, since there was no proof that it had avoided war while it has certainly been a cause of war.

Similarly, according to Morgenthau, to argue for the balance of power as an efficient instrument for conflict limitation was inadequate, because its functioning presupposed it being commonly accepted as such. This last point should be stressed. Besides some passages on the balance of power covered in the next chapter, and besides his attempt to produce a theory of International Relations based on universal categories, for which he has become both famous and criticized, Morgenthau argued that the balance of power was not mechanical, but emanated 'from a number of elements, intellectual and moral in nature':

> Of the temperateness and indecisiveness of the political contests, from 1648 to the Napoleonic Wars and then again from 1815 to 1914, the balance of power is not so much the cause as the metaphorical and symbolic expression or, at best, the technique of realization. Before the balance of power could impose its restraints upon the power aspirations of nations through the mechanical interplay of opposing forces, the competing nations had first to restrain themselves by accepting the system of the balance of power as the common framework of their endeavors . . . Where such a consensus no longer exists or has become weak and is no longer sure of itself, as in the period starting with the partitions of Poland and ending with the Napoleonic Wars, the balance of power is

---

[4] This does not mean that he does not privilege in the last resort military preparedness or war as the ultimate bases and practices of international power politics. Yet, Morgenthau is also a foreign policy analyst; and here the military factor is not the only, or necessarily the most important one.

incapable of fulfilling its functions of international stability and national independence.

(1948: 163–5)

In the tragic twentieth century, this code of conduct is under permanent attack by the incompatible and uncompromising forces of nationalistic universalism. 'While the democratic selection and responsibility of government officials destroyed international morality as an effective system of restraint, nationalism destroyed the international society itself within which that morality had operated' (1948: 189). Therefore, any international system, if it is to be ordered and thus peaceful, must rely on normative mechanisms. Morgenthau distinguished three different mechanisms, in rising order of actual impact: ethics, including mores and law; then world public opinion; and finally, international law. If their creation fails, the system will always fall back on the brute clash of national forces. These struggles will establish balance mechanisms, that, in turn, ask for normative mechanisms to function, and so on. National power politics and the balance of power are the fall-backs of any international system: this is the basic realist position – one cannot avoid the struggle for power. But for avoiding major tragedies in an era of universalist nationalism, for making the balance of power function as a restraint of war, normative arrangements or institutions must take the place of the declining aristocratic code of conduct.

With all his analytical stress on the inevitable struggle for power and the necessary balance of power, the policy-concerned Morgenthau reserved a role for norms and public control which was far from insignificant; it was the necessary cultural (normative) force that enabled a balance of power system to work as a peace-preserving mechanism. Since international politics has been democratized, the new foreign policy élites must learn to follow the established roles. Since one can no longer rely on aristocratic tradition, the enlightened observer has to convince these élites of a foreign policy that reflects and reproduces the traditional diplomatic culture. This is the basic tension between the analytical Morgenthau and the policy-concerned Morgenthau, a tension which is fundamental with many realists. On the one hand, Morgenthau understands diplomatic culture as the product of a particular socio-historical tradition. As a tradition, it is practically acquired. On the other hand, present diplomacy is conducted by practitioners with no such tradition. For these policy-makers, acquiring the maxims of traditional diplomacy requires endless rational justification. For making tradition meet reason, the temptation is great indeed to turn these maxims, the lessons of history, into scientific laws.

In later editions of his book, Morgenthau upgraded the scientific approach. The new introduction gave the entire enterprise a more one-sided outlook, despite Morgenthau's historical subtlety throughout the rest of the book. The regularities of international relations and the permanence of human nature became necessities to which all rational foreign policy, in the national interest, must conform. Morgenthau needed to adapt the picture of realist practices to the academic and political discourses of its mainly American audience. In his very attempt to communicate realist lessons, he changed them. He turned realism from the historical experience and shared knowledge of a diplomatic culture to a social science theory which is understood as 'governed by objective laws that have their roots in human nature.'

CONCLUSION

The historical context of Munich and appeasement gave realism, as opposed to the idealist approaches prevailing in the inter-war period, an enormous appeal. Carr and Morgenthau contributed to undermining the basic principles of what was dubbed idealism (Carr's Utopianism). Morgenthau was crucial in securing the ascendancy of realism in the newly founded academic specialization of International Relations.

Carr used realist scepticism to criticize a great power of his day, his native Britain. He debunked the apparently universal harmony of interests as a *status quo* power ideology. Yet Carr's scepticism produces a restless circle of criticism which is, as he acknowledged, self-contradicting. Moreover, Carr's scepticism is neither able to define his exact mix of realism and idealism, nor to positively propose a coherent policy.

Morgenthau, in his attempt to teach the diplomatic lessons of the past, was torn between his earlier criticism (1946) of idealists who confounded politics with science, and his own attempt to replace idealism by a claim to the scientific superiority of realism (1948, 1960). The result is a theory which must find conceptual bridges starting from the eternal laws of human nature, via the state as a unitary actor, to a necessary balance of power theory. It is much more complex and contradictory than usually acknowledged. To take just one example, Kenneth Waltz (1959) proposed a famous distinction between three images for understanding the causes of war. The first image is based on human nature, the second on the nature of the political regime, and the third on the specific characteristics of the international realm (anarchy). Waltz plainly placed Morgenthau within the first category. Yet, although Morgenthau derived power, and hence the essential characteristics of all politics including war, from human nature, he could also qualify for the other two images. He argued that the typical war of the gruesome twentieth century was a result of the democratization, and hence nationalization of international politics. This was how he called the shift to mass societies whose rulers have to respond to large constituencies. This is a form of a second image explanation. And finally, although it is true that politics is about the struggle for power based on human nature, the specificity of the international realm, what he called multiplicity, explains why the warlike struggle for power, while tamed at the domestic level, is endemic to the international level.

How can Carr and Morgenthau, so different in style and content, and whose approaches are filled with so many internal tensions, become major reference points for one school of thought? Obviously they were perceived mainly through what they had in common, the critique of idealism and the priority given to power and politics. Hence, this chapter should also serve as a warning: as much as idealism was often idealized to allow a realist critique, realism has often been demonized by its adversaries and misused by reactionary friends. The binary opposition of realism and idealism more often serves to provide observers and practitioners with an identity than it does to provide analytical clarity.

The realist world-view wants to be pragmatic, not cynical. Its main purpose is the avoidance of great war through the management and limitation of conflicts by a working balance of power supplemented by normative arrangements. Nevertheless, for realists, the struggle for power will always arise. Conflicts cannot be abolished. For realists, foreign policy often brings choices that nobody wants to make. Diplomats might at times have to gamble, but not because they like doing it. On the stage of world politics where brute forces can clash unfettered, diplomats enter a theatre of tragedy. This is the fate of the statesman, who, in the writings of Morgenthau, but also Kennan and Kissinger, appears as a romanticized heroic figure. Often misunderstood also by self-proclaimed realists, realist policy is not the external projection of a military or even reactionary ideology; it is the constant adjustment to a bitter reality. For realists, Realpolitik is not a choice that can be avoided, it is a necessity which responsible actors have to moderate.

3 The evolution of realist core concepts during the second debate

The first debate within the discipline of International Relations, between realism and idealism, took place between the wars and immediately following the Second World War. The 1960's witnessed a new great debate, this time not about central theoretical tenets, but about the scientific status of the discipline. Generally, scholars in International Relations had cut their teeth in international law and diplomatic history. During the heyday of the behavioralist revolution in the social sciences, however, this traditional International Relations came under severe fire. Behaviouralists attacked what appeared to them as unreflected assumptions and woolly hypotheses. Without the rigour of a scientific approach, the critique run, traditional International Relations was nothing more than either purely descriptive history or normative theory.

The resulting dispute, on account of its chief protagonists, was called the Bull-Kaplan debate or the traditionalism versus scientism debate, and more briefly the 'second debate'. This debate brings us back to the problematic identity of International Relations as an independent discipline (see Chapter 1). The first debate succeeded in separating International Relations from other academic fields in terms of its specific subject-matter. It failed, however, to provide a methodological demarcation. As a consequence, International Relations always reflected the methodological fads of other disciplines, in particular those of American political science.

Against the background of this debate, realists of both stripes scrutinized the central concepts of anarchy, the national interest, the balance of power, and indeed, power itself – either to show how a realist behaviourial science of International Relations could be constructed, or to refute this very enterprise.

INTERNATIONAL RELATIONS TURNS SCIENTIFIC

The scientific approach was based on three assumptions. First, the language and approach of systems theory, in particular its cybernetic version, were applied to International Relations. Second, the understanding of scientific work became empiricist. Morgenthau still held that universal historic laws or human nature explained the empirical world. Now, empirical correlations were to provide the starting point for establishing laws of human (or, here, state) behaviour. Third, science was demarcated from ideology, arts, and history by the provision of a methodology, inspired by Karl Popper, with which its laws could be 'falsified'.

Yet these three assumptions of the scientists at the time were not necessarily at ease with each other. System theory was criticized for not being falsifiable, but merely a descriptive taxonomy (Reynolds 1973: Chapters 2 and 3). Some approaches were of such an empiricist nature that they assumed a direct access to the real world, an approach Karl Popper would have sternly criticized.

These strands will therefore be treated separately. After an introduction into the assumptions of falsificationism, the turn to an empirical science will be exemplified with the increasing reliance on the security dilemma, and not human nature, as the underlying cause of international power politics. Then, one of the central debates of this period, the polarity–stability debate, will illustrate the ambivalent mix of behaviouralism and systems theory. In a final section, Morgenthau's ambivalent position in the debate will be taken up again so as to prepare the following conceptual critique by his fellow realists.

Falsificationism

Falsificationism is a methodology. That is, it indicates one particular standard through which an academic discipline can hold certain propositions to be valid or true.

Falsificationism is based on a method whereby one tries to subsume a particular event under a general law (deductive-normative approach). That is: starting from a general law, one should develop hypotheses, and state the criteria for the possible test of these hypotheses. If a test is unsuccessful, the hypothesis is considered falsified, and can be taken as an indication that the general law may be false as well. The standards are not standards of absolute truth, but of scientific method (Hempel 1965). Take the following example:

General law: The law of gravity. Any object is attracted towards the centre of the earth.

Particular case: A stone is thrown. What will happen?

Hypothesis: If the stone can be considered an object, if its movement is not hindered, then it will be attracted by the mass of the earth. It will fall down.

Experiment: The stone is thrown.

Result: It falls. The general law has not been falsified. The particular case can be seen as an incident of the general law.

This approach implies a particular validity claim, that is a contingent truth claim. It assumes that there exists an objective nature outside, independent of the interpretation of the observer. If it is raining, you become wet, whether you think it is raining or not. Few authors would go so far, however, as to think that the general laws discovered correspond to an eternal truth. They are only an approximation and must necessarily remain axiomatic, that is, impossible to verify.

Falsificationism castigates two main fallacies, or logical mistakes. Both make falsification impossible. One is the fallacy of the so-called infinite regress. Let us take an example from the literature in the political theory of power which opposed the élitist and pluralist school (Dahl 1958) in community power studies:

Our state is governed by a ruling élite.

The analysis finds out that those usually held for the élite are not prevailing in the most important decisions.

Counter argument: this is so, because behind this élite of façade there is another élite that actually rules.

Counter analysis: this élite does not exist, because there is no clear-cut pattern that the group prevails in decision-making.

Counter argument: this is so, because behind this élite of façade there is another élite that actually rules; and so on.

This means that if theory and findings do not coincide, the empirical research (and not the theory) was wrong. Consequently, the theory is immune to critique and can shift the weight of justification to the empirical findings. No falsification is possible.

The second fallacy is tautological or circular reasoning. This is the result of an imprecise articulation of the test. For a test to work, the hypothesis should state a relation between one independent variable (cause) and a dependent variable (effect). Circular reasoning occurs when the two variables are actually not independent from another, i.e. the result is already included in the assumptions. Take an example, still from the analysis of power:

The often tacit assumption of power analysis is that being powerful means possessing the means to prevail in conflicts. Being powerful and the control of outcomes are assumed identical.

Hypothesis: if two actors meet in a conflict, then the more powerful will prevail (i.e. the law of the strongest).

Test: if the expected powerful did not prevail, it does not invalidate the hypothesis, but can be saved by showing that since the other side prevailed, it was the really powerful one. Hence, since power and outcome-prevailing are circularly defined, there can be no incidence to falsify this theory.

The advance of the third image: the security dilemma

In an international realm that is characterized by multiplicity (Morgenthau), one actor's quest for security through power accumulation cannot but exacerbate the feelings of insecurity of another actor, who in turn, will respond by accumulating power. 'Since none can feel entirely secure in a world of competing units, power competition ensues, and the vicious circle of security and power accumulation is one' (Herz 1950: 157). The system of self-help engenders a spiral of competition, aimed at making each individual actor more secure, but producing overall insecurity: this is the famous security dilemma.

In this account, it is not an innate human drive for domination, but a national drive for survival under conditions of anarchy which provides the foundation of International Relations. Power politics in its international version is thus not an anthropological, but a social problem (Herz 1950). It appears only when there is no stable normative setting, such as a world government. In an anarchic system, security cannot be entrusted to anyone but one's self. The context triggers the 'inevitable' nature of power politics.

Compared with a first image explanation, such a grounding of International Relations offered two advantages. First, the security dilemma was more amenable to a scientific understanding of the discipline. For Morgenthau, the conflict-ridden character of international relations ultimately derived from human nature. Yet, few behaviouralists followed him with what were perceived as metaphysical assumptions about innate power instincts. Attempting to upgrade International Relations to the level of a science, they preferred the apparently more empirical concept of the security dilemma.

Second, the security dilemma, referring to the basic cause of war as strictly international, helped to solidify the demarcation of International Relations as an independent discipline. Moreover, the security dilemma allowed realists to keep a unified vision of politics. The distinctive contexts, namely the lacking international correspondent to the domestic government, became now a qualitative difference between sovereignty inside and anarchy outside. The theoretical starting point of international anarchy provided the undisputed territory of the discipline, whereas its actual subject-matter, the study of war, was shared among many sciences analysing conflict, such as politics, sociology and psychology.

Scientism in practice: the polarity–stability debate

The scientific approach is often equated with the increasingly quantitative nature of International Relations. The usual textbook example for this trend is the famous correlates of war project. This project compiled an ongoing database covering a vast number of known historical wars. This database serves as a control for empirical correlations between certain variables and the occurrence of wars (for a more recent assessment of its findings, see Vasquez, 1987).

But seeing behaviouralism solely in terms of quantitative research is slightly misleading. The underlying thrust was rather to model International Relations, a method, which would then offer the possibility to subsume certain empirical events under established models. As such, the so-called polarity–stability debate is a good example of this moment.

The starting point is the security dilemma and its assumptions. States want to survive. They have to compete in an anarchical system with no arbiter. But the modelling goes further. It distinguishes between different types of anarchical systems, according to the distribution of power. The scientific aim is a partial theory of international behaviour. Although one cannot predict individual events, it should be possible to predict a patterned behaviour within a particular kind of international system. At the same time, 'the theory should be able to predict the conditions under which the system will remain stable, and conditions under which it will be transformed, and the kinds of transformations that may be expected to take place' (Kaplan 1969: 292. An earlier version of the article was published in 1957).

The approach runs as follows.[1] In good behaviouralist manner, the models are concerned with the regular empirical patterns that might exist between particular environments (inputs) and the behaviour of states (outputs). In this particular debate, the models establish a relationship between certain distributions of power (polarization) and the stability of the international system. The latter term had been used in two different ways. Whereas Kaplan is more interested in the stability of the system as such, whether bipolar or multipolar, the polarity debate often understood stability in terms of low conflict or even peace.[2]

Hence, in a first step, given the assumptions of the security dilemma, the analyst establishes different models of behaviour according to different constellations of power. For instance, in a bipolar world, one could expect that states will think in zero-sum terms: every gain of one side is seen automatically as a loss for the other side. As a result, each will be concerned with every single small change in the distribution of power. The system will be rather war-prone. In other words the analysis is concerned with deducing propositions from the distribution of power that have a particular impact on the rational calculus of the agents (states), which, in turn, renders the system either stable or not. We get a causal account of the following kind: if there is bipolarity, and given the assumptions of rationality and

---

[1] For the classical texts, see Waltz 1964; Deutsch and Singer 1964; Rosecrance 1966. For an excellent discussion of the debate, see Huysmans 1992.

[2] In this respect, Waltz's (1993: 45) recent restatement is coming closer to Kaplan's initial formulation. Here, the definition of stability is no longer twofold, as in 1964. He drops 'the peacefulness of adjustment' and keeps the 'durability of the system itself'.

self-help in an anarchical system, the effect on the rational calculus of actors will be patterned so that a high probability of (in)stability results.

Consequently, establishing these patterns allows the analyst to deduce hypotheses which, and this is the second step of the approach, can be tested against further empirical cases. Here, a form of falsification is possible. Should a particular event, which was subsumed under one of the models, not display the expected patterned behaviour, then either the model needs to be refined, or, if this unavailable, dismissed.

It is interesting to note that the two scientific analogies on which stability was modelled were, methodologically speaking, very different. The first is a homeostatic analogy. Similar to the way the temperature of human bodies is regulated, an equilibrium is not a static result, but a constant process. Cybernetics, that is the science of information flows, is a holistic account which makes sense of the way particular patterned reactions happen by referring to the function they have in an overall system. After a stimulus (e.g. heat) perceived and processed by a central node (e.g. the brain), the body reacts (sweating), which functions to control the temperature (homeostatic equilibrium). Kaplan uses this analogy when he writes that 'the international system is not only stable but . . . ultrastable. That is, it acts selectively toward states of its internal variables and rejects those which lead to unstable states' (Kaplan 1969: 293).

The other model is the market and its equilibrating price mechanism, an individualist approach. Here the equilibrium is the unintended consequence of rational individual action without the influence of any steering centre. Applied to International Relations, this analogy sees equilibrium as the result of the individual states' attempts to protect themselves which inevitably ends up balancing their respective powers (Kaplan 1969: 296; for an earlier analysis of this analogy, see Haas 1953: 455).

Morgenthau's concepts read more scientifically

Morgenthau's (1946) early diatribe against the social engineers of the interwar period already encapsulated many of the criticisms traditionalists advanced against the scientist approaches (Bull 1969). First, scientists misread the nature of international relations:

> To be successful and truly 'rational' in social action, knowledge of a different order is needed. This is not the knowledge of single tangible facts but of the eternal laws by which man moves in the social world . . . The key to those laws of man is not in the facts from whose uniformity the science derives their laws.
>
> (Morgenthau 1946: 219–20)

Second and related, International Relations, if it was to be a policy-relevant discipline must rely on the same intuitive insights of history as do statesmen. The art of politics requires historically informed wisdom, not some ahistorical empirical correlations. Finally, politics is inherently normative. Morgenthau claimed that the scientific turn in International Relations which he saw in the inter-war period:

> produced as its inevitable result the substitution of scientific standards for political evaluations . . . The quest for and the defense of power then become aberrations from the scientific attitude, which looks for causes and remedies . . . There is essentially nothing to fight for; there is always something to analyse, to understand, and to reform.
>
> (Morgenthau 1946: 101)

Morgenthau himself was, however, not innocent in regard to the progress of less historical and less normative approaches. Already in his earlier writings in international law, he advocated the scientific standards of philosophical positivism and proposed a legal position, called 'realist', more positivistic, so he claimed, than that of Kelsen himself (Morgenthau 1936).

More consequential for the discipline of International Relations were his famous six principles of realism, which he added to later editions of his textbook. The first three of these have made him the father of a more scientist-like realist approach. The first principle states Morgenthau's assumptions about what theories are about, that is, his metatheoretical assumptions: 'theory consists in ascertaining facts and giving them meaning through reason . . . Political realism believes that politics like society in general, is governed by objective laws that have their roots in human nature'. The first part of this principle could mean that Morgenthau endorses empiricism, that is, believes that with our senses we can apprehend facts, and only then we make sense of them. The second part gives his theoretical starting point, human nature. This, given its fundamental immutability, provides the bases for a science with objective laws, and thus the possibility of limited prediction.

The second principle gives the central concept of political theory, namely the 'concept of interest defined in terms of power'. This concept permits a demarcation of the political sphere from other spheres of social action, and makes political behaviour intelligible.

Morgenthau's third principle, built upon his second, introduces the pivotal concept of the national interest defined in terms of power. It is pivotal because it allows bridging between the analytical and the prescriptive level of his realist theory. It is both the ideal type which can be used to explain behaviour, and a guide to a rational foreign policy formulation. The analytical level is mainly an analysis of the means–ends relation of action, based on Weber's *zweckrationalem Handeln* (instrumentally rational action). The prescriptive part of the concept is similar to the traditional concept of *raison d'état* as formulated by Friedrich Meinecke, a historian Morgenthau admired and whose definition he accepted as being analogous to his own:

The 'reason' of a state thus consists in realizing itself and its environment and to derive from this understanding the maxims for action . . . For every state in every situation, there exists one ideal logic of action, one ideal raison d'état. This to recognize is the insistent attempt of the acting statesman and the reflecting historian.

(Meinecke 1965 [1924]: 1)

Kindermann, a leading figure of the Munich School of neorealism (not to be confused with Waltz's later approach) has given a description of Morgenthau's objective notion of interest which was explicitly accepted by the latter:

Seen objectively, i.e. as a reality independent of reflection, the national interest can be understood as the essence of possible behaviour whose realization in a concrete historical situation maximizes particularly the existential [interests] of a state [security, power, wealth].

(Kindermann 1986: 20, my translation)

In every case, according to the logic of national interest, there exists an optimal rational choice, independently of whether or not the actor is aware of the options.

It is in this context that one must see the more mechanical understanding of the balance of power, described by Morgenthau (1948: 28) as 'a universal instrument of foreign policy used in all times by all nations who wanted to preserve their independence'. Morgenthau's approach shifted to a science made of laws assuming phenomena as naturally given, and using objective concepts such as national interest; a science which could be used both to explain and to advise political behaviour in the international sphere. Despite his own ambivalence as mentioned in the last chapter, he therefore contributed to the advance of the behaviouralist and increasingly mathematical research he so much despised (Morgenthau 1970).

THE SECURITY DILEMMA REVISITED: THE REALIST QUALIFICATION OF ANARCHY

Since many classical realists have expressed dissatisfaction with the attempt to subsume international relations under a pure power politics model, the assumption of anarchy in the security dilemma has been repeatedly refined. The concept of anarchy was qualified in two ways. On the one hand, critiques contended that the security dilemma did not apply to all subsystems of International Relations. This prompted a conceptual distinction between forms of pure and mitigated power politics. On the other hand, an entire approach was founded qualifying anarchy as such, implying that the international realm, although lacking central government, could not be likened to the Hobbesian state of nature, from which the grimmer versions of power politics were derived. As a result, the security dilemma, which rests upon an unqualified concept of anarchy, sees its explanatory thrust much diminished. For some classical realists, no necessary behaviour could be deduced from it.

The qualification of anarchy: amity/enmity

The most common path traditionalists took for qualifying international anarchy was to introduce two distinct types of International Relations under anarchy. Indeed, Morgenthau himself introduced such a distinction. By referring to the European Concert system, where diplomacy could rely on a shared framework of interests and values, he accepted that the struggle for power, albeit not its temporal permanence and spatial universality, could be mitigated (Morgenthau 1946: 107–8).

These two different types of international system were further elaborated by Henry Kissinger in his doctoral thesis on the working of the European Concert system inaugurated by the Congress in Vienna of 1815. Kissinger distinguished between a legitimate and a revolutionary international order, depending on whether or not the major powers share a common code of conduct:

> A legitimate order does not make conflicts impossible, but limits their scope. Wars may occur, but they will be fought *in the name of* the existing structure . . . Diplomacy in the classic sense, the adjustment of differences through negotiation, is possible only in 'legitimate' international orders.
>
> (Kissinger 1957: 1–2)

In contrast, a revolutionary order always occurs when one or more powers not only want adjustments within the system, as any revisionist actor does, but an adjustment of the system itself:

> But the distinguishing feature of a revolutionary power is not that it feels threatened – such feeling is inherent in the nature of international relations based on sovereign states – *but that nothing can reassure it.* Only absolute security – the neutralization of the opponent – is considered a sufficient guarantee, and thus the desire of one power for absolute security means absolute insecurity for all the others . . . Diplomacy, the art of restraining the exercise of power, cannot function in such an environment . . . And because in revolutionary situations the contending systems are less concerned with the adjustment of differences than with the subversion of loyalties, diplomacy is replaced either by war or by an armaments race.
>
> (Kissinger, 1957: 2–3)

In other words, the feeling of insecurity and threat is inherent only for some specific orders, as, for instance, the US–Soviet Union relations at the height of the Cold War. Others are, in Aron's words, a historical compromise between the state of nature and rule of law, as the Concert of Europe in the nineteenth century and, more recently, the relations within the European Common Market (Aron 1962: 143).

Aron himself used a similar distinction between 'système homogène' and 'système hétérogène'. Homogeneous systems are characterized by states of a similar kind which, moreover, share the same conception of politics. In contrast, heterogeneous systems are made up of states that are organized according to different principles and that endorse contradicting value-systems (Aron 1962: 108).

At first, Kissinger and Aron seem to differ. Whereas Aron seems to imply a direct causal link between the domestic organization of the political system and the nature of the resulting international system (this is the first part of his definition of heterogeneous systems), Kissinger analyses the existence of an international code of conduct which could be distinctive from the national rules of legitimacy. For Kissinger, different social systems can agree to settle their interstate relations following rules that differ from those that function in their domestic spheres. This carries the public–private distinction of liberal domestic policies into the international realm. In this distinction, individual states are allowed to pursue their own faith in their private domestic realm, but must refrain from imposing it on the international community.

But in fact, Aron and Kissinger share a rather similar view. Both agree that there are exceptions to their categories, and these exceptions tend to overlap. Aron argues that before 1917, the heterogeneity of principles of domestic legitimacy was compatible with a profound cultural homogeneity of the European powers (Aron 1962: 111). Here, Aron takes exception to the direct link between the domestic political organization and the international system. Conversely, Kissinger does at times assume that states with similar political regimes tend to produce a legitimate international order. He quotes Versailles as an example of an international system which has been resented as oppressive by one of the actors (and therefore revolutionary), despite the fact that the Republic of Weimar followed lines of domestic organization similar to the victorious states (with the exception of its sovereignty, curtailed in the Versailles Peace Treaty). Similarly, Aron (1962: 112) describes as 'perhaps the most frightening heterogeneity' the one which 'develops out of a basic community'.

Thus, the domestic system cannot give more than an indication of the resulting international order. A decisive characteristic is the existence of irreconcilably contradictory values which are pursued at the international level. These distinctions between a pure power political realm and a mitigated one, can be used to differentiate the international realm both in time and in space. Over time, one can distinguish between different historical systems belonging to one or the other category, as for instance, the European Concert as a period of a mitigated security dilemma. In space, it can also be applied to judge whether or not the security dilemma reigns in every part of the world; some subsystemic relations, as for instance in Western Europe, could be said to form a 'security community' (Deutsch *et al.* 1957).

These qualifications of the security dilemma through distinctions of different anarchical systems have a profound theoretical consequence. These distinctions show that anarchy does not create the same imperatives, and thus the same effects, in all international systems. The distribution of power is hence insufficient to qualify different international systems. While using another distinction, namely between enmity–amity, another realist, Arnold Wolfers, very early spelled out the theoretical consequences:

> One consequence of distinctions such as these is worth mentioning. They rob theory of the determinate and predictive character that seemed to give the pure power hypothesis its peculiar value. It can now no longer be said of the actual world, for example, that a power vacuum cannot exist for any length of time; a vacuum surrounded by 'satiated' or '*status quo*' states would remain as it is unless its existence were to change the character of these states and put them into the category of 'imperialist', 'unsatiated', or 'dynamic' states'.
>
> (Wolfers 1962: 86; for the same argument, see also Griffiths 1992: 61)

If this is true, there is no one single type of security policy, based on power, which would be the most rational in all cases. Wolfers distinguished between international systems according to a continuum from a pole of power to a pole of indifference. In the first case, power politics are needed. Attempts to treat an imperialist power like Nazi Germany as just another member of the international community will produce hopeless appeasement policies. At the pole of indifference, however, where no amount of opportunity for successful attack could induce a state to launch it, 'nothing could do more to undermine security . . . than to start accumulating power of a kind that would provoke fear and countermoves' (Wolfers 1962: 160). This is exactly the kind of argument used these days with regard to the possible Russian reaction against an eastward enlargement of NATO in Europe. Wolfers concluded, that 'after all that has been said, little is left of the sweeping generalization that in actual practice nations, guided by their national security interest, tend to pursue a uniform and therefore imitable policy of security' (Wolfers 1962: 156).

The qualification of anarchy: the 'anarchical society'

If anti-idealism is a defining criterion for being realist, the so-called English school of International Relations certainly qualifies. Yet, possibly the most representative author, Hedley Bull, argued that the very starting point of realism, namely the Hobbesian state of nature, is misleading.

After analysing Hobbes' account of the features characteristic for a state of nature, Bull rejected this analogy for the international system. He found that neither the non-existence of legal and moral rule, nor the absence of trade, industry (in the Hobbesian sense), navigation, nor, finally, the state of war portray the international realm convincingly (Bull 1966a).

The international order differs from Hobbesian anarchy for four reasons. First, the international realm is characterized by economic interdependence. Second, states are less vulnerable than individuals. Third, equal vulnerability of every person to every other makes anarchy intolerable. Therefore, for Hobbes, too great a discrepancy in power naturally moves anarchy to hierarchy. Yet the international system, although characterized by the permanence of great and small powers, does not become hierarchical. According to Bull, the differentials of power are supposed to have a cooperative and stabilizing impact on state behaviour.[3] Finally, states are materially more self-sufficient than individuals.

Bull defined the international realm instead as an 'international society', i.e. a venture among sovereign states to regulate conflict and cooperation without overarching government. War, far from being an expression of the dysfunction of the international society, is one of its institutions, as much as are the balance of power, great power politics, diplomacy, and international law (For a detailed account of these institutions, see Hedley Bull 1977: Chapters 6–10.). Neither reducible to domestic societies, nor to a total lack of governance, the international system should be understood as a society alone in its genre, best comparable to some primitive societies explored by anthropologists.

Bull refers to this special conception of an international society as the 'Grotian tradition', so named after the Dutch Hugo Grotius, a famous international lawyer of the seventeenth century. The English School of International Relations can be recognized both through its early attempt to divide International Relations theories not into two schools (realism and idealism), but three, and by being the defender of this very middle category, called the Grotian or rationalist tradition (Wight 1991).

Once Bull had defined the international society as a type of its own, where institutions and norms permanently exist, he clarified where these norms come from. Again, he strove for a middle position between Hobbesian realism and idealism. He distinguished between two versions of the Grotian tradition, a solidarist and a pluralist one. Their respective treatment of the issue of foreign intervention can clarify their central difference. The solidarist version, as represented by Grotius himself, still stands in the natural law tradition. This implies that in the name of solidarity with human beings, international law can overrule national sovereignty. Grotius justified intervention for the just cause (*ius ad bellum*). The pluralist version, defended by Oppenheim, another famous international lawyer, stands more in the legal positivist tradition which bases law on the actual agreement of the contracting parties (the states). Oppenheim was very cautious

---

[3] In this respect, Bull agrees with Kenneth Waltz who wrote that 'extreme equality is associated with instability' (Waltz 1969 [1967]: 312).

about normative justifications of war besides those generally accepted by the warring parties. He concentrated more on the means that were allowed in warfare (*ius in bello*). In opting for Oppenheim, Bull remained closer to the realist position:

> The view of pluralists is not to be dismissed as a mere rationalization of state practice; it is a conception of international society founded upon the observation of the actual area of agreement between states and informed by a sense of the limitations which in this situation rules may be usefully made rules of law . . . But it may still be held that the method [Oppenheim] employed of gauging the role of international society in relation to the actual area of agreement between states is superior to one which sets up the law over and against the facts.
>
> (Bull 1966b: 71–3)

Bull's compromise was the following. By presupposing a society, i.e. a larger area of agreement which is possible by the specific characteristics of the international realm, he included the idealist position of a substantial role of norms in international affairs. Yet by deriving them from the actual authorization of the states and their respective power, he fundamentally endorsed the power–materialist position of realism.

Hence, although anarchy remains undoubtedly a central feature of the realist approach, many classical realists contested the uniformity of the security dilemma, as well as its conspicuous explanatory weight assigned by more positivist realists. On the one hand, anarchy was differentiated so as to allow for periods of time and/or parts of the international system, that would not be ruled by the necessities of the security dilemma. On the other hand, the English School insisted that anarchy in the international system had to be interpreted as a particular form of political organization: it is an international society which does not correspond to a Hobbesian state of nature understood as a permanent state of war.

THE CLASSICAL REALIST CRITIQUE OF MECHANICAL AND OBJECTIVE REALISM

The traditionalist side in the second debate criticized the two models on which the scientific turn in International Relations relied, system theory and economic theory, and their attempt to make causal input–output analyses of state behaviour. The critique was mainly levelled against two concepts: the balance of power as the objective constraint (macro-level) and the national interest as the objective best rationale for foreign policy (micro-level).

Self-regulatory mechanisms: the balance of power

All realists agree on including the concept of the balance of power in their theories. The same cannot be said for the actual meaning of the concept. Morgenthau, for instance, gave four different meanings. For him, it could be understood as 'a policy aimed at a certain state of affairs; an actual state of affairs; an approximately equal distribution of power; any distribution of power' (Morgenthau 1960: 167, fn.1). As already mentioned, he also used it in a fifth meaning, described by Ernst Haas (1953) to be a universal law and by Inis L. Claude (1962: 27ff.) as balance of power 'as-a-system', a kind of self-regulatory mechanism.

These two critics find four general categories for the usage of balance of power. When referring to a situation, it is a descriptive category (see Morgenthau 2–4); when proposing a policy it is a prescriptive category. Used as a central theoretical concept, it is an analytical category, and since it mixes all these levels to suggest a link between description, analysis and prescription, it is an ideological category, a symbol and tool for political propaganda.

The following discussion will focus on the critique of the analytical and prescriptive categories in Morgenthau's approach, in particular since the balance of power was considered a universal law of realist International Relations, and hence a central piece in a more behaviourial theory. The starting point of the debate was Morgenthau's famous definition of the balance of power (Morgenthau 1947: 125):

> The aspiration for power on the part of several nations, each trying either to maintain or overthrow the *status quo*, leads of necessity to a constellation which is called the balance of power and to policies that aim at preserving it. We say 'of necessity' advisedly . . . It will be shown . . . that the international balance of power is only a particular manifestation of a general social principle to which all societies composed of a number of autonomous units owe the autonomy of their component parts.

The critics could not exactly pin down in which sense this balance of power was indeed 'of necessity'. Leaving aside the hollow sentence that 'any configuration of power distribution' was necessary, Morgenthau claimed to use the term in the meaning of equilibrium. This, according to Inis Claude, would be patently false. Even assuming that the balance of power worked as Morgenthau described, the British balance-of-power policy in the nineteenth century did not resemble it. This policy has been aptly described as 'balance for the continent and power for Britain' (Morgenthau 1947: 125). Britain's foreign policy served as an arbiter which could step in to stop a continental challenger by tipping the balance to the defender's side. Only when Germany perceived itself strong enough to equate or even overtake its opponents plus Britain, did the balancing policy fail. A stalemate situation with an arbiter interested in the *status quo* is a better description for this epoch than 'equilibrium'. Nor can balance of power mean a policy directed towards equilibrium. By the very assumptions of realism, since the struggle for power is not limited at any given point, every power seeks superiority, not equilibrium. Finally, balance of power is not 'of necessity' unique for the management of peace and war in the international system, because Morgenthau himself suggested other techniques, such as international law or diplomacy.

Therefore, in Claude's analysis, Morgenthau's balance of power is synonymous with power politics; or, as Claude put it, the balance of power is essentially a redundant concept in Morgenthau's theory (Claude 1962: 25–37. For a short restatement and actualization, see Claude 1989). For Morgenthau, the striving for power was a necessary act in the international system. The *raison d'état* required that the nation should be as strong as possible. But this was obviously only an iron law if in any case where one country was not as strong as its possible challengers, this power vacuum would inevitably be filled, or where any expansion of power would be inevitably matched. Yet, as realists like Wolfers argued, states fail to do what the balance of power would require, nor should they do it under circumstances of amity or legitimate order. Hence, since Morgenthau cannot prove any necessity for an equilibrium, all that the concept of the balance of power says, is that states, in their search for security, will accumulate power which, in turn, might be sometimes used for balancing each other. If there is no need for an equilibrium, all that is left is a description somewhat 'synonymous with the state-system itself' (Wight [1946] 1979: 179).

Consequently, the more classical realists, as well as Morgenthau in some passages of his textbook (see Chapter 2), understood the balance of power as a diplomatic practice. Here, the balance of power is one of the *institutions* of international society. It is a conscious and culturally circumscribed practice by the (initially European) society of statesmen, not a 'natural' mechanism from which one could deduce political analysis (Bull 1977: 111–12).

Objective laws and national interest

The critique of the balance of power targeted the homeostatic analogies of more scientific approaches to International Relations. But realists also criticized the analogy with the neoclassical market equilibrium. Here, the market and its equilibrium correspond to the balance of power and the striving for utility maximization corresponds to pursuing the national interest expressed in terms of power. In an anarchical context, without a central sanction mechanism, the impulse to survive pushes actors to maximize power at least as an intermediate goal, power that can be later converted into other final ends. Therefore, power becomes comparable to money in neoclassical theory. The aggregation of the individual striving for power results in an international competitive order which, as do market prices on individual economic actors, sets external constraints on national actions. The national interest represents utility maximization in this context: it corresponds to the Pareto optimum in neoclassical economics.

Raymond Aron explicitly attacked this economic analogy. First, he considered power as too ambiguous an end upon which to found an economic approach. If power is treated as the main foreign policy goal which allows the rationalist articulation of the theory, then the definition of power becomes crucial. Yet, Aron found three different definitions, none of which would be able to carry this explanatory weight. For him, neither 'power-as-resource', nor 'power-as-force' (actually mobilized resources), nor finally 'power-as-coercive capacity' could encompass or synthesize all foreign policy goals. Instead, Aron (1962: 28–9) developed a triad of foreign policy goals: power (puissance), security and glory/ideals. He emphasized that it was not possible to reduce foreign policy behaviour to one of the three. Moreover, there is no reason to assume that the quest for power or security were a behaviour which all diplomats should share. In view of the plurality of foreign policy goals, there is no single means–ends relationship, no single most rational foreign policy, no single national interest.

The second reason for which Aron denied the applicability of an economic approach to International Relations was its dependence upon power as a central explanatory concept. Power is not as fungible as money. The term fungibility refers to the idea of a movable good that can be freely replaced by another of the same class. Goods that are fungible are universally applicable or convertible in contrast to those that retain value only in a specific context.

This assumption, plausible for the role of money in monetarized market economies, does not fit the role of power in International Relations well. Here, a power resource which is decisive in one context might be inconvertible for influence in another context. An atomic threat might not necessarily be useful for inducing another state to sign a convention on environmental protection.

Aron recognized that economists cannot know exactly all the particular preferences of economic actors. Yet they are able to reduce the multitude of preferences to one utility function. They can do so because of the existence of money as a general standard of value and medium of exchange. Such a standard does not exist in politics: it is a qualitative, not quantitative difference. For Aron, the empirical differences between money and power made it impossible to model political science explanations by substituting utility for national interest or security and money for power. For Aron, the invention of money revolutionized the real world economy and allowed economists to model marginal economics. Only because there is a market economy based on money can neoclassical economic theory be used. There is nothing within real world politics which can take the place of money (Aron 1962: 98).

From this critical analysis, Aron derived two conclusions. First, he criticized Kaplan's approach of system modelling. Since power was no unequivocal foreign policy goal, it could not stand for the basic drive to survive. Similarly, the distribution of power cannot suggest one single pattern of state behaviour. Hence, neither of the two conditions of the distribution of power and the individual drive for survival are sufficient to elaborate a model for the functioning and evolution of the international system (Aron 1962: 140, 154). Second, therefore, theorization in International Relations is limited to a framework of analysis that justifies the focus and selection of certain variables considered to be significant and to the understanding of particular historical constellations of world politics (Aron 1962: 140). For Aron, there can be no theory of International Relations which can be modelled in analogy to neoclassical economics (Aron 1962: 102).

CONCLUSION: METHODOLOGICALLY DIVIDED REALISM

The debate about the scientific status of realism affected the meaning of its central explanatory concepts. Not human nature, as for Morgenthau, but the security dilemma explained the origins of conflict (and war). With this focus on international system as the main cause of war and main field of study, scholars scrutinized the exact nature of the systemic level. Here, anarchy was as much an answer as a restatement of the problem. Many classical realists attempted to differentiate different types of international anarchies, or, as the English School proposed, to replace the concept of anarchy by international society for its particular societal features. Finally, many realists did not agree with the attempt to remodel core concepts in order to suit the needs of applying economic or system theory. Neither power, nor national interest, nor the balance of power were deemed able to carry this explanatory weight.

But one should not infer from this conclusion that traditionalism won the second debate. Although realism was not easily converted into a scientific theory, the status of traditional diplomatic maxims was no longer self-evident. Realism became divided into three main camps consisting of: those who pursued the behavioralist programme without much change, although increasingly resorting to economic utilitarian theory. They were opposed by the traditionalists, best represented by the English School of International Relations, where International Relations is studied as the history of the international society and its expansion, through an analysis of its norms. Finally, there was the middle road of historical sociology (Meyers 1984), a school which seeks to avoid both empiricist diplomatic history and scientific theory, but is instead inspired by normative theory and Weberian sociology. This school is represented by the writings of Raymond Aron, and Stanley Hoffmann (1965), but also to some extent by Richard Rosecrance (1977 [1963]), who made an attempt to combine the language of system theory with a historical sociological analysis.

4 Realism and the US policy of containment

The following chapters will explore how realist thought developed in parallel with US foreign policy formulations. The policy concept of containment is the main subject of this chapter. The concept is commonly used in two different ways. Generally, containment designates the official US foreign policy approach in the Cold War, from 1947 to its end. But it is also used as a particular foreign policy principle which was part of every US East–West policy during the Cold War.

These two aspects will be covered in four steps. First, the historiographical debate around the Origins of the Cold War provides the context for analysing the origination of containment, that is, how the understanding of the post-war era, guided by at least some realist concepts, influenced US foreign policy formulation. Second, the theoretical analysis of the content of containment will mainly refer to its spiritual father, the realist George F. Kennan. Third, some salient cases, including the Marshall Plan, the Truman Doctrine and the Vietnam War, will be examined to illustrate the ambivalent application of containment. Finally, the chapter touches on the reformulation of containment during détente, which will be analysed in detail in Chapter 7.

THE ORIGINS OF CONTAINMENT: THE RIGA AXIOMS PREVAIL

In the 1940s, two strategic conceptions fought each other in the Roosevelt and Truman Administrations. Daniel Yergin called them the Yalta axioms and the Riga axioms, in a way much reminiscent of the realist–idealist opposition (Yergin 1978). It was only between 1944 and 1947 that eventually the latter prevailed.

The Yalta axioms and the Riga axioms

President Roosevelt is often presented as a modern version of Woodrow Wilson. During the Second World War, his foreign policy was fiercely opposed both by traditional isolationists or by those who wanted a tougher stance against the Soviet Union. Roosevelt gained a distinct reputation for having a penchant for idealism. According to John Lewis Gaddis (1982), the story, however, is less clear cut.

Roosevelt's general conception of world politics was as anti-isolationist as Wilson's. For him, any possible hegemony on either its transatlantic or transpacific front (i.e. Germany and/or Japan) was a security threat to the US which foreign policy had to prevent, if necessary by war. Moreover, he was convinced that the non-entanglement policy after 1918 (with the US not joining the League of Nations), and the attempted disengagement from World affairs (with the notable exception of the financial sphere) constituted major reasons for the failure of the collective security system.

Roosevelt's perception of the USSR was largely pragmatic. Although he was explicit about his disdain for the Soviet dictatorship, he did not believe that the Soviet Union should be treated as an outsider to the international system. Since the Soviet Union was the largest power in Europe, no functioning international system could exist without it. This, in fact, was a central tenet of realist diplomacy. Were states unable to find ways to make their claims heard (Carr 1946), they would be forced to take means which are not necessarily peaceful. Similarly, Kissinger (1957) had been criticizing international orders which were based on isolating particular states. Again, this could push these states to question not just the *status quo*, but the very rules of the game. In such a situation, diplomacy could no longer function.

Moreover, Roosevelt did not hold that the ideology of the Soviet Union made it automatically expansionist and hostile. Totalitarian regimes could very well be pragmatic and defensive in foreign affairs. It seems as if he interpreted hostile Soviet foreign policies as a reaction to allied anti-Soviet acts since 1917. There were many of these: first, the allied military intervention into the Russian Civil War at the end of the First World War, meant to reverse the communist revolution; second, the installation of a *cordon sanitaire* (buffer zone) in central Europe; third the Western policy of diplomatically isolating Soviet diplomacy in the 1930s; and fourth the long refusal of France and Great Britain to accept an alliance with the Soviets against Hitler; and finally fifth the conference in Munich which, with the Soviets excluded, allowed Hitler to draw nearer to the Soviet border.

To overcome the legacy of Western policy directed against the Soviet Union, and later also impressed by the Soviet war effort, US foreign policy had (for Roosevelt) to demonstrate its goodwill and its acceptance of the international weight of the USSR. In other words, the Soviet Union should be treated as a traditional great power, less directed by ideological aims than by pragmatic considerations of national interest. One 'could do business' with it. Roosevelt wanted to offer the Soviet Union participation in the new international order and to recognize its spheres of influence such as to 'build confidence', to use a recent expression, in exchange for Soviet moderation. This vision was opposed by those who subscribed to what Daniel Yergin named the Riga axioms, so called for the Soviet Service installed in Riga in the twenties when the US had not yet officially recognized the USSR. In Riga, which after the Bolshevik Revolution had turned into a minor St Petersburg, a small group of Kremlinologists attached to the US Embassy was responsible for gathering and analysing information from the USSR. The most prominent figures were Loy Henderson, Charles Bohlen, and George F. Kennan.

Their perception of the actual Soviet policy was quite different from Roosevelt's as described above. First, they felt that the totalitarian character of the Soviet regime was reflected also in foreign affairs; the USSR was expansionist and profoundly anti-democratic. Second, the ideology, far from being only a propagandistic mock-up for traditional power-politics, was the coherent reference of Soviet foreign policy. Third, Soviet diplomacy is only a subordinated means for this end. The Riga group was emphatically against making pragmatic bargains with such a state. Politics built upon long-term confidence or trust relations were illusory. Traditional diplomatic manoeuvres were useless, if not dangerous.

Riga axioms prevail: the three phases

The climax of Roosevelt's diplomacy was Yalta. During this conference, Roosevelt got the Soviet Union to accept the United Nations (with a veto right in the Security Council), to join the allied war against Japan, and to sign the Declaration of Free Europe, with an implicit recognition of spheres of influence.

But the ambiguities of Roosevelt's policy quickly surfaced. Since he tried to avoid the fate of Wilson's policy, he carefully mobilized a domestic consensus behind US intervention abroad. In doing so, he had to use moralistic themes appealing to the US public. The Atlantic Charter envisaged one world without spheres of influence and without blocs and alliances; an open-door policy would universally open markets. The US population rallied behind foreign intervention, 'to make the *world* (nothing less) safe for democracy', as Kennan (1967: 323) sarcastically noted in his memoirs. This created a contradiction between a domestic (idealist) and a foreign (more pragmatic) foreign policy (Loth 1983: 32; Yergin 1978: 57, 68). Roosevelt died on 12 April 1945 before he could in some way resolve this ambiguity.

The hopeful atmosphere of Yalta was quickly followed by a disappointment on both sides. Roosevelt had raised expectations at home which were flatly contradicted by Soviet behaviour in Poland. The Polish compromise of Yalta could not be realized: the Polish government could either be (roughly) freely elected or friendly to the USSR, but not both. The Soviet government made the latter option prevail. On the other side, the Soviets were concerned about the endless delays of the Western allies in opening a second front against Germany:

From the Marxist viewpoint, the Allies were doing exactly what they should be doing – namely postponing the second front until the Soviet Union and Germany had exhausted each other. Then the two Western powers could land in France, march bloodlessly into Germany, and dictate the peace to both, Germany and Russia . . . destroy both their two major ideological opponents at one and the same time.

(Spanier 1980: 16ff; this could, in fact, also be a realist viewpoint)

In 1945, seemingly adding insult to injury, the Truman administration abruptly cut the Lend-Lease agreement with the UK and the USSR, which latter had always considered it as financial compensation for the Soviet manpower within the allied war efforts. Whereas Kennan (1967: 266–70) defended this cut, recent interpretations have tended to see it as a diplomatic mistake (Herring 1973). This loan was a potential economic carrot; instead of unilaterally cutting it, its renegotiation after the war could have been used to influence Soviet behaviour. This cut happened exactly when the credits were most wanted, when the war was over and the Soviet Union urgently needed money to reconstruct its country on whose territory much of the war was waged. Given this timing of the move and the lack of prior consultation, the Soviet government must have perceived it as aggressive.

Even if Truman had not been a newcomer in international matters, it would have been difficult to slide smoothly into Roosevelt's very personalized foreign policy. Taking Roosevelt's declarations literally, he could not but feel disappointed and even cheated by Soviet behaviour. The Riga axioms, increasingly defended by members of the State Department, gained influence in the whole administration. Only two persons still believed in Roosevelt's foreign policy: Byrnes, the Secretary of State, and Hopkins, personal adviser to Roosevelt and now to Truman. Byrnes was forced to give up searching for a compromise during the first Foreign Minister Conference in London (11 September to 2 October 1945) to avoid being labelled a politician of appeasement. After having completed a journey to Moscow, Hopkins died in January 1946.

At this point, one could speak of a second phase of the introduction of containment policy: the uniformization of the perception of the Soviet Union (February 1946–February 1947). In February 1946, the State Department made an innocuous request to the US Embassy in Moscow to analyse Soviet intentions. This came after a rather aggressive statement by Stalin on 9 February and the Soviet decision not to join the IMF/World Bank. The answer was the famous long telegram (8,000 words!) by George F. Kennan from 22 February. Kennan deemed the Soviet Union, no differently from its predecessor Russia, to be an expansionist power. He argued that communist ideology was only a fig leaf for traditional Russian expansionism, though he did caution that it played a major rule in the domestic legitimacy of the Soviet rulers. Kennan filled the conceptual void in the US administration: he likened Soviet policies neither to a traditional great power behaviour (as had Roosevelt), nor to a new kind of totalitarian foreign policy, but to the imperialist tradition of the Tsars, in which the communist ideology was used for legitimating and tactical purposes. At the same time, as Leffler (1992: 108–9, 191) notes, Kennan tipped the balance to view the USSR as an enemy, and not just as an unreliable ally. This allowed the transfer of images, symbols, but also policy options, from the former enemies – in particular Nazi Germany – to the USSR.

In the eyes of the US administration, the events supported Kennan's views when the Soviet government intervened into the crisis in Iran (February–March 1946) and when in August 1946, Stalin asked for a change of the Montreux Treaty regulating the access to the Dardanelles. The Soviet Union appeared overtly expansionist. Moreover, the Republicans' victory to the Congress stiffened domestic pressure for a policy change.

The new policy, formulated in the third phase, was containment. On 21 February 1947, the United Kingdom told the US administration that for lack of resources, they would have to end military assistance to Greece and Turkey and pull out British troops. Great Britain declared its retreat from being a superpower and the US was left to take its place in the eastern Mediterranean. This it did. The Greek resistance was seen as a new wave of communist expansionism, even though historians of the Cold War now agree that Stalin did not in fact encourage them (Loth 1983; Yergin 1978: 288ff.; Gaddis 1972: 355). Afraid of the effects the fall of Greece and Turkey could have for free Europe (another example of a domino theory), the Truman Administration committed itself to protect anti-communist regimes in the international struggle between the free world and totalitarian communism. In his famous speech of 12 March 1947, Truman set up a guarantee for all anti-communist forces. The Truman Doctrine signalled US assumption of its superpower role toe-to-toe against the Soviet Union (or world communism) in a subsequently bipolar world.

In July 1947, under the pseudonym of Mr X, George Kennan published an article in *Foreign Affairs* entitled 'The Sources of Soviet Conduct'. It quickly became the analytical underpinning to a new policy against the Soviet Union, based on the long telegram's proposed perception of the USSR and applied with the Truman Doctrine. In a passage later to become central for the strategy of containment, Kennan wrote:

In these circumstances, it is clear that the main element of any US policy toward the Soviet Union must be that of a long term, patient but firm and vigilant containment of Russian expansive tendencies . . . a policy of firm containment, designed to confront the Russians with unalterable counterforce at every point where they show signs of encroaching upon the interests of a peaceful and stable world.

(Kennan 1951: 119)

CONTAINMENT: THE POLITICAL CONCEPTION OF
G. F. KENNAN

George F. Kennan based his conception on a specific analysis of Soviet foreign policy, on its traditions, its ideology, its ends, and means. He proposed a policy which would contain Soviet expansionism such as to induce change at home (see Gaddis 1982: 25–53 for concepts underpinning the following section).

The analysis of Soviet foreign policy

Kennan looked back in time to find a more geopolitical logic to understand Soviet foreign policy behaviour. For him, Russia has always been a country of open lands exposed to multiple invasions by hostile neighbours. This has created a collective memory within the Russian – later Soviet – psyche of a traditionally inimical foreign world, and an instinctive feeling of acute insecurity.

Kennan considered the Soviet ideology of lesser importance for the explanation of actual foreign Soviet behaviour. Though he noted that Marxist/Leninist dogma served as a force of legitimation for the political system and for its expansion within the country, he did not assume that the ideology profoundly guided Soviet foreign policy. The USSR was above all pragmatic: ideology could be and was adapted to strategic and political needs. In a certain sense, the ideology depended on Soviet policy aims – and not vice versa. 'This means that truth is not a constant, but is actually created for all intents and purposes, by the Soviet leaders themselves. It may vary from week to week, from month to month' (Kennan 1951: 117). Kennan mentioned a task given in a Russian language course at the Soviet group in Riga, where participants were asked to draft a newspaper article in which the introduction of capitalism in the Soviet Union would be presented as a tremendous triumph of socialism (Kennan, quoted in Yergin 1978: 20).

With regard to the means employed by Soviet foreign policy, Kennan noted that the Soviets simultaneously used official and unofficial levels of international political action (Komintern, Kominform). All methods that improved the relative correlation of forces were to be used. In the domestic sphere, this meant increasing the strength of the Soviet Union, whether militarily or industrially. The external borders of the USSR were to be expanded whenever necessary. In addition, every opportunity to weaken the enemy was to be taken, whether by exacerbating the domestic and intra-capitalist struggles, or by helping all progressive (i.e. anti-imperialist) forces.

Also, Soviet foreign policy aims reflected only the tactical rather than the fundamental place of ideology. The main aim was, according to Kennan, indeed expansionism. Yet, this expansionism was considered in the Tsarist imperialist tradition and to be understood as the attempt to create security zones and spheres of influence politically dependent on the USSR. Military

expansion was no end in itself, but at best a means to this political hegemony. Briefly, the aim of Soviet policy, as Kennan saw it, was a political
hegemony rather than outright conquest, let alone a Soviet-led world
socialist revolution.[1] Territorial annexations are considered generally costly
and less controllable. For Kennan, the Soviet leaders were basically flexible
in their reaction to political realities:

> [the Kremlin's] political action is a fluid stream which moves constantly,
> wherever it is permitted to move . . . toward a given goal . . . [but] there is
> no trace of any feeling that the goal must be reached at any given time . . .
> [The Soviet diplomacy] is more sensitive to contrary force, more ready to
> yield on individual sectors of the diplomatic front when that force is felt
> to be too strong, and thus more rational in the logic and rhetoric of power.
> (Kennan 1951: 118–19)

Here, Kennan gave a realist account of what appears to him as a largely
realist policy. Soviet foreign policy is perceived as a form of power politics,
flexible, patient and pragmatic with untouchable spheres of influence. Such
a policy did not follow any ethical considerations, nor recognize international law, at least in the Western sense. Rather, Kennan argued, Soviet
politicians decide only in due analysis of its interest and the actual 'correlation of forces', used in its Soviet sense (see Chapter 6).

The US response: stasis for change

Once the US had a coherent explanation of Soviet behaviour, it could devise
its own coherent security policy. Kennan elaborated on two basic building
blocks of US foreign policy with the Soviet Union during the Cold War:
containment and change.

The policy of containment is the first and necessary ingredient of any US
foreign policy towards the USSR. Its exact status stems from the peculiar
role the US played in the post-war system. On the one hand, only the US
was able to oppose a possible Soviet expansion. On the other hand, its
resources were not unlimited. As a result, Kennan proposed a limited or
particularistic approach, where only five regions of the globe were judged
of vital interest for US national security: the US, Great Britain, Germany,
Japan, the USSR. The USSR should remain isolated; its reach should not
extend to the other regions. Furthermore, since the USSR was expansionist
for traditional imperialist motives and not for its socialist ideology, and
since the national security policy is defined in terms of the balance of
power, the US policy should be anti-Soviet and not anti-communist (For
a different position which stresses the universalist and military aspects of
Kennan's approach, see Wright 1976). Finally:

[1] This assessment of Soviet aims is corroborated by the massive demobilization of Soviet army
manpower after the end of the war which left just enough to deal with the subjugation of the
Eastern European satellites. See Ulam 1968: 403–4.

it is a *sine qua non* of successful dealing with Russia that the foreign government in question should remain at all times cool and collected and that its demands on Russian policy should be put forward in such a manner as to leave the way open for a compliance not too detrimental to Russian prestige.

(Kennan 1951: 119)

Keeping these conditions of a successful US foreign policy in mind, the actual policy should be conceived in three stages, applying first pressure from outside in order to eventually induce change from within (Gaddis 1978).

The first priority was to reestablish the confidence of those countries directly threatened by Soviet (political) expansionism. This could be done by financially and economically strengthening potential allies. In addition, the US could help to insulate these countries from Soviet influence by exploiting intra-socialist splits and anti-Soviet nationalism.

In the second stage the US should help to create a stable and multipolar balance of power. It would need allies for the long struggle:

It is clearly unwise for us to continue the attempt to carry alone or largely singlehanded, the opposition to Soviet expansion. It is urgently necessary for us to restore something of the balance of power in Europe and Asia by strengthening local forces of independence and by getting them to assume part of our burden . . . the present 'bi-polarity' will, in the long run, be beyond our resources.[2]

In the third stage of policy implementation, containment should help to bring about a long-term change in Soviet perceptions of International Relations. Containment was fundamentally a means to this ultimate end:

The US has in its power to increase enormously the strains under which Soviet policy must operate, to force upon the Kremlin a far greater degree of moderation and circumscription than it has had to observe in recent years, and in this way to promote tendencies which must eventually find their outlet in either the breakup or the gradual mellowing of Soviet power. For no mystical, Messianic movement . . . can face frustration indefinitely without eventually adjusting itself in one way or another to the logic of that state of affairs.

(Kennan 1951: 127–8)

From early on, Kennan based his policy on the hope that internal reform would overcome dictatorship and expansion (Kennan 1951: 136–43). Indeed, in later writings, when the external front was fixed, he insisted that the real competition between the two systems should be fought on the domestic front. The victory in the Cold War depended not on what both systems

---

[2] George F. Kennan, in PPS 13, 'Résumé of World Situation', Nov. 6, 1947, FRUS 1947, I, pp. 772–7 as quoted in John Lewis Gaddis, 'The Strategy of Containment'.

could realize with their fancy weapons in space, but on their respective capacity to resolve their domestic problems and to realize the respective ideals. Asked where the US should oppose the Russian danger, he stated that it should start with those problems it did not yet solve and was ashamed of, such as, for example, the race issue, the misery in US cities, general and political education (Kennan 1958).

Yet as an approach that attempted to both confront and reform an opposing system, containment would often have trouble keeping on a steady course. Sometimes containment policies were used to increase outside pressure on the Soviet society with the goal of forcing a collapse. For the fact of mutual nuclear deterrence, this more typical Cold War posture avoided open military conflict. But it pursued competition on all other levels, as, for instance, in the arms race, and competition for welfare state systems. At other times, containment was simply a form of détente policy based on the hope that the Soviet government would eventually adapt to a non-expansionist policy. This posture did not entail a relaxation of vigilance, but it relied on a long-term learning process. In the long years of the Cold War, containment as a long-term strategy has oscillated between these two poles. It comes as no surprise in the post-Cold War period, that the historical debate centres around whether the USSR collapsed from external or internal pressure.

THE APPLICATION OF CONTAINMENT

The first measures: the Marshall Plan and the Truman Doctrine

The direct outcome of Kennan's approach was the Marshall Plan. On 5 May 1947, a special policy planning committee within the State Department was set up and ordered to elaborate a financial and economic aid programme for Europe. The director of this committee was Kennan himself. His aim was to diminish the impact of the post-war economic distress which made Europe appear vulnerable to side with the Soviet pole. In order to avoid the individual handling of individual countries' requests, European receiver countries were united in the Organisation for European Economic Cooperation (OEEC, later OECD) which divided the money before it was distributed. Hence, by tying aid to a political collaboration Kennan attempted to start a coordination process among European countries. This move was also consistent with Kennan's strategy to develop a possible burden sharing in the future multipolar balance of power in Europe. In other words, in response to a political – rather than military – Soviet threat, the Marshall Plan attempted to use aid to restore economies and bolstering self-confidence.

Quite differently conceived than the Marshall Plan, was the Truman Doctrine from March 1947, a kind of Western declaration of the Cold War. The US President proclaimed, 'I believe it must be the policy of the US to support free peoples who are resisting attempted subjugation by armed minorities and by outside pressures'. Rather than follow the lines of a geopolitical struggle against the Soviet Union, Truman asserted a broader ideological struggle against communism.

Kennan (1967: 320 ff.) describes his consternation when he heard about Truman's speech. Although a speech of strength, it shared with Wilson's idealist approach a universalist character by offering a blank cheque to every possible movement in the World that claimed to be anti-communist. He further criticized the anti-communist and not anti-Soviet outlook of the policy, and the military aspect of the doctrine against what was primarily a political threat. Therefore, the Truman Doctrine and the policy labelled containment made out of the first means of US national security policy, containment, its only aim. The doctrine lacked Kennan's criterion for winning the struggle: bringing about a change in the Soviet approach to foreign policy. Moreover, by alluding to the anti-communist character, it strongly supported the Manichean character of US foreign policy; in other words, the struggle between good and evil, so characteristic of the different strategies of roll-back or liberation that emerged in the first term of the Eisenhower Administration. As with the military outlook of the Truman Doctrine, Kennan always opposed NATO which he saw as the wrong answer to the threats in Europe. He felt that the only assured effect of the Alliance was the rigidification of the division of Europe.

Kennan's own approach is, however, not without internal tensions. He himself admitted that his 1947 article could be interpreted in a militarist and universalist way (Kennan 1967: 359). There he wrote, to repeat the quote, that containment is 'designed to confront the Russians with unalterable counter-force at every point where they show signs of encroaching upon the interests of a peaceful and stable world'.

The problem is not purely stylistic, however: it is also conceptual. As this quote illustrates, it was not far-fetched to presuppose containment as resulting in a strategy which left the political initiative to the USSR and committed the US, be it for the psychology of power Kennan constantly emphasized, to become the fire-fighter countering revolutionary bushfires around the world. Moreover, in a new world of bipolarity, it was much more difficult to stay calm when power shifted, or was perceived to shift: every Soviet gain could be interpreted as a Western loss.

Kennan wanted to build up a multipolar system for greater sharing and more flexibility. The problem was that containment had to work until such a situation could be realized. Wherever dominos fell, the US perceived itself alone in countering them. As the Berlin crisis and Korean War were soon to demonstrate, Kennan's approach to containment could not easily discriminate between vital and less vital interests. For practical purposes, defending against the worst case scenario in any given situation entailed involvement in every given situation. The result was a fairly universalistic policy. In fact, Kennan was in favour of military deployment in Greece. He was afraid of the domino-effect of decolonizing Indonesia in Southeast

Asia. He warned of a possible bandwagon-effect in Europe, i.e. European countries joining in the wake of the major European power (USSR), if communist parties were allowed to stay in power. Therefore, he favoured both overt and covert action in France and Italy (Leffler 1992: 195–6, 206, 214, 260, 503). Indeed, he helped to reverse the US policy towards Franco's Spain. Whereas the US administration had been calling for the Spanish people to overthrow Franco, in late 1947 Kennan urged, for security reasons, to reconsider this policy (LaFeber 1993: 65).

Finally, having repeatedly insisted on the uselessness of diplomacy with the Soviet Union, Kennan did nothing to prevent the 'we-do-not-negotiate' mentality of several US administrations. There is some justification in US Secretary of State Dean Acheson's failure to understand why Kennan so vehemently opposed NATO; it seemed to him congenial to Kennan's containment concept. Leffler (1992: 144, 180–1) insists that both the administration and Kennan had the same analysis of a political threat of the USSR. The administration thought, and Kennan sometimes as well, that this needed to be countered by means which could not exclude military ones.

Vietnam – the final collapse of containment?[3]

The US involvement in Vietnam, which Kennan opposed from the beginning, can be seen as the final collapse of the militarized or Cold War version of containment. But before coming to the political (or even conceptual) and military failures, some fundamental characteristics of US foreign policy from 1947–68 should be briefly covered.

The starting point in discussing US foreign policy during the Cold War is the perception of a basic bipolarity of the international system. As mentioned, bipolarity invites thinking in terms of a zero-sum game. By seeing the world in terms of a two-way contest between liberty and totalitarianism, Truman and his successors made the US the world policemen in defence of freedom everywhere (including when that meant helping US-friendly authoritarian regimes). Assuming the leadership of the anti-totalitarian front, the US was held responsible for managing the border between the two blocs. In policy terms this meant global deterrence, the building up of military pacts around the Soviet hemisphere, as with the pactomania of Secretary of State John Foster Dulles. Eventually, every conflict at the borders between the two blocs, borders that could cross within countries, assumed the status of a frontier war.

The US was trapped in its own logic. After extending guarantees globally, the US felt it needed to honour all of its commitments if it was to maintain credible deterrence. The failure to honour a commitment in one area might be seen by the rival as an indication that another commitment might not be honoured and induce him to test US determination. Each new

[3] John Spanier, *American Foreign Policy*, p. 140.

commitments, whether eagerly sought or reluctantly accepted, became a matter from which it is perceived virtually impossible to withdraw without dangerous consequences. The fall of one frontier could be the beginning of the fall of a whole region (the domino theory). Furthermore, the US could not allow too visible a compromise or defeat, because the perception of power and its credibility, is as important in peace as in war. So, in order to control the psychological factor of power, repeatedly stressed also by Kennan, the US found itself maintaining a universal obligation to maintain the *status quo* (for more details about Kennan's position on the Vietnam War, see Smith 1986: 185–8).

Three conceptual (and political) failures can account for the US disaster in Vietnam, where the giant lost to the little man. First, the idea that the defence of South East Asia was crucial to the maintenance of world order was flawed. It was linked to the inability to make a distinction between vital and peripheral interests. US credibility was actually more shaken by the shape that the actual commitment in Vietnam took: Vietnam was not important enough to engage early with massive forces, and later, after a piecemeal build-up, it became too important to disengage once committed. Second, the US problems in Vietnam were compounded by the *status quo* approach to containment. A policy of stability which identifies instability and communism is eventually obliged, by the very logic of this interpretation, to contain in the name of anti-communism all manifestation of popular dissatisfaction and all reformism. So, supporting dictatorship becomes a last possible solution of a policy that wants freedom, but is based on stability. Finally, the US administration acted sometimes as if unaware of the limits even of vast US resources. In Vietnam, the succeeding administrations had problems to bring means and ends in a calibrated relationship and were consequently criticized, including by realists. Also, the drain of US resources into the Vietnam conflict finally undermined the legitimacy of the domestic social contract, initially strengthened through President Johnson's design of a 'great society'.

Although not necessarily linked to the conceptual mistakes, and thus to the relationship with realist theories of International Relations, for the sake of a more complete presentation, it is worth briefly examining the flaws of US military policy in Vietnam. Broadly speaking, these stemmed from the doctrine of flexible response, introduced under the Kennedy–Johnson administrations for handling the strategic relations between nuclear superpowers, but ill-adapted to fighting a guerrilla war. Flexible response was conceived as a doctrine of calibration. In Vietnam, this meant first retraining Saigon's military and security forces in counter-guerrilla warfare; and second, broadening the public support of the South Vietnamese government in its struggle against communism. This was to be done with an economic and political reform programme. In addition, US administrations attempted, by mounting ever-increasing military pressure, mostly in the form of bombing campaigns, to convince North Vietnam that it was in its own interest to cease aiding the Vietcong.

But this policy was limited by a whole set of restraints. Action was to be strong enough to prevent further deterioration of the situation, but not so violent that it would knit the North Vietnamese people closer together, nor so threatening that it would provoke Chinese intervention (as had happened in Korea), nor so brutal that it would arouse world public opinion, nor so embittering that it would preclude opportunities for an eventual negotiated settlement.

A policy so constrained could easily fail. It did so, because the initiative passed to the other side. To proclaim that one intends to do only what is necessary to counter aggression and nothing more is, after all, to yield initiative to the aggressor. This policy did not secure South Vietnam, but somehow 'vaccinated' North Vietnam. It misunderstood the nature of guerrilla warfare. Guerrillas win wars by capturing the power of the government from within, eroding the morale of the army and undermining popular confidence in the government. They typically use hit-and-run tactics, engaging only smaller and weaker governmental forces that they can defeat. In Mao's words, 'fight if you can win, march if you can't'. By presenting themselves as liberators from colonialism or foreign rule, by decrying the despotic local government, and by being seen as the enemies of social injustice and economic deprivation, guerrillas gain the support of the peasantry. The proclaimed US strategy of bolstering domestic support for the Saigon regime notwithstanding, US counter-guerrilla tactics concentrated on military efforts at the expense of winning the psychological struggle. A force whose operational doctrine was to search and destroy was unlikely to win hearts and minds.

In a nutshell, Vietnam was a failure of a foreign policy of the *status quo*, a policy of the world policeman which turned out to be, as Kennan had warned, 'in the long run, beyond our resources'.

CONCLUSION: DÉTENTE AS A CONSEQUENCE OF THE VIETNAM WAR

The Vietnam War, which represented the defeat of the more Cold War version of containment, was certainly not the only factor that caused the US to pursue a détente policy. The roots of this shift predated the debacle. Yet Vietnam affected US policy-making in many important ways.

On the strategic level, the Nixon Administration redrew the distinction between vital and peripheral interests in order to avoid being dragged into all frontier challenges. As the victory of the guerrilla tactics implied the potential for successful application elsewhere, the US started to pick its fights more selectively. The new US policy was less concerned with preventing every potential communist gain everywhere. It opened up to a broader vision of world politics, looking beyond the zero-sum game with the Soviet Union, and adopting flexibility as a watchword.

The effects on Vietnam on US foreign policy were not only reflected in the group of high-level policy-makers considering where they had gone wrong – on the domestic political level, the post-War bipartisan consensus in international affairs all but evaporated. This in itself brought a new set of constraints. The US Congress made a concerted attempt to curb presidential power in foreign affairs (as, for instance, in the War Power Act). Richard Nixon, well aware of his difficult mandate in foreign policy long before Watergate, was very conscious of domestic sensitivities. The Carter Administration was not even able to recreate the consensus within its own ranks, combining such different political personalities as Cyrus Vance (Secretary of State) and the hardened National Security Advisor Zbigniev Brzezinski.

The US was seen more and more by international opinion as an imperialist and anti-reformist power. The Soviet Union tried to exploit this situation, accelerating the arms race, launching a diplomatic offensive in the Third World, and for instance wooing India. The US response, in turn, was to attempt to reestablish a certain legitimacy, as for instance with President Carter's Human Rights Policy.

The new détente approach of the US, spurred if not caused by the failure in Vietnam, did not actually stray from the core concepts of containment, as envisaged by Kennan. The new policy of President Nixon and Henry Kissinger (first National Security Advisor and later Secretary of State), was simply a reversion to the less military mode of containment, and came close to Kennan's initial ideas in several respects (Gaddis 1982). It implied a greater awareness of the limited means of US global policy. Rather than committing itself to provide direct conventional military support to every regime threatened by communist aggression, the Nixon or Guam Doctrine (so named for the location of his speech in July 1969) attempted to regionalize conflicts, and to limit direct US involvement:

> First, the United States will keep all of its treaty commitments. Second, we shall provide a shield if nuclear power threatens the freedom of a nation allied with us or of a nation whose survival we consider vital to our security. Third, in cases involving other types of aggression, we shall furnish military or economic assistance when requested in accordance with our treaty commitments. But we shall look to the nation directly threatened to assume the primary responsibility of providing the manpower for its defense.
>
> (Nixon, quoted in Gaddis 1982: 298)

Aside from its more measured approach to US commitments, détente involved a more flexible diplomacy, attempting to transcend the costly zero-sum struggle with the 'united' communist bloc in favour of a more manageable multipolar system. By distinguishing a particular Soviet threat as at least partially distinct from an overall communist threat, the

US would be able to play the USSR and China off against each other. In other words, it became possible to deal with the communists against the communists. As we will see in Chapter 7, Kissinger's policy, however, was not free of the ambiguities of Kennan's containment project.

5   The turning point of the Cuban missile crisis: crisis management and the expanding research agenda

With hindsight, the Cuban missile crisis can be seen as representing a turning point both for East–West relations and for the realist definition of the discipline of International Relations. The crisis was perceived by both superpowers as the climax of the Cold War. Before the crisis, the spirit of Cold War policies had reversed the famous Clausewitzian formula: that the conduct of politics in peacetime is the continuation of war by other means. Containment had turned from a means of foreign policy into an end. Strategic thought often stopped short at the different military scenarios possible in the age of nuclear war. When superpower competition was resolutely conflictual, and where war was not possible, the international crisis became an endemic feature of world politics, and crisis brinkmanship a possible bargaining strategy.[1] The nuclear risk during the Cuban missile crisis reminded the two superpowers of the original Clausewitzian formula which urged statesmen to consider the long-term political aims to which military means are subordinated. In the nuclear age, war is a pathological state of affairs; the permanent risk of escalating crises is the common enemy. Statesmen were given another chance to find out the political imperatives of their strategic doctrines.[2]

Graham T. Allison's in-depth analysis of the Cuban missile crisis (Allison 1971) ended up redefining the research agenda of International Relations; it also represented a turning point in the discipline of International Relations. His book epitomized the interplay between US foreign policy, the evolution of realist thought, and the criteria of the academic discipline of International Relations. Facing a potential nuclear disaster, crisis management was first and foremost a political imperative not just an item for research. Allison's study aimed not only at understanding how statesmanship once gambled

---

[1] There is a vast literature on crisis (management) analysis. As a general introduction to the literature, see Williams (1976). For a recent text of one of its main scholars, see Michael Brecher (1993).

[2] For a realist critique of the tendency in the deterrence literature to reverse Clausewitz's formula, see Raymond Aron (1976).

with, yet ultimately avoided disaster, but also how to diminish the risk that such an event recur. Far from being a dangerous intrusion into normative concerns, Allison's goal was not only normatively legitimate, indeed required, but also scientifically acceptable. Cognitive interests are always influenced by values. According to the prevailing Weberian epistemology in International Relations, science is only at risk when the explanation tautologically derives final results from initial commitments. Allison did, however, clearly state the assumptions of his three frameworks of analysis, and openly discussed the limits of these explanatory models – so much so that many scholars overlooked the policy-inspired character of the book.

Whereas during containment, realism influenced US foreign policy, here US foreign policy concerns, such as controlling the risk of nuclear war, influenced the research agenda of International Relations. Realist theories focus on the explanation of state behaviour. As long as realism assumed the distribution of power to be the determining characteristic of the international system, it could argue for a unique rational policy in the national interest. As long as it assumed a unique 'national interest', it need not be concerned with domestic politics except as a possible obstacle to the application of *raison d'état*. Foreign policy was following rules of its own, and therefore legitimated its status as the designated domain of the diplomatic, and not the domestic, expert. But Allison further relaxed the rationality assumption in the national interest of realist International Relations theories. He convincingly showed the endemic, and not just occasionally constraining, impact of domestic politics on foreign policy. Finally, his research was devised in a way which both acknowledged the necessity of model-building for interpreting diplomatic history, and restricted its scope to a kind of Weberian ideal-type or analysis framework, not a behaviourial theory. If realism was about the explanation of state behaviour, Allison's book suggested that the decisions which underlie foreign policies needed a conceptual apparatus and a variety of variables largely neglected by realists. Foreign policy analysis should have been the obvious core of a realist theory of International Relations. But, rather than attempting to explain the origins of foreign policies, realists more often than not took them for granted. Consequently, Allison's framework made the research agenda of International Relations explode. It redefined the boundaries of the discipline, and thus threatened the overlap between realist assumptions of world politics and the identity of International Relations.

This chapter largely follows Allison's approach. After each model, the text will explore the hypotheses generated by Allison to analyse the Cuban missile crisis.[3] Allison's hypotheses aim at answering three questions:

---

[3] For the sake of a more coherent exposition of the explanatory models, I simply refer to Allison's account. For an early and concise survey of its factual (and methodological) weaknesses, see Steve Smith (1980). With the opening of some of the former Soviet archives, today's accounts are less US-centred.

why did the Soviet government decide to install missiles in Cuba, why did the US administration opt for a blockade, and why did the Soviet government remove the missiles from Cuba? John Steinbruner's (1974) approach complements Allison's three models. Hence, a first section will show the basis for combining the two. A final section discusses in detail the possible challenges by foreign policy analysis thus understood for realist theorizing in International Relations.

CONSTRUCTING FOUR MODELS OF FOREIGN POLICY DECISION-MAKING

Graham T. Allison and John Steinbruner make mutual references which justify a combination of their models. Allison (1971: 255) acknowledges a possible fourth, the cognitive model, while Steinbruner (1974: 77, 142, fn. 13) explicitly refers to Allison's models as being equivalent to two of his. Combining both writers' works, there are four general models for the analysis of decision-making.

The analytic paradigm (rational actor model I) assumes the traditional realist world-view where foreign policy is analysed according to the ideal of the most rational foreign policy understood as the national interest. The model assumes domestic factors of decision-making to be constant, and therefore neglects their analysis.

The cybernetic paradigm (organizational process model II) understands decisions not as the outcome of instrumental rationality, but as the result of a decision-making process under the constraints of organizational inertia. This applies to the information-gathering necessary for a correct evaluation of threats; for instance, a bureaucracy has only certain boxes available for classifying and understanding events. It also applies to the implementation stage, where rational choices can be precluded by the limited range of prepared options.

The governmental politics model (III) treats decisions as the outcome of group bargaining. It is similar to model I to the extent that it relies also on a rational actor assumption (therefore Steinbruner subsumed both under one approach). They mainly differ in regard to the levels to which they are applied. Whereas in model I, the choice is caused by systemic constraints and the strategic interaction of states and their representatives, model III looks at intra-governmental politics for understanding decision-making.

Finally, Steinbruner added a fourth model, the cognitive paradigm. Here, for psychological reasons, decisions might not reflect instrumental rationality. Neither perception, nor the processing of information is necessarily guided by rationality. The models can be summarized as follows (see Table 5.1).

Table 5.1 Foreign policy analysis models (Allison/Steinbruner)

	rational	*non-rational*
impersonal	model I: rational actor (foreign strategic causality)	model II: organizational process (bureaucratic causality)
personal	model III: governmental politics (domestic strategic causality)	model IV: cognitive process (psychological causality)

THE ANALYTIC PARADIGM: THE RATIONAL ACTOR MODEL

Assumptions

In the analytic paradigm, national behaviour is explained as a rational choice for given aims under determinate circumstances. After a cost–benefit analysis, the optimal choice consists in finding the solution that maximizes the relative value of multiple aims. The decision is analysed at the individual level in strategic interaction. Strategic interaction means that value-maximizing choice in the social world must by definition refer to the aims and actions of other actors. This involves both anticipating others' actions and reacting to them. The model assumes that alternatives and consequences of actions are known, though not necessarily all information is available, or that the calculus of consequences cannot be wrong. What is important in terms of the analytic paradigm is that the decision is made in this calculating (rational) way, not that its outcome necessarily turns out to be the most rational way to make ends meet. Given the prevailing assumptions of psychological warfare, and the aim of shortening the war, it was probably rational for the allied forces to destroy both Dresden and Tokyo with massive bombardments. As it is now known, this military strategy did not have the expected effect.

In this model, individual behaviour must reflect intention. Behaviour is consistent and explicable. The model's explanatory appeal derives from its logical coherence which posits one actor, only one rational value-maximizing action (at a single time) and the fusion of what an actor wants to do (objectives) with the reasons for doing it (motives). In particular:

> The models' rigor stems from its assumption that action constitutes more than simple purposive choice of a unitary agent. What rationality adds to the concept of purpose is *consistency* among goals and objectives relative to particular action; consistency is the application of principles in order to select the optimal alternative . . . '*Rationality refers to consistent, value-maximizing choice within constraints*'.

(Allison 1971: 28–30)

For actual foreign-policy analysis, there are two further, more operational, assumptions which set the possibilities and limits of the applicability of the model in empirical research. First, the less information outside observers, whether politicians or academics, dispose of, the more they adopt this model for anticipating actions or for retrospective explanation. This creates a tendency to slide toward worst-case analyses based on the most unfavourable assumptions of the other's behaviour (Allison 1971: 19). Second, this model has only a limited explanatory value. It can provide a summary of general tendencies by identifying the weight that the relative strategic gains/losses had in the actual behaviour and by focusing on the aims in question. It determines the range of possible actions.

Cuba: the first interpretation

On the basis of the first model's assumptions, Allison deduces hypotheses for explaining the Cuban missile crisis. In all cases, his theoretical strategy consists in checking the relation between means and ends in order to know if a given hypothesis seems plausible. The first hypotheses apply to the question of why the Soviet government installed missiles in Cuba in the first place.

First, there is the possibility that the Soviet Union wished to create a bargaining chip to be exchanged for the withdrawal of US missiles in Turkey. According to Allison this implies that the two installations were of equivalent strategic importance. The large number of missiles installed in Cuba, however, belies this explanation. Also, the relative increase in Soviet nuclear power with the Cuban missiles, particularly for a possible first strike, was strategically much more important than the Turkey-based missiles were to the US.

Another hypothesis constructs the deployment as a provocation aimed at triggering a US attack against Cuba. This would serve to isolate the US in world opinion, to split NATO, and to open the way for the Soviets to equal the aggression by taking West Berlin. Yet, presupposing the intention of war contradicts the final Soviet withdrawal before attack. Furthermore, the comparison with Berlin appears rather weak; a US attack on Cuba could indeed have turned world opinion against the US, but not necessarily enough to give the Soviets *carte blanche* in Berlin. A Soviet attack on the city would most likely have meant a general war.

Allison's third possible explanation would shift the origins of the deployment back to Cuba. After all, it was Castro who had asked for the missiles to defend his regime. But that begs the question as to why the Soviet Union did not install tactical (that is, short-range) missiles. They are easier to hide, but have the same defensive effect. Most of all, tactical missiles were unlikely to have provoked the same reaction in Washington as did the larger ones. It seems unlikely that the Soviets practised such high brinkmanship for the rather limited end of Cuba's defence.

Allison discusses a fourth hypothesis, which analyses the crisis as a further example of Cold War politics. Along this line, the Soviet deployment was simply a probe of US resolve and intentions after the Bay of Pigs disaster and the Geneva meeting between Khrushchev and Kennedy. Missiles in Cuba would then correspond to an attempt to gain further psychological advantage in the superpower competition. Again, this does not explain why IRBMs (intermediate range ballistic missiles) were installed, which made retaliation much more probable, and therefore could be expected to diminish the psychological effect of an unanswered tactical deployment. Similarly, if psychological effects were the aim, Allison questions the choice of Cuba, instead of Berlin, as a test case.[4]

Allison has a final hypothesis deduced form the assumptions of model I as to why the Soviets deployed missiles in Cuba: the Soviet government was trying to improve its missile power on the cheap. 'MRBMs [medium range ballistic missiles] and IRBMs based in Cuba would provide a swift, significant, and comparatively inexpensive addition to the Soviet capability to strike the United States' (Allison 1971: 52–3). The time it would take for Soviet missiles to reach the US would be reduced from 30 to 3 minutes. The short range would also allow for higher precision and it would make Khrushchev's plan to achieve missile parity more probable. This, according to Allison, accounts for the presence of IRBMs not explained by any other hypothesis.

Four main puzzles regarding the Soviet deployment remain that the rational actor model cannot convincingly answer. First, why were MRBMs installed before the surface-to-air missiles (SAMs) were operational? This failing in time coordination contradicts the rational-actor view which must reconstruct the installation as a carefully planned effort. Similarly, the Soviet military inexplicably failed to camouflage the missile sites. It seems moreover unreasonable to proceed with the installation of missiles and to expect these to remain unseen despite regular US surveillance overflights. Finally, the question is left as to why the Soviet government pursued its plans in the face of repeated and explicit US warnings.

Allison then deduced hypotheses of model I with regard to his second question, namely why did the US opt for a blockade (called diplomatically a quarantine). This is the one question the rational actor model has little trouble answering. This decision appears as a straightforward rational choice in a bipolar nuclear world, where a path must be found between nuclear war that has to be avoided and inaction that leads to enemy expansion. The quarantine was exactly the kind of middle-of-the road solution that allowed for time and crisis management. It was more than a diplomatic manoeuvre, less than a military attack for military purposes. The blockade was both a strong signal, indeed an act of war, and yet left time and room to

[4] Here, I think Allison's dismissal is too quick. One could imagine an incremental change where the provocation should be public, yet not too important to generate resistance. Continuous small humiliations are often a better tactic than a single big one.

halt a further escalation of the crisis (a principle which would become central for the US strategy of flexible response). The only other limited military option, the surgical strike, was deemed impossible, because it could not guarantee the destruction of more than ninety per cent of the missile sites. This would have left the Cuban capacity to retaliate diminished but intact.

Following this model, the Soviet decision to withdraw, Allison's third question is straightforwardly explained through the blockade backed by an ultimatum. But several questions remain, such as why the Soviet government did not understand the different signals that should have deterred its installation of the missiles in the first place; why it did not expect them to be recognized before everything was completed, and why it reacted with such panic once the blockade was announced.

THE CYBERNETIC PARADIGM: ORGANIZATIONAL PROCESS

Assumptions

The organizational process (Allison) or cybernetic paradigm (Steinbruner 1974), model II of this chapter, concentrates on the role of routine procedures in decision-making. The mechanism of the cybernetic decision works following the principle of a recipe. Decision-makers have a given repertoire of operations ready for implementation. A course is followed after checking the outside world for the status of a particular crucial parameter. If one repertoire will not improve the value of the crucial variable, then others are activated sequentially. In this approach, decision-makers activate certain options rather than consciously choosing them after a cost-benefit calculus. The result, the final output, corresponds to the end of a sequence and not to a single moment or choice. In a certain way, the process, once initiated, reacts blindly to the environment with some automatic adaptation procedures.

The classical physical example is the way temperature is controlled by a thermostat. The thermostat can activate a repertoire of two options. It checks the environment for the parameter of temperature. Should the latter fall below a certain threshold, the thermostat activates heating. Should this input into the environment have the expected result and the temperature rise to the threshold, the thermostat activates the other option and stops the heating. The central point of every cybernetic system, and its analysis, is this closed feedback loop (for the classical application of cybernetics to political science, see Deutsch 1966).

How does such a recipe approach to decisions apply to politics? In politics, decisions are at times complex. Confronted with an abundance of often contradicting information and incompatible aims, the decision-maker can, if no time constraint is given, avoid an immediate choice and transform it into a process; politics becomes a process.

The first principle of processing could be called fragmentation for simplicity. The decision is fragmented in little parts, whose bits are less conflictual and can be aggregated to the final procedural decision. The organization of modern bureaucracy is a logical outlet of this phenomenon. The decision-maker is then constrained by the routines that bureaucracies use when collecting and distributing information.

The second principle of processing is closely linked to the now famous concept of the so-called standard operating procedures (SOPs). These are routines which constrain decision-makers either by limiting the possible interpretations of existing information, or by offering only particular options for the implementation of choices. Two historical examples might provide good illustrations of a fixed repertory of action. On 7 December 1941, repeated information about Japanese preparations for an attack on Pearl Harbour was always implicitly interpreted as attack from within, i.e. sabotage. The measures taken were against the expected action, leaving the base utterly exposed to the Japanese air raid. Another sadly famous example was the Russian response to the German/Austrian ultimatum to Serbia following the assassination of the Habsburg Crown Prince. Since a partial mobilization did not exist in the standard military procedures, a total mobilization was initiated, which was one of the triggers of the First World War.

The third principle of processing says that internal evolution occurs as instrumental learning. As we have seen, information is always decoded so as to fit a pre-established feedback channel. Should the input require another reaction, other SOPs are applied sequentially. An adaptation of the procedures only occurs if the sequence of SOPs yields no satisfactory results.

The fourth and final principle of processing is coordination. If complex organisations aim at producing coherent decisions, it is necessary that the fragmented activities be coordinated at a certain level. Coordination does not mean integration, only that routines have a certain logical coherence. Yet, since the simplicity of the individual decision is needed to process the information, the coordination is rather rigid, inflexible and strongly structured. Once installed, routines die hard.

Cuba: a second interpretation

By 24 October 1962, there were six MRBM field sites with four launch and reload positions. Of the maximum 48 missiles, 42 were present. They had a range of 1,100 nautical miles. There were furthermore three fixed field sites of IRBMs with reload, that is, potentially 24 missiles with a range of 2,200 nautical miles. The US could detect 42 IL-28 jet bombers, 42 MIG 21 fighter aircrafts, 24 SAMs, the most modern 'Snapper' anti-tank missiles, as well as 22,000 Soviet soldiers and technicians.

The timing and implementation of the various components of this missile installation presented numerous puzzles. SAMs that would protect against intelligence flights started to work only after the installation of offensive missiles. There was no radar before the 24th October, two days after the US had imposed the blockade. There was no camouflage. The missile sites looked exactly like the ones the US knew from their intelligence photos taken in the USSR, making them easily identifiable. Instead of concentrating on one missile type, making it operational as soon as possible, the simultaneous building of MRBMs and IRBMs was strategically not very convincing. Similarly, the reloads seemed questionable as the sites were not hardened, and thus very vulnerable to a counter-strike by the US. The presence of anti-tank missiles adds a touch of the absurd to the list of puzzles.

Most of these puzzles, many of them left over from the rational actor model, can be convincingly solved within the organizational process model by analysing the Soviet military SOP for the structure of battle regiments and missile installations: all the above listed items were the standard parts of a Soviet missile site, yet implemented in a totally different environment. A first radar set was also there from the start, but the insufficient standard one. Only the timing of SAMs remains still unexplained.

Allison's second question about the US decision for a blockade can also be elucidated by the second model. The decision for the blockade was influenced by two bureaucratic or organizational constraints. It was made at a time where it was already too late to avoid shipments to Cuba, yet early enough to avoid a military reaction, because the missiles were still not operational. Hence, the question is why, despite different hints from the French secret service and from Cuban emigrants, the sites were not recognized sooner. Besides the risk of a U2 being shot down over Cuba, a further 10-day delay was caused by different bureaucracies quarrelling over the responsibility for this flight. The second influence resulted from a US armed forces' SOP. The army had classified the MRBMs as movable and then made the appropriate calculations. In this case, 10 per cent of the missiles were considered able to resist an attack. They deduced that a surgical strike could not be strategically effective, as some missiles could be expected to stay intact and be used for retaliation. Only later did civilians resurrect this option by showing that movable meant within five days.

With regard to the last question, the cybernetic model would concentrate its analysis on the question as to why the blockade found the Soviets so unprepared. Within 36 hours, British Intelligence knew that the US knew, and by Saturday 20th, two journalists (Alfred Friendly and James Reston) knew it as well. One can only presuppose that the Soviet Union must have known. The model cannot give any further answer why it did not anticipate any reaction.

GOVERNMENTAL POLITICS

Assumptions

For the government politics model, decisions are the outcome of intra-governmental strategic interaction. Governmental action is seen as a collage of relatively independent decisions. The analysis starts from the positioning of the main decision-makers. From these positions with their different respective weights and roles, analysts can infer perceptions and preferences to make reliable predictions. The analysis focuses on the interplay of rational actors. It is an interactionist or strategic approach. The decision is conceived by analogy to force vectors in physics. It is the resultant vector of respective bargaining power, based on bargaining advantages, skill, and will, as well as the other players' perception of these factors.

The explanatory power of the governmental politics model is achieved by displaying the strategic interplay: the action-channel, the positions, the players, their preferences, the bargain. In other words, it captures the interplay and conflict between different leaders. Model III's relation to model II (i.e. in organizational process) can be varied. On the one hand, model II can highlight the reasons for the difficulties leaders face when they try to force organizations to work against their established routines and goals. On the other hand, leaders have autonomy of action insofar as they influence which organizations should play out which operating procedures.

Cuba: the third interpretation

Since at the time of the study, no information was available about the internal political struggle within the Soviet élite, Allison's third model can only shed light on the second question, the US decision for a blockade. Its thesis is that:

> A series of overlapping bargaining games determined both the date of the discovery of the Soviet missiles and the impact of the discovery on the administration. An explanation of the politics of the discovery is consequently a considerable piece of the explanation of the US blockade.
>
> (Allison 1971: 187)

The main decision-maker was President Kennedy. The model looks at how the interplay of forces was articulated around him. The President's choice had to be made in a highly critical domestic context: the Bay of Pigs fiasco had already shed doubts about Kennedy's foreign policy judgement; the Republicans, led then by Senator Barry Goldwater, threatened to use the Administration's do-nothing – politics as a weapon in the mid-term Congressional elections, and there was uncertainty about his pragmatic, less anti-communist policy. On top of all the domestic pressure, Khrushchev had lied to Kennedy by repeatedly assuring him that no missiles or other offensive weapons would be deployed in Cuba. Kennedy seemed resolved to play tough.

Allison reconstructed that the President's most trusted advisors, his brother Attorney-General Robert Kennedy, the Secretary of Defence Robert McNamara, and his personal adviser, Theodore Sorensen, all opposed a military solution. Others criticized the option of a blockade since it would simply postpone the eventually inevitable intervention. Worse, it would give the Soviet Union time to make their missiles operational and hence reduce the credibility of the threat of an air strike (because of possible retaliation near the American border and not in Europe). 'The rapid abandonment of the nonmilitary path resulted less from the balance of arguments than from the intra-governmental balance of power' (Allison 1971: 202).

On Wednesday, 22 October, when the blockade showed no signs of working (that is, there was no reaction from the Soviet government), the President ordered the massive invasion of Cuba. At 1.30 p.m. a Soviet proposal reached the White House through the chief of the KGB station in Washington. It offered a withdrawal, under UN supervision, for a guarantee that the US would not invade Cuba. At 6 p.m. a secret letter from Khrushchev offered the same deal. On Saturday, a new official letter offered an exchange of the Cuban missiles for the US missiles in Turkey (which Kennedy had already earlier ordered to be dismantled). When a U2 was shot down over Cuban space, the President decided not to retaliate. Being offered different options by the Soviets, he decided to answer the more favourable of the two letters. The Soviet government accepted. The crisis was over.

COGNITIVE PROCESS

This is not the place to introduce the literature on cognitive approaches in foreign policy analysis. The argument here does not dwell on the distinction between group-psychological and individual approaches, nor on the study of perceptions (Jervis 1976), or the active force of belief systems (Little and Smith 1988). Rather, this short section simply aims to illustrate some ideas that have been developed in direct connection to, and complementing, Allison's models.

Assumptions

Steinbruner's approach concentrates on the psychology of the individual decision-maker and represents the last of the four models outlined above. The basic starting point of this model is the recognition of the human mental capacity to impose structure on data which would remain otherwise diffused, and that this capacity is a fundamental force in the decision-making process. One could call this the 'ordering principle of mind'.

There are two main assumptions here. First, the model assumes that decisions can be made without any conscious direction. Second, there exist regularities in cognitive operations which determine the (cognitive) decision-making process. These do not regard the content, but rather the structure of thought; in other words, they deal with the way thoughts become interconnected and how information is managed with regard to already-held beliefs.

Application with regard to Allison's models

Cognitive approaches are most useful in crisis situations or more generally situations of high complexity. There are different conditions of complexity. The first is the condition that individuals are confronted with choices where two or more of their values are incompatible. They face a dilemma. To a certain extent, the present discussion about NATO enlargement is a case in point. On the one hand, the enlargement is bound to undermine the aim of keeping the Russian federation in the common European security system and can be expected to produce adverse effects in some of the countries neighbouring Russia. On the other hand, the aim of stabilizing central European societies makes NATO member states sensitive to the central European claim that only NATO can provide them with a security guarantee.

The second is the condition of uncertainty, that is, the imperfect correspondence between the information and the environment. It applies to all situations where probabilities have to be included into the decision. Finally, there is the condition of dispersion, where decision-making power is scattered among a number of individual actors and organisational units. Therefore, crises and crisis management where time constraints reinforce all these factors, can be seen as good empirical cases for studying decisions under complexity.

In situations of high complexity, cognitive processes tend to resolve dilemmas by denying their existence: the mind disconnects the alternatives and pursues them separately. So, instead of meeting trade-offs in values by integrating them, the mind can impose order by disregarding, at least temporarily, one of the alternatives. This imposes a clear-cut and categorical judgement. It contrasts with a classical rational decision where conflicting aims must, at least in a limited way, be made commensurable along a common utility measure.

Allison's third model handles the individual decision-maker. Under conditions of complexity, the cognitive process model would generate different expectations and ask for new data to be taken into account. Allison's governmental politics model views decisions as resulting from an intra-governmental bargaining where decision-makers are assumed to be rational actors. For the theory of the cognitive process, this rationality cannot be assumed. The common search for a compromise is rendered difficult by the cognitive aspects of the decision. In particular, the cognitive dispositions of the more important decision-makers can make a difference. Thus, the decision-making will be less coherent than if it had happened as a series of mutual adjustments between analytical players. Bertjan Verbeek (1992), for instance, has shown how British decisions during the Suez crisis can only be understood by including a cognitive analysis of its leading politicians.

A CRITIQUE OF REALISM?

Allison's approach is considered as a critique of prevailing International Relations explanations, and (hence) of realism in particular. Since some form of realism is close to the rational actor model I and since this model proved least useful for understanding the actual decisions during the Cuban missile crisis, Allison's models are often read as a departure from realism. Bureaucratic politics, as the combination of models II and III was called (Allison and Halperin 1972), became increasingly associated with a non-realist position. Yet, this statement needs to be heavily qualified.

To see just how much of an attack on realism Allison's models actually are, it is crucial to clarify whether his models were meant to be complementary, contradictory or mutually exclusive. If they are complementary, then realism might be saved by taking the results of the other models into its analysis. If they are contradictory, then realism might be preferable for some explanations, less for others; this can be determined through empirical analysis, but realism need not be rejected from the outset. Finally if the models are meant to be mutually exclusive, this would imply that there is no logical overlap between them. In this case, the last models cannot serve to falsify the first. Realism would be saved again. The only point all three visions have in common is that realism loses its exclusive theoretical status: it just becomes one theory among others; realist theorizing as such is not shattered, but its defining status for the discipline.

Complementary models?

Although not explicitly stated, these four approaches can be interlinked in three ways. First, as four models of continuously restricting focus: model I shows the general context of a decision, model II the organizational routines which 'produce' information, alternatives and actions. Model III focuses within model II on the individual leaders and the bargaining between them. Model IV focuses on the cognitive processes within the mind of the respective leaders (Allison 1971: 258). Second, the models can be linked according to the ascending complexity of data needed in actual research. Third, the four models are suited for a rising complexity of decision: model I for easy straightforward decisional situations; model II for conflictual, but not urgent decisions; model III for crises (when bureaucratic decision is too slow); and model IV for immediate and individual decision (when crisis management is too slow).[5] This would allow for them to be used in a complementary manner.

Indeed, Allison (1971: 24) accepts the explanatory power of model I and defends its usefulness in all those situations where little data is available and the analyst has no choice but to argue and think in terms of a decisional black box. He insists, though, that 'it is not itself a full analysis or explanation of an event and cannot stand alone' (Allison 1971: 255). In this reading, model I realism remains valid, albeit within certain limits (for a similar interpretation, see Waltz 1979: 126 ff).

Contradictory models?

If the models are contradictory, rather than complementary, the relevance of realism comes under question – if realism is understood as a theory of strategic state interaction for explaining state behaviour, as exemplified by model I. There are good reasons for this interpretation of Allison's text. If the models were to be understood as complementary, then model I determines a range of different explanations which is further narrowed by the subsequent models. Therefore, explanations excluded by the rational actor model should not turn out as being still possible by looking to the other models. Yet, certainly the latter *is* a possibility. The assumption of an anarchical system is that states which do not follow the best track (rational policy) will suffer. Assuming that foreign policy decisions might be the outcome of non-rational processes, it is, however, no longer obvious that a deviation from the so-called national interest will inevitably be punished by the international system.

Although it shares the effect of rendering impossible a rational determination of (one) national interest, this argument is slightly different from the differentiations of the international system that have been introduced by realist writers like Aron, Kissinger, and Wolfers (see Chapter 3). These writers distinguished between different types of international environments, such as legitimate versus revolutionary, or heterogeneous versus homogeneous, which explain different strategies for an optimal foreign policy. By insisting on the impact of organizational and cognitive processes, these foreign policy models require the prior analysis not of different international contexts, as for classical realists, but of processes independent of the international structure. This approach is based on the analysis of specific national foreign policy traditions that are, to some extent, idiosyncratic and which provide the background for foreign policy actions.

Had the concept of containment and the underlying analysis not been taken as a general model for treating communism, Kennan's approach would qualify as such a contingent approach; indeed, it was conceived as a

---

[5] For an elaborate statement when cognitive factors are assumed to play a more important role during decisions, see Ole R. Holsti (1976: 30).

plea not to apply US standards of rationality for interpreting Soviet foreign policy. Similarly, some more recent foreign policy analysts rely on national security discourse analysis to understand state interaction (Wæver 1990). That foreign policy is not left alone to scientific analysts, but systematically relies on area or country specialists is an indicator that practitioners in fact rely less upon model I than some observers.

The implication of the argument is not that the international anarchical system sets the range of rational options eventually qualified by foreign policies, but the other way round: the interaction of foreign policy traditions sets the range of individually rational options. This argument, innocuous at first sight, is of major importance. The discipline has long been aware of the uneasy mix of explanations which privilege either the international or the state level (Singer 1961). As a practical compromise it has often pursued a two-step division of labour which is similar to the vision of supplementary models mentioned above: after an analysis of the international constraints, the analysis moves downwards to the level of states to delineate concrete foreign policy choices. The implication of the argument pursued here is that the sole reference to the international structure might actually hide possible explanations. Or, formulated more sharply, explanations led by external versus internal factors are not necessarily two phases of one and the same analysis, but two competing explanations. Thus, foreign policy analysis in its integration of governmental and domestic politics, if taken to its more historicist roots, is certainly a major criticism of the scientific and systemic realism used during the second debate (and today in neorealism, see Chapter 9).

Mutually exclusive models?

Were Allison and Steinbruner arguing that model I and the others were mutually exclusive? Since they clearly show many features untouched by model I, would this imply its rejection? Whereas Allison elaborates his models in order to understand a particular historical event, Steinbruner illustrates his theoretical argument with an empirical case. Allison uses his models as Weberian ideal types, that is, as heuristic instruments, so as to understand state action. He does not use them as an *end*, that is, a scientific theory from which to deduce generally testable propositions (for such a Weberian understanding of Allison, see Aron 1984: 29–30). Allison tries to show that the traditional realist approach systematically blends out important causal factors and produces many puzzles in the analysis of the Cuban missile crisis. He offers models to understand the underlying dynamic of these causes which point outside model I. He does not say that they are laws which always apply. They are causes which remain hidden as long as our conceptual and analytical apparatus are confined to model I. What he suggests is not that all studies within model I are wrong, but that, at a minimum, 'analysts should be encouraged to put on model II and model III spectacles in searching for hypotheses about any issue' (Allison 1971: 264).

To recall a distinction introduced in Chapter 1: though admittedly some passages in Allison's work might give a different impression, it is more coherent to interpret Allison as being primarily interested in the constitutive, and not in the instrumental functions of theories. He looks at how models contribute to construct an interpretation, and not how models can become more general theories. 'I explore the influence of unrecognized assumptions upon our thinking about events like the missile crisis. Answers to questions . . . must be affected by basic assumptions we make, categories we use, our angle of vision' (Allison 1971: v).

In such a reading models can be mutually exclusive, because the underlying logic for the perception and interpretation of reality might be qualitatively different. This is indeed Steinbruner's explicit claim. But this does not necessarily imply the rejection of one of them, if by this we mean empirical falsification. Empirical cases do, however, certify the necessity of having more than one model at hand: no model can claim to be sufficient. Empirical analyses are not tests which can falsify theories.

Similarly, the hypotheses that are derived from the model are not thought in terms of testable propositions of a more general law, but are theoretically justifiable research hypotheses, 'conceptual lenses' as Allison calls them, which may, or may not, be applicable depending on the empirical case. He argues that they are applicable to the case of the Cuban missile crisis. Hence, a recent study which proposes to show that Allison does not have a strong case for his attempt to devise tests to falsify rational choice theories (Bendor and Hammond 1992) is based on several misunderstandings. First, Allison's rational actor model was intended to challenge the realist assumption of rationality, and not rational choice theories as such. Indeed, his model III far from being entirely anti-rationalist, includes many items of an interactionist bargaining approach. Similarly, this critique is misleading because it implies that Allison's models are not meant as heuristic devices for understanding, but testable theories. Allison wrote:

> In arguing that explanations proceed in terms of implicit conceptual models, this essay makes no claim that foreign policy analysts have developed any satisfactory, empirically tested theory. In this study the term *model* without qualifiers should be read 'conceptual scheme or framework'.
>
> (Allison 1971: 4)

But realists following model I would also commit a categorical mistake to believe that since Allison's models do not falsify, we can go on with model I as if nothing happened. This is no longer possible. Allison's and Steinbruner's models can show that model I provides only a very limited apparatus to analyse (let alone predict) historical events which systematically blends out possible causes. Furthermore, it cannot claim any explanatory priority, and must accept a status of being at best one theory among others. Realism has lost its unique status.

CONCLUSION

The Cuban missile crisis was a turning point in Cold War history. Similarly, it seems that the rising awareness of the risk of nuclear brinkmanship also affected research in International Relations. Allison's study was, of course, not preordained by the events. But it had a profound impact. The models made the discipline much more aware of the constituting function of theories. The entire study changed the role of realist explanations, at least of those solely based on the security dilemma, that is, a systemic theory where state behaviour is primarily caused by the effects of strategic interaction of states within the international anarchical system (model I). Most importantly for the discipline, realism appeared just as one theory among others. In itself it could no longer be assumed to understand international events sufficiently. It was challenged by domestic and governmental politics, indeed psychological factors. Since the discipline was defined by its paradigm, realism, this stretches considerably the borders of the discipline. And because the internal history of the discipline, the evolution of its central concepts and assumptions, was so closely linked with the central and unchallenged role of realism, the crisis of realism was and is also a crisis of the discipline's identity.

6 Epilogue: Soviet theories of International Relations

It is worth taking a pause from the analysis of realism as it developed in the West. A chapter on Soviet theories of imperialism is, of course, not essential for looking at the evolution of realist thought within the discipline of International Relations as it developed in the US. Hence, readers might immediately turn to the interlude. There are, however, three reasons, why such a chapter might be useful for the argument of this book. First, it can serve as a comparative epilogue to realist theories in the US, because it shows in a more extreme manner how superpower competition during the Cold War affected scholarly thought. It scrutinizes how Soviet theorizing adjusted analytical tools, initially Marxist, to the new global interests of the USSR. Second, it stands for the remarkable fact that Soviet theories of imperialism, increasingly divorced from their Marxist origins, display a sometimes astonishing conceptual convergence with realism.[1] Finally, it serves to make the reader at least superficially acquainted with concepts that, redefined in later Western neo-Marxist writings, have spurred the interest of some realist writers in International Political Economy (see Chapter 11).

This chapter will first introduce classic Marxist thought on imperialism and then its Soviet development. Marxist thought outside the Soviet reach will be presented in Chapter 11.

CLASSICAL IMPERIALISM

Classical Marxist theories of imperialism all share a basic tenet, namely that the inherent contradictions of capitalism prompt capitalist states to territorially expand, which eventually leads to their direct military confrontation. The different approaches, however, display a considerable variety in identifying the exact location of these contradictions and the basic causality of imperialist expansion.

---

[1] A further, more personal, reason is my witnessing of the astonishing revival of geopolitical thought and teaching in central and eastern Europe. Asked about the reason, the almost inevitable answer is that realism appears as the obvious and logical continuation of the theories used in central and eastern Europe during the Cold War.

The legacy of Marx

Although Marx did not develop a grand theory of imperialism or of International Relations, Marxism does assume expansion to be a basic characteristic of capitalist states. The underlying reason for capital to expand abroad was Marx's 'law of the rate of profit to fall'. For Marx, surplus value (profit) is obtained from the difference between labour power and labour value. But as competition increases the share of capital in the production process at the expense of the labour component, the surplus shrinks (for a critique, see Brewer 1990: 33–5; see also Barone 1985). Firms can meet this tendency by expanding into other branches of industry or into new markets.

Overall, the question of imperialism in Marxist thought was treated from the perspective of capitalist states; the Third World, into which such expansion might be expected, is relatively speaking not a major subject in Marx's analysis. Where he did consider it, Marx shared, up to a point, the views of major liberal thinkers regarding the progressive impact of capitalism on pre-capitalist societies. Up to the industrial revolution, capitalism's external relations were mediated through merchant capital. The latter drew other societies into the world market, but did not necessarily transform these societies. Once industrial capital had taken charge, however, capitalist conquest was able to play a progressive (though brutal) role in initiating industrialization.

The most important legacy of Marx's ideas can be found at the paradigmatic level. In view of the fact that basic economic forces of change do not know any borders, Marx redirected attention to the transnational nature of international relations (Merle 1982). This was, to some extent, achieved at the expense of losing the phenomenon of nationalism as a possible factor of change in the context of International Relations. But in this regard, other theories of International Relations also do not necessarily score any better.

Classical imperialism

The late nineteenth century was the historical context of classical imperialism. There were several characteristics that featured prominently in Marxist historical analysis of capitalism. There was, first, the extreme rapid growth (in the core countries) and tremendous colonial expansion. Second, Marxists focused attention on features of monopoly capitalism, such as cartels, trusts, and the rising importance of large banks. Some thinkers focused on the return of tariffs. Finally some of them analysed a change in the very nature of the bourgeois class which increasingly collaborated with governments whose functions incessantly expanded.

Marxist methodology makes two fundamental assumptions. First, the analysis must be historically contextualized. Historical materialism sees distinct phases or stages of the development of modes of production. Any analysis of capitalism must be carefully circumscribed as to specify which stage of development, in which part of a country, in which part of the world. Second, Marxism is a dialectically materialist theory. Its basic assumption is that the material stage of the relations of production determine human consciousness, and also as the political and judicial structure of societies (Marx [1859] 1987: 13). By fixing the mode of production, the theory is able to delimit the significant social actors, the classes. In a bourgeois capitalist society there are two main classes, the owners of the means of production, and the proletariat. The class struggle determines the superstructure, and in particular, the capitalist state. Internal contradictions of the capitalist mode of production impel the expansion of the state(s) which eventually leads to the outbreak of intra-imperialist war.

Beyond these two assumptions, two main schools for the explanation of imperialism can be distinguished. The first view, embraced in particular by Rosa Luxemburg, saw imperialism as nothing more than an aspect of the most advanced stage of capitalism. Imperialism resulted from underconsumption, that is the idea that demand within the capitalist world falls short of meeting the pace of its productive expansion. For her, the colonialist scramble showed the desperate need of capital, using the vehicle of the state, to spread capitalism to the last remaining parts of the non-capitalist world, so as to realize a surplus that could no longer be realized at home. The second view, which won wider adherence under the banner of Lenin, saw imperialism as the result of a special new stage of capitalism, called monopoly capitalism, where heightened competition must include the entire world.

Luxemburg derived the need for expansion from the inherent underconsumptionist feature of capitalism. Her basic assumption was that capitalism cannot exist without its non-capitalist environment; it always had and required a systematic exchange with non-capitalist social strata and societies. Were capitalism's internal dynamic self-sufficient, capitalism would be a limitless process which, according to Luxemburg (1985 [1921]: 445), contradicted the Marxist thesis of the eventual and inevitable economic crisis of capitalism. In her critique of Marx she argued that the capacity of capitalist systems to reproduce themselves in ever increased size (expanded accumulation) cannot be realized within a closed capitalist system. Neither the level of consumption, nor the demographic increase of the consumers (the workforce) can keep pace with the output of production. This underconsumption has two implications. First, some products will not be exchanged for money. Hence, part of the surplus value cannot be realized which would be the necessary condition for expanding to a new and bigger cycle of accumulation, that is, for investing in greater productive capacity. Second, knowing that demand is insufficient, capitalists have no incentive to increase their production.

Luxemburg concluded therefore that expanded accumulation required by necessity the existence and exploitation of non-capitalist social strata or societies. Such strata represented a market for consumer and capital goods and a reservoir for labour (Luxemburg [1913] 1985: 316–17). This expansion proceeds in three steps. First, primitive or self-sufficient economies and their social ties are uprooted, a process which inevitably involves violence (Ibid. 319). Secondly, these societies are integrated into commercial exchange (Ibid. 334), as for instance China following the Opium Wars. Capital accumulation at the international scale is channelled mainly via international loans. These loans place surplus capital, and, through the conditions attached to them, increase the foreign demand for goods from lender countries, as well as the forced industrialization to pay the interest. The massive investment into infrastructure (railways) has a similar aim. Eventually, expansion will use the vehicle of political and direct physical violence, as in revolutions and wars. 'Imperialism is the political expression of the process of capital accumulation in its competition for the leftovers of the non-capitalist world' (Ibid. 391, author's translation). Among the classical Marxist thinkers, Rosa Luxemburg had the most to say on the impact of imperialism on pre-capitalist societies, the destruction of the natural economy, the appropriation of the means of production, and the proletarization, or expansion of wage-labour. However, her views on this subject were limited to the impact of foreign capital and even she excluded 'any consideration of internal forces and contradiction within the pre-capitalist mode of production' (Barone 1985: 34).

The underconsumptionist thesis was criticized by Bukharin and Lenin at the time. In particular, Luxemburg was attacked for neglecting the dynamic adjustments of the capitalist production process – today's overproduction can be absorbed by tomorrow's level of consumption.

Monopoly capitalist theories use a series of causal links to explain imperialism. The following section will present the relationship between classes and states, the causal links between capitalist states and expansion, and finally the link between expansion and war (see Fig. 6.1).

The link from class to state is made though the central concept of monopoly and finance capital as a new stage of capitalist development. Traditionally, the state was understood as reflecting the diverging interests of the bourgeois class. Marxist thinkers of this monopoly school saw a historical shift in capitalism when competitive markets fell prey to huge trusts. Monopoly capitalism meant the increasing concentration of production and cartelization of markets in advanced capitalist countries. Rudolf Hilferding argued, moreover, that financial and industrial capital were fused into finance capital. Thus, the industrial economies were not dominated by a large bourgeois class, but by its élite, a small monolithic group. The state acts in their interest – which can sometimes be against the interests of other bourgeois strata, but objectively never against the interests of the bourgeoisie and capitalism as such. As Bukharin noted, this allows for a conceptual simplification because state behaviour can indeed be reduced to the interests of a tiny class. Hilferding analysed in detail how states

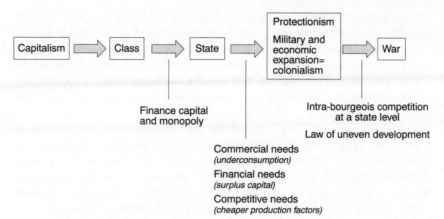

Figure 6.1 Monopoly capitalist theories of imperialism (Hilferding, Bukharin, Lenin)

were pushed to mercantilist policies to protect home markets from foreign monopolies, but also to allow the expansion of domestic trusts in order to sustain the process of monopolization. This came at the expense of smaller national producers. Lenin considered the simultaneous development of monopolies and increased state intervention to be the basic features of state-monopoly capitalism, and imperialism to be the consequence of having reached this highest stage of capitalism.

Since the state is not an autonomous actor, but rather a vehicle of the ruling class, the monopoly bourgeoisie is the driving force of expansion/colonialism. Hilferding based his explanation on the domestic finance capital whose attempts of cartelization would eventually overcome the anarchy of capitalist production (markets) and economic crises, yet fail to resolve the contradiction between the bourgeoisie and the proletariat. He explained imperialist expansion in terms of the needs of monopoly capitalists searching for cheaper raw materials and labour for higher profits, opening new markets for the excess of goods, and finally, finding outlets for investments. In other words, expansion occurs for financial, commercial, and competitive needs. Imperialism is understood here as the internationalization of a tamed domestic intra-bourgeois competition.[2] Finance capital required a strong state whose policies supported the monopoly capitalist's world-wide competitive struggle for markets. In order to mobilize enough domestic resources for imperialism, the state was increasingly to rely on an ideology of imperialism reinforced in times of fierce international competition: a mixture of

---

[2] There is a certain similarity to Morgenthau's idea that the struggle for power, tamed at home, only re-emerges in worse form abroad. Both approaches see in the consolidation of the nation state and its economies at the end of the nineteenth century the origins of unforeseen international rivalry.

racism, nationalism, and militarism. Similarly, Bukharin insisted that the growing internationalization of capitalism went hand in hand with a growing nationalization of politics. On the domestic level monopoly capitalists could not necessarily rely on a strategy of divide-and-rule because of the counteraction of trade unions. On the international level, however, they could mobilize the nationalist loyalty against another monopoly–capitalist state.

This leads us to the final link, namely the explanation of war. Writing in 1916, Lenin expanded the antagonistic view of inter-state relations previously proposed by Hilferding and Bukharin to the phenomenon of war. As to the origins of war, Lenin's writings were ambiguous. Some scholars sustain that he failed to analyse the exact cause of imperialism (Barone 1985: 53). He was probably not an underconsumptionist. He argued as if he did not question Marx's tendency for the rate of profit to fall as the primary cause of imperialism (O'Connor 1970). Yet he was adamant that the tendency toward domestic monopolies cannot be replicated at the international level. In other words, he refused the vision of a world trust, which would brutally rule the world, but avoid intra-capitalist war. This was, according to Lenin, due to the surplus of capital and the law of uneven development.

Because of the uneven development of different industrial branches and countries, monopolies do not eradicate competition. Capital is driven from the most developed branches and countries, and where the rate of profit is the lowest, to those where the profit is highest. That is, capital movements to other branches and countries become the most important feature of capitalist imperialism. Not commercial, but financial needs lead to an international competition between monopolies on a world-wide scale, a redivision of the world among the most powerful countries. This argument is levelled against another famous Marxist theory, namely Kautsky's thesis of ultra-imperialism (in disagreeing with which Luxemburg and Lenin concur). Kautsky, the leading figure of the German social-democratic party (which was still Marxist at that time), argued that the bourgeois would be rational enough to divide the world without incurring the risks (and costs) of wars. This ultra-imperialism meant the joint exploitation of the world by an alliance of monopoly capitalists. Lenin's insistence on uneven development implied that such a compromise, should it happen, was not viable in the long run: the fastest growing state monopoly will inevitably try to reverse the alliance (for some good reasons why Lenin's and Bukharin's attacks on Kautsky's thesis are not convincing, which do not imply that Kautsky is therefore right, see Brewer 1990: 131–2).

SOVIET THEORIES OF INTERNATIONAL RELATIONS

Marxist theories of imperialism are the basis of Soviet approaches to International Relations. The evolution of Soviet theories displays, however, a disproportionately close link to the practice of Soviet foreign policy. Reinterpreting the laws of Marxism, the theory is supposed to interpret the past, to guide present decisions, and to forecast the future. Yet, if foreign policy behaviour fails or the international system does not demonstrate the expected features, politics was not blamed, but the theory adjusted. In a world of truth, theory and practice must be in harmony.

Even though Soviet analysts spent a considerable amount of effort in refuting Western approaches (as if Marxism was anything else), some Western analysts have stressed the conspicuous similarity of some of its major concepts with tenets of US theories and foreign policies during the Cold War (Light 1988; Lynch 1989).[3]

International anarchy: correlation of forces versus balance of power

A Soviet analyst gave the following definition of 'correlation of forces' as the relation:

> among the totality of economic, political, legal, diplomatic and military contacts and interrelationships among peoples, among states and state systems, and among the main social, economic and political forces and organizations functioning in the world.
>
> (Dimitry Tomashevsky quoted in Lynch 1989: 91)

These relations constitute 'the objective circumstances in which both world politics as a whole and the foreign policy of individual states are developing' (Lynch 1989: 91). The correlation of forces calculates class, material, and moral forces and assigns to them a central explanatory role for foreign policy analysis (micro-level) and international politics (macro-level). It takes into account every possible state, transnational, and domestic actor, as well as the nonintentional or unconscious consequences of their actions.

The correlation of forces is conceived in dynamic terms. It can change either through objective forces, as international factors are called, or subjective forces, referring to internal political demands for the use of force. This distinction has the important theoretical consequence that it preserves the explanatory power of the approach: should the objective forces fail to materialize in a conflict, the subjective element can explain why the potential forces were in fact not actually used. Avoiding the internal inconsistency of having a subjective element in a theory supposed to be entirely objective, this subjective element is, in turn, sometimes derived from objective forces. In other words, the lacking resolve of a state actor to use power is itself the result of economic processes and the domestic class struggle.

[3] Since I am not a Soviet specialist and do not read Russian, the following section relies heavily on secondary literature – as presented by Western writers. I would therefore expect realist analogies to reflect not only similar attitudes, but the conceptual biases of the Western writers to whom I refer, including my own.

Understanding the change of the correlation of forces was a major topic of Soviet analyses of the international environment following the Second World War. The main objective changes which allegedly shifted the correlation of forces to the detriment of imperialist interests were the rise of Soviet military power; the increase in Japanese and West European economic power, and the development of movements of national liberation. Given the subjective US unwillingness to use force during and after the Vietnam war, the decline of US power was more important than the actual rise of Soviet power. This change was then used to explain US behaviour: Soviet atomic parity coupled with European pressure forced the US to accept détente.

The concept of the correlation of forces consciously attempts to avoid some of the shortcomings of the balance of power concept and policy. The latter is criticized by Soviet analysts first for increasing the propensity to use force (whereas the correlation of force invites consideration of aspects of power other than military). Second, concept and policy of the balance of power are accused of reinforcing the ideology of the *status quo* (whereas the correlation of forces implies change). Finally, balance of power theory is faulted for merging all types of expansionist foreign policies, thus disregarding the qualitative difference between imperialist and anti-imperialist policies.

Soviet critiques notwithstanding, a comparison of the correlation of forces and the balance of power reveals many similarities between the two (see Light 1988: 286 ff.). Both end up with a zero-sum view of power where gains for one side automatically imply losses for the other. Theoretically speaking this zero-sum conception of power is not necessary for either approach. Yet, by reducing the balance of power or the correlation of forces to two main poles, zero-sum arguments easily follow. Moreover, both concepts are absolutely central to their larger schools of thought, respectively realism and Soviet theories of imperialism. The balance of power and the correlation of forces are objective factors that limit the range of possible outcomes in international politics and the possible rational (and legitimate) behaviour of states.

Beyond the obvious similarities of the two concepts, not all of their invoked differences are real. Despite Soviet claims to the contrary, balance of power theories also provide rather exhaustive lists of the range of components of what makes up power and forces. The military or single factor fallacy is, at least theoretically, avoided. Both approaches are also well aware of the fallacy of permanent power, that is, the erroneous assumption of a permanent efficacy of certain power resources to achieve outcomes (for both fallacies, see Morgenthau 1947: 114 ff.) Similarly, for Lenin, power without historical process was useless (against the tide of the time). It also seems that Soviet theories are not necessarily biased for change. In fact they assume, as realists do, a repeated tendency towards an equilibrium and *status quo*. This tendency, in turn, is conceived as the independent variable through which foreign policy behaviour and international politics is explained – and legitimated. When change affected the respective sphere of influence, as, for instance, the Cuban revolution and the 1956 Hungarian revolution, both theories have been used to legitimate the suppression of change during the Cold War.

It is a question of conviction as to whether differences between US imperialist expansion and Soviet anti-imperialist expansion are substantive or semantic. Perhaps economic ends are more important for Western foreign policies, typified by the priority placed on controlling for instance Middle Eastern oil. But as the USSR never lacked primary resources, it would be difficult to prove that theoretical differences were the exact reason for its relative restraint in the region. China's recent foreign policy of claiming as its own some small but oil-rich islands seems to indicate that socialist countries can also have economic aims. Certainly, the US could (and can) use international economic institutions to its advantage in a way socialist countries could not. The question is whether these differences are the result of the different logics of capitalist and socialist foreign policies, or just the result of different opportunities or values.

Not even the inclusion of the category of social classes, theoretically prior to states, does, when applied, go far enough to differentiate between Soviet theories of imperialism and balance of power theories. Theoretically speaking, the integration of the class actor can allow more refined explanation: even when states attributes do not change, the correlation of forces might do so. Hence, Soviet theories of imperialism can conceive of change where an exclusive focus on the state would not see it. In practice, Soviet analysts, when establishing the correlation of forces, increasingly emphasized the relations between states at the expense of the initial focus on classes. Consequently, the integration of the class actor into Soviet theory resembles the integration of transnational actors into balance of power theory, or the integration of market forces in more recent theories in International Political Economy. The following discussion of the concept of peaceful coexistence will show that the integration of these two levels of analysis, classes and states, is far from unambiguous.

Transnational versus inter-state politics: peaceful coexistence and containment

Peaceful coexistence, as well as containment, is a policy between two superpowers and their allies, based on a strategy of simultaneous cooperation and confrontation (see Chapter 4). Even though the reasons for war are to be found in imperialism, the socialist camp can accept living with imperialist forces, at least temporarily.

Peaceful coexistence corresponds to a strategy of tactical cooperation. It is based, first of all, on the decoupling of international competition from the military sphere and redirecting it to the economic and ideological spheres.

Moreover, peaceful coexistence implies the reciprocal acceptance of the principle of non-interference. Finally, it is made possible by the existence of common goals, indeed it is imperative for the avoidance of mutual nuclear destruction.

At the same time, peaceful coexistence does not deny the continuing international confrontation between imperialist and anti-imperialist forces. Its long-term goal is the victory of the latter. In other words, peaceful coexistence should provide a peaceful environment for consolidating international socialism while changing the existing political and social *status quo* through transnational relations. This is not dissimilar to the mix of antagonistic and cooperative politics that containment in its détente version was supposed to realize (see Chapter 7).

Unfortunately, the double twist of this approach became, in its Soviet realization, self-contradictory in two important arenas of international politics. The first problem relates to Soviet policy toward the Third World. In order to harmonize the tactic of inter-state coexistence with the strategy of trans- or international anti-imperialism in the Third World, Brezhnev declared that peaceful coexistence did not apply to national liberation movements. Yet, expansion of the USSR in the Third World (and the implicit shift in the balance of power) was exactly what triggered US reaction and an attempt to link this Soviet foreign behaviour to other levels of Soviet–US relations (see Chapter 7). Additionally, in regard to promoting domestic class struggle in the West, help for anti-imperialist forces manifestly clashed with the principle of non-interference. In this latter case, the Soviet Union often let inter-state interests prevail over class solidarity. Between security and proletarian internationalism (international class relations), the Soviet Union chose whatever appeared to serve best its own perceived interests regardless of its stated ideological responsibilities.

With all of its qualifications and exceptions, was peaceful coexistence nothing more than a mirror image of containment policy? At the psychological level, both presupposed the driving force for war to be the adversary's expansionism. At the foreign policy level, both conceived politics in terms of limiting conflicts. Thus, they generally accepted the respective spheres of influence (and *de facto* the Brezhnev and Monroe doctrines), and only occasionally, if the risk was limited, interfered in each other's. The hope to change (win) was not forgotten but delayed; if there were to be a decline of one superpower, then it was not to be the result of direct military pressure alone. The change should, if possible, come from within. The 'impossible war and improbable peace' (Aron) pushed both to divert their efforts from inter-state to intra-state foreign policy. Foreign policy became 'total' (Krippendorff 1963). Through a policy of containment, at least as George Kennan saw it, the US aimed at bringing about domestic reform in the USSR. By sustaining the international class struggle, Soviet peaceful coexistence endeavoured to undermine capitalism. As a consequence of this convergence, diplomacy was able to recover a central role.

Conclusion

The evolution of Soviet theories of International Relations was marked by an assumed close link between theory and practice in Marxism. Since Marxism was used to legitimate Soviet political action, Soviet theories were obliged to continuously readjust Marxism to the requirements of Soviet foreign policy. Since the early days of socialism in one country, the focus on class struggle and Marxist proletarian internationalism was increasingly replaced by a focus on inter-state conflict. The interests of socialism were equated with those of the USSR. Anti-imperialist struggles by Third World nationalist bourgeois forces were seen as good (for a vitriolic Marxist critique of Lenin, see Warren 1980), whereas socialist turmoil in the West was to be avoided, for it could upset Soviet relations with its key antagonists during a phase of particularly peaceful coexistence.

Similarly, some of the central concepts in Soviet theories of International Relations developed in such a way as to make them nearly indistinguishable from realist (power materialist) approaches. This could be theoretically justified: for Soviet theorists, neither domestic regime changes (as in China), nor Third-World anti-imperialism created the new international socialist relations, but only an international socialist subsystem. For the time being, the international system in its totality was capitalist and could be analysed accordingly. Allowing for the rift between domestic socialist evolution and socialism at the international level creates a space, the international realm, for which laws other than the socialist apply. As already seen, peaceful coexistence was not dissimilar to realist views: force, correlation of forces, spheres of influence in a bipolar zero-sum competition with antagonistic and cooperative elements, where diplomacy prevails over merely military relations. It also shared with realism all the pitfalls concerning the exact definition of central concepts, the difficult integration of transnational factors, and an outlook which increasingly privileged the *status quo*, in particular within respective spheres of influence.

Interlude
The crisis of realism

7 The policy of détente: Kissinger and the limits of concert diplomacy

After the Cuban missile crisis, the Soviet government reversed its previous policy of trying to match US power through (mainly nuclear) strategic shortcuts (Carrère d'Encausse 1984). Disposing of Khrushchev, the new Soviet government embarked on a policy of massive rearmament and accelerated its policy of world-wide projection. The US became engulfed in the quagmire of Vietnam, draining its forces abroad, and undercutting consent and legitimacy at home. By the end of the sixties US superiority, so tangible only a decade before, was vanishing: the USSR, it could be claimed, had reached strategic parity.

It was in this context, that the Nixon Administration took office. It proposed a new strategy which, only slightly paradoxically, would turn the new military parity into a diplomatic asset. The US was ready to acknowledge equal status with the Soviet Union, a former international outcast, if this was accompanied by Soviet foreign policy moderation. The USSR could become a legitimate member in the club of superpowers on the condition it behaved like a traditional power in a revised version of the nineteenth century Concert of Europe. US foreign policy would provide both incentives and sanctions for achieving this shift from a revolutionary to a legitimate policy.

Henry Kissinger, as National Security Advisor (1969–73) and later Secretary of State (1973–77), had elaborated a set of geostrategic assumptions, which was one of the inspirations of this new policy, the US version of détente. His approach was a historically based realism. He proposed updating the principles of nineteenth century European statecraft and applying them to the circumstances of his time. Yet already, after Kissinger's first years at Nixon's side, this task proved not only to have been self-consciously heroic and neoromantic (Hoffmann 1978), but also unrealizable. It did not succeed in accommodating the emancipation of new states, outside the direct control of the central bipolar concert, and the independence of the economic sector of international relations, outside the reach of the classical diplomat. Kissinger's efforts represent both a grandiose attempt to invigorate the codes of nineteenth century diplomacy, and the limits of such an attempt.

Whereas Chapter 5 attested some of the anomalies of realism as an explanatory theory, the failure of Kissinger's project bears witness to the limitations of reapplying realism understood as a diplomatic practice. As the next chapter of this interlude will show, the crisis of realism as a theory and practice in the main country of International Relations, not only eventually led to a fragmentation of the US foreign policy establishment, but also of the academic discipline.

KISSINGER'S GENERAL APPROACH

Kissinger applied a historical approach to the study and practice of diplomacy. His major political endeavour consisted in devising an international order which could combine the flexibility and, indeed, generosity of nineteenth century diplomacy with the changed circumstances of the twentieth century. Vital to the functioning of the European Concert was the existence of what Kissinger calls a legitimate order. A legitimate order, not to be confused with a just one, is an order whose principles are agreed by all of its participants (for more detail, see Chapter 3). This section will treat in detail what Kissinger perceived as a series of major problems needing to be addressed in order to realize such an updated concert system.

International politics was for the first time global. Originating from Europe, international society now included many new states outside it. The revolutionary character of many polities in the new states render a Concert system problematic. 'Our age has yet to find a structure which matches the responsibilities of the new nations to their aspirations' (Kissinger 1969: 54). With the decline of imperialism, the world had become finite: European conflicts could neither be exported, nor compensated abroad. Finally, rising global interdependence linked up decisions and their effects world-wide. All events fed back onto the central balance, but were not necessarily subordinate to it. Politics had been globalized.

Diplomatic flexibility has now been undercut by international and domestic developments. International diplomacy has been frozen into the bipolar nuclear order. In this system, politics was easily conceived in zero-sum terms where the gains of one side were automatically translated as losses for the other. Kissinger saw a political multipolarity rising in the sixties, which diminished the rigidity of the militarily still bipolar order, but also reduced its manageability (Kissinger 1969: 57). Similarly, the domestic system increasingly reduced diplomatic options, because of the bureaucratization of politics which produces damaging constraints in the form of vested interests and organizational inertia (Kissinger 1969: 20–3).

Another problem in the application of a new concert system was the lack of a transnational class that shared a similar socialization and rules of conduct and which would be in control of foreign policies. The aristocracy no longer served this function; hence the smooth reproduction of established policy practices could be jeopardized with the changing recruitment and shifting attitudes of new foreign policy élites. Kissinger's insistence on the attitudes of the US foreign policy élite was not simply a self-directed spotlight for featuring his own historical training and perspective, or a vehicle for criticizing his supposedly less trained bureaucratic adversaries, as for instance Secretary of State William P. Rogers (Kissinger 1979: 31). The existence of shared attitudes across different national foreign policy élites was a major prerequisite of the (old) European Concert. It allowed long-term diplomacy. The clash of incompatible domestic structures leaves much less room for manoeuvre than the domestically insulated 'aristocracy international', as Morgenthau called it.

Given his approach, Kissinger was deeply concerned about the diversity, and often incompatibility of leadership types as they arise out of different domestic systems. He provided a slightly impressionistic typology of leaders in the twentieth century. The US foreign policy élite represents the bureaucratic-pragmatic type of leadership. Recruited mainly from law and business, this élite tended to privilege *ad hoc* decisions when problems arise, and there is not much place for history: 'Nations are treated as similar phenomena, and those states presenting similar immediate problems are treated similarly' (Kissinger 1969: 33). Neither does the ideological type of leadership, as represented by Soviet politicians, nor the revolutionary leadership of many new nations, provide a base for such a shared code. They all share the propensity for short-term policy conceptions.

Similar to a thesis elaborated in detail by Bertrand de Jouvenel (1972 [1945]), Kissinger sees that modern societies with their reliance on mass support, be they democratic, authoritarian or totalitarian, have reinforced central authority and can mobilize a hitherto unprecedented power. But they have also become prisoners of a 'domestic need for success at all times' (Kissinger 1969: 46), undermining the possible generosity of aristocratic diplomacy.

This links up with another epochal change which threatens to jeopardize a legitimate order. The twentieth century is, to use Bracher's phrase, an 'era of ideologies' (Bracher 1982). Ideologies provide identity and purpose for nations and their foreign policy. One of the implications of the necessarily popular legitimacy in modern societies is the more probable link between domestic structures and foreign 'revolutionary' behaviour (see Chapter 3). Whenever the legitimacy of domestic systems rests upon ideologies which are of potentially universal scope, the problem is exacerbated. Indeed, communism is difficult to handle within the traditional concert system, because it is not based on inter-state but inter-class relations: its borders pervade state borders and its transnational nature makes the insulation of foreign policy from domestic politics impossible (Kissinger 1979: 68). 'When domestic structures–and the concept of legitimacy on which they are based– differ widely, statesman can still meet, but their ability to persuade has been reduced for they no longer speak the same language' (Kissinger 1969: 12).

Kissinger's reference to a common language was not fortuitous. His central concern was how to recreate a 'common culture' which would allow diplomacy to play its role. At one point Kissinger (1969: 57) even wrote that the greatest need of contemporary diplomacy is an agreed concept, that of 'order'. Thus, it is a necessary condition for diplomacy in a legitimate order that a common language be established despite all the structural misgivings of contemporary politics. At the same time, diplomacy is the means through which such a common language can be found. This circle is necessary for Kissinger's approach (Hoffmann 1978).

A problem in creating a common diplomatic language was the advent of nuclear weapons which eroded the direct link between power and policies, or power and influence. As he repeats in his writings, power has become both more awesome, and more 'abstract, intangible, elusive' (Kissinger 1969: 61; and 1979: 67). Here Kissinger is not primarily interested in the explanatory value of the concept of power. He is rather concerned with the communications of diplomats who, in handling international politics, need to come to a shared understanding of power, independent of its use. Otherwise, power and power rankings would only be accessible through constant conflicts, a situation which would contradict the very purpose of balance-of-power diplomacy. To make the traditional balance-of-power politics and diplomacy work, the central coordinates, references and symbols, such as national interest or power, must have a translatable meaning. For compensations cannot be used to ease tensions if their value is deeply contested; nor can balancing diplomacy have its effect of moderating conflict if there is no common understanding of the term equilibrium.

In a nutshell, Kissinger held that elaborating abstract plans whose realization would herald a stable international order was a futile effort. Instead, diplomats must accept the task of devising a code of common understandings which, in turn, would make an international order possible. The existence of nuclear weapons leaves little time for this task. 'We must construct an international order before a crisis imposes it as a necessity. This is a question not of blueprints, but of attitudes' (Kissinger 1969: 49).

NEGOTIATED CONTAINMENT

When Kissinger took office he was in a unique position to make international affairs come closer to meeting his vision. Inheriting both the problems and the possibilities of a superpower, he could use US foreign policy as a means to turn US enemies, if not into friends, into partners for an updated legitimate international order.

The philosophical origins of détente

Kissinger derives his détente policy from three major philosophical insights, as he would call them. Foreign policy must draw on the lessons not only of the Second, but also of the First World War. The international order had to be based simultaneously on a balance of power, so as to avoid the appeasement of the thirties, and on diplomatic control over military planning, such that unintentionally sliding into another 1914 could be ruled out (1982: 237–8).

The major powers that had to be entangled into this order were the Soviet Union and the Peoples' Republic of China. Kissinger saw China as lesser problem, because it was 'in the great classical tradition of European statesmanship' (Kissinger 1982: 50). From this, it is clear that Kissinger did not find communist ideology *per se* a problem. A bigger problem was the USSR where communist ideology was accompanied with military capabilities and their world-wide projection. The Soviet Union, although not necessarily a revolutionary power, behaved like one. In a way much reminiscent of Kennan (see Chapter 4), Kissinger describes Soviet foreign policy as 'ruthless opportunism' (1979: 119), which nevertheless could adjust to the expediences of the moment, because it does not follow any particular schedule (Kissinger 1982: 51).

Finally, Kissinger wanted to base US foreign policy on a sober analysis of the international order, and not the moral crusades that have been its traditional characteristic. He tried to establish a foreign policy which would go beyond the analogy of domestic or international morals and politics. He opposed the moralism of American foreign policy, that is, either isolationist ('we do not dirty our hands in the quagmire of foreign policy'); or messianic ('we save the world by teaching everyone else to be as we are'). For him, these traditional US foreign policies were equally unsuited to face the Soviet challenge:

> In every decade the alternative to policies of sentimental conciliation was posed in terms of liturgical belligerence as if the emphatic trumpeting of anti-Communism would suffice to make the walls come tumbling down. . . . The liberal approach treated foreign policy as a subdivision of psychiatry; the conservative approach considered it as an aspect of theology.
>
> (Kissinger 1979: 123; 1982: 239)

Since not the ideology of communism, but the capabilities and motives of Soviet foreign policy, were responsible for the present conflictual relations, Kissinger's main strategy is close to Kennan's original project: containment where necessary, cooperation where possible. A robust military and political posture was accompanied by incentives to change Soviet foreign policy with the aim of turning it into a legitimate power, that is, one that shares the codes of conduct of international society. Economic and financial help, recognition of equal status and prestige were made dependent on the international behaviour of the USSR. Détente is a sequentialized and flexible mix of confrontation and collaboration, of deterrence and coexistence. Its accommodating character is meant to keep containment working when public opinion turned increasingly reluctant to follow the Cold War rhetoric:

> To be sure, détente is dangerous if it does not include a strategy of containment. But containment is unsustainable unless coupled to a notion of peace. The remedy is not to evade the effort to define coexistence; it is to give a content that reflects *our* principles and *our* objectives.
>
> (Kissinger 1982: 241–2)

Also similar to Kennan, Kissinger (1979: 120 ff.) sees Soviet weaknesses as mainly domestic: no mechanism for succession, a weak economy and increasing domestic strains for the privileges of the nomenclature regime. Initially his policy aimed at a shift in Soviet foreign policy priorities so as to make them consonant with his vision of international order. In this he differs from Kennan's approach by holding a much more important place for negotiation in US–Soviet relations. For him, US containment policy was too militarily conceived (Kissinger 1969: 86).

Later, he accepts Kennan's long-term goal of preparing an end to the Cold War through domestic changes in the USSR. Although détente could lull the West into believing that competition might be over, Kissinger was convinced that domestic weaknesses and an increasingly hollow legitimacy made détente a higher risk for the Soviet Union. He called this a 'historical bet' (1982: 243). Kissinger's détente can be best summarized as an 'effort to resist expansionism and to keep open the option of historical evolution – in effect, to combine the analysis and strategy of the conservatives with the tactics of the liberals' (Kissinger 1982: 240).

Linkage and its application

Kissinger portrays a multidimensional balance of power in contemporary International Relations. Power resources are qualified by their specific areas. Nuclear weapons might provide status and prestige and serve to deter other nuclear weapons, but they are not always very helpful in opening markets or running the world currency. This conceptual move restored economic statecraft to a central place in US foreign policy. Also, with multiple dimensions, power ceases to be a zero-sum concept. The loss of power in one field can be redressed in another (Gaddis 1982: 277). Obviously such a conception had a certain attractiveness for the economic giant whose military credibility was undermined in Vietnam.

Kissinger's multidimensionality implied the existence of several (central) balances of power. The military balance became a triangle with the US opening to the Peoples' Republic of China. The economic balance was a triangle composed of Japan, Europe and the US. Being the only member of both triangles, the US would play a central role because it could link them up and extort advantages in both directions: using the economic balance for military containment against its adversaries and using the military dependence of its allies for economic concessions. Being aware of the global and interdependent character of international politics, linking up or linkage becomes the central concept of Kissinger's foreign policy of détente applied both to friends and foes. Indeed, détente can be defined as a containment policy of negotiated linkage.

Linkage policy consisted in intermingling policy areas in order to obtain a leverage for diplomatic advance on multiple fronts. Its main target was the USSR government. In fact, it implied two seemingly contradictory elements. On the one hand, it attempted to integrate the Soviet economy into that of the Western international system to such an extent that the USSR would have few motives for upsetting the international *status quo*. This represents Kissinger's repeated concern that another Versailles peace 'disorder', which he thought responsible for pushing too many central actors out of the legitimate circle, be avoided. On the other hand, it tried to induce Soviet political cooperation by extending economic concessions only as a reward for good behaviour.

To make this difficult project float, Kissinger tried to use geopolitical constraints to induce domestic and foreign actors into accepting and sharing a political conception of the world in terms of the balance of power (understood in classical realist terms). Most importantly, Kissinger referred to the necessity of avoiding nuclear disaster. Initially a proponent of the 'limited' nuclear war option, in the aftermath of the nuclear brinkmanship in Cuba, he came to doubt the possibility of fine-tuned nuclear escalation.

One task within this consisted in educating the US public (1982: 50) in the necessity of a sober balance policy, or diseducating it of the notion of a final victory. Similarly, he stressed the necessity of direct talks with other foreign policy leaders for furthering a common analysis with the other major powers. This is most visible in his discussions with the then Chinese premier Zhou Enlai:

> Precisely because there was little practical business to be done, the elements of confidence had to emerge from conceptual discussions. Zhou and I spent hours together essentially giving shape to intangibles of mutual understanding . . . [Zhou] understood that if the United States and China could articulate parallel analyses of the world situation, compatible actions would follow automatically, while if we failed to do so, verbal assurances meant little.
>
> (Kissinger 1979: 746; 1982: 52)

To obtain the time for such discussions (and the right pressure), he used a mix of military sticks and economic carrots. On the stick side, opening to China was an undefined threat to the USSR and to North Vietnam alike. On the carrot side, the USSR, in turn, was offered most-favoured-nation trade status.

Since this required a very flexible and independent foreign policy, Nixon and Kissinger together isolated foreign policy from certain negative influences. First, they reduced external commitments that overburdened US government capabilities. This is exemplified by the disengagement from Vietnam, and especially the Guam (or Nixon) Doctrine (see Chapter 5), and also the shift from overt military interventions to covert action (as, for example, in Chile). In this vein, the administration also toughened its stance on the size of the contribution that US allies should make to the common cause, a move not without frictions within the alliance. For the US, Japan and Europe were usually welcome partners for burden sharing, but unwelcome for power sharing. This attitude had a parallel in Europe's feelings towards the US, which was welcomed for its role as the provider of security and for permitting diplomatically the Europeans to play the progressive Western part, but resented for recurrently confusing particular US interests with more general ones.

Furthermore, Kissinger tried to insulate foreign policy from internal (bureaucratic) constraints. He extensively used diplomatic back-channels, that is, running parallel sets of negotiations on the same issue, one public, one secret. To a certain extent, therefore, his first position as the relatively low-profile National Security Adviser was more congenial to his conception than his later promotion to Secretary of State, which exposed him to more domestic criticisms and control.

Kissinger readily admits that the policy turned out to be too ambitious, at least during the time of the Vietnam and Watergate disasters. He leaves open the question of whether the project was doomed to failure or could have succeeded under other circumstances.

PROBLEMS OF LINKAGE

With the hindsight of two decades, it seems that from the outset, an updated Concert diplomacy could have only a very limited scope at the end of the twentieth century. The main reason is that many issues that vitally affect international order are outside the direct reach of great power management. It is no longer possible to oppose nationalist or anti-colonialist movements with the same legitimacy as Metternich did. Market forces, crucial for the social contracts everywhere, eschew state command. Consequently, a foreign policy which privileges the central (military) balance of power as the means to impose or indeed, change the order (to a legitimate one) can be successful only there where this balance in fact controls events. His diplomacy privileged those theatres where diplomats could still make a difference. They exist. But this diplomacy is relatively helpless where impersonal forces and their management are at stake (Hoffmann 1978).

Concert diplomacy cannot revert to times of domestically insulated policy-making. Similarly, since direct control of allies now effectively requires intruding on their domestic affairs, something that can be expected to provoke resistance, allies cannot be expected to toe the line in such a way as to permit the flexibility of linkage. Finally, subordinating the new emerging nations, as Kissinger called them, to the central military balance, misreads independent political dynamics.

In other words, to make a new Concert system work, the realist Kissinger needed not only to cage the Soviet bear, but impose an exclusively geopolitical logic on an international order which is no longer malleable to such an approach. His policy remains, in the last resort, imprisoned by the *idée fixe* of keeping the central military balance. Subordinating all to the competition with the USSR, even if this was meant to educate it, Kissinger's containment policy provided an inadequate 'intellectual focus for dealing with the growing number of issues that lay beyond that sphere' (Gaddis 1982: 336).

US dependence on domestic politics for the control of linkage instruments

The Vietnam War removed the US Executive's traditional free hand in the foreign policy sphere, an area where it had enjoyed relatively most independence. The War Power Act requires approval from Congress for any foreign policy intervention exceeding sixty days. If military sticks implied long-term commitment, this could become a problem.[1]

Also, the apparently flexible economic carrots turned out to be a rather more complicated means of foreign policy. A mercantilist foreign policy was not possible in times of peace during the twentieth century where the Executive's control over the economy was shared with the Congress and, much more so, with private actors. The Congress is important whenever international trade and aid is concerned. When Kissinger tried to use the most-favoured-nation clause as a bargaining chip to mitigate Soviet foreign policies, he was hamstrung by the Jackson amendment which linked the clause to Soviet emigration policy. Kissinger makes generous use of his legendary sarcasm on what for diplomats of his sorts must have appeared as a clear misunderstanding of the possibilities of foreign policy in superpower relations (1982: 250–5, 984–98). In Kissinger's view, one could expect the Soviet Union to change its foreign policy, but not its internal affairs. His hands however were tied by the final decision of the Congress in this case.

Another example which shows the impact of private actors and lobbies was the obviously strong bargaining chip of grain sales to the shortage-prone Soviets. In Kissinger's times they were not even negotiable, because of the strong reaction by farmers and the Department of Commerce. When, in the aftermath of the Afghanistan invasion, the Carter administration decided on a grain embargo against the USSR, it was sabotaged in its implementation.

The basic flaw in Kissinger's approach lies in an overestimation of the possibility of isolating foreign from domestic politics. Although Kissinger

[1] Indeed, during the second Gulf War, US intervention passed only very narrowly the Senate.

might be right in his sarcasm about the Jackson amendment, it is also unrealistic to base a foreign policy on a capacity to isolate foreign means
from domestic interests and lobbies, not only, but particularly in the US.

Mishandling relations within the alliance

Since linkage politics ties every political change to the central balance and
implicitly to the politics of the central actors, flexibility for the US government, as the leader of the alliance, meant discipline for the rest of the
alliance. Kissinger was aware of the necessity to tie the alliance together.
He launched a major diplomatic initiative, the Year of Europe in 1973.
He generously offered the Europeans to pursue their regional interests
while the US had global interests. This came close to a division of labour
where the Europeans were asked to contribute more to European security
(the main military front against the USSR), and the US was left alone to
handle all other international issues of Western interest. Needless to say,
the Year of Europe was a diplomatic disaster.

Similarly, carrots and sticks that might be useful for an opponent power
are not easily used with or against allies. In the Cyprus crisis of 1974, the US
did not succeed in stopping the Greek intervention (replacing Makarios)
and had to accept the biggest strain on its military alliance since its
existence. Undoubtedly the most important decision was to break up the
Bretton-Woods system (see Chapter 12). The allies were not consulted,
the *ex post facto* agreement on an international monetary order was not
held. Finally, Japan was not even informed about the Chinese–American
rapprochement before Kissinger's first trip to China in July 1971.

Non-interference in the domestic politics of allies has not been exactly a
sacred law of US policy. The US intervened heavily in Mediterranean politics with its excessively strong reaction against Eurocommunism (stirred up
even more after the Portuguese Revolution of 1974) in Spain, Portugal and
in particular in Italy where the Communist Party became for a short while
the strongest party in the country. The Christian Democratic Party (DC) in
Italy, when thinking about a great coalition with the Communist Party
(PCI), was pressured back. At the Group of Seven (G7) meeting in Puerto
Rico in 1976, the then German Chancellor Helmut Schmidt warned the
Italian government on behalf of the others that should they make a coalition
with the PCI, this would have consequences for Italian membership in
NATO. European politics were reduced to a two-camp vision which has
been arguably either counter-productive or useless (in Portugal and Spain,
it was not US nervousness, but Western European economic help which
did much to stabilize the systems during the democratic transition).

In their need to control all events for tipping the central bipolar balance in
the right direction, both superpowers confronted alliance problems, the
USSR, of course, in a much more pronounced version. The Soviet Union's
approach of peaceful coexistence and the correlation of forces does not give

a clue how to handle intra-socialist relations, which should accept both the sovereignty of its members, and the requirements of international socialism in the anti-imperialist struggle. In practical politics, there was little quibbling, however, as witnessed by the crushing of the Hungarian uprising in 1956 and the bloody end to the Prague Spring of 1968. The USSR held the monopoly for defining these requirements of international socialism which came at the expense of sovereignty, when the latter implied freedom from communist rule.

US dependence on the Soviet Union for the maintenance of stability in the Third World

The Third World was the region where the Soviets declared that the principle of peaceful coexistence did not apply (see Chapter 4). Kissinger, aware of this tension, tried to link up economic and political bargains on the central balance between the United States and the Soviet Union with Soviet behaviour in the Third World. Sometimes it worked. In 1970, Moscow agreed not to build a submarine base in Cuba. The Soviet client Syria was induced to withdraw from Jordan. US pressure on Moscow helped to avoid India's invasion of west Pakistan in 1971. Yet, generally it did not work (Gaddis 1982: 329 ff.). The major reason is the underlying overestimation of Soviet will and, again, the limited possibilities of the central balance in general to control their allies. The primary example of linkage's failure to utilize the central balance to influence Third World events was perhaps where the US needed it most, in Vietnam. Even had the Soviets been willing – and they may have been – for something in return, there was not much they could actually do to rein in the Vietcong. Likewise, the strategy failed in Cambodia, where the Vietnamese themselves had little control over the Khmer Rouge.

Misconception of North-South relations

For Kissinger, multipolarity did not include the more independent stance of countries outside the central balance. Of course, the US had a long-standing tradition of treating Latin America as the courtyard of US influence, a tradition also revived during the Nixon–Kissinger years (Chile 1973). But also outside this courtyard, a rather rigid zero-sum calculation was applied to emerging countries, where short term strategic losses meant long-term gains for the USSR. In other words, Kissinger treated the Third World as an appendix of the central triangular balance and was by this logic forced back in the contradictions of traditional Cold War policies. Indeed, his insistence on linking all world events made it increasingly difficult to isolate vital from peripheral conflicts. Since each contest could be read as a test-case for US resolve to contain Soviet expansion, and since any change of the *status quo* could tilt the central balance in Soviet favour, by his geopolitical logic

Kissinger was compelled to overcommitting US forces. He just pursued, and did not correct, mistakes of earlier administrations he had so rightly denounced.

US policy engaged its resources to contest Soviet threats in many areas of the Third World, often little aware of the political consequences of such action in the region. The US administration supported the white governments in Southern Africa at a time when Angola and Mozambique were decolonizing, and South Africa and Rhodesia were under internal strain. To please the Chinese government, traditionally worried about its Indian neighbour, which could also be seen as a Soviet ally, US policies helped Pakistan in the crisis of 1971, even though Pakistan had violently suppressed the Bangladeshi upheaval. Putting short-term interests first, the US administration allowed unlimited arms sale to Iran, without getting much in return. Moreover, although Kissinger was, at least in his writings (1969: 82), perfectly aware of the potential political backlash of an unequal modernization policy, as for instance, in Iran, nothing was done to pressure governments for domestic reform. In the civil war in Angola, during and after its independence from Portugal in 1975, the US supported two fractions which were, in turn, supported by the Zaïre and South Africa government – not exactly popular in Angola or elsewhere in Africa at that time. All this could be justified by Kissinger's beloved reference to geopolitics, but all also diminished the ideological and political appeal of US policies. The legitimacy of its role undermined, the US provoked more resistance towards its foreign policy and had to expend greater effort, often coercive, to ensure its aims prevailed. This put additional strain on maintaining the US's power position.

In an ironic turn, the attempt to perceive all Third World dynamics in terms of the central balance blinded US diplomacy from conceiving preventive action: whenever crises were out of the central control of the superpowers, the US was left with little more than exactly those *ad hoc* options Kissinger himself so deplored.

CONCLUSION

Détente is both the conclusion of containment policy and the breakdown of a traditional diplomacy for handling a new international order. Gaddis (1982) rightly notes the similarity between Kissinger and Kennan's original outlook of containment policy: the 'disideologicalization' of international affairs, the central concept of containment implemented through a mix of cooperative and conflictual postures, and the attempt to integrate and thereby to moderate the Soviet Union, without appeasing it. As in Kennan's conception, these features were (partly) cleaned of their typically US exceptionalist overtones they had acquired during the earlier Cold War era. Because Kennan and Kissinger tried to avoid the two typical poles of American foreign policy, the oscillation between moral integrity and isolationism and moral responsibility and intervention, they might indeed be called realist – similar to the Realpolitik of nineteenth century Europe.

But Kissinger symbolizes also the limits of Concert diplomacy. He did try to update the system. He integrated the economic sphere to the level of high politics. Yet, he reserved space for the economic sphere where it still appeared entirely controlled by state diplomacy, something later administrations had to relinquish. Although Kissinger alluded to the multipolarity and the increasing elusiveness of power, he still believed in the great powers' capacity to manage the international order, or, at least, he did his best to make his hopes come true. But the state has, however, lost control over international events and the aggregation of states does not constitute the international system any more (if it ever did). A central balance between the superpowers cannot rule international relations, and the military depen- dence of the allies does not automatically entail the superpower's authority. External relations cannot be managed in isolation from domestic politics, as foreign policy would preferably require. International Relations and politics have become more complicated than a realist model can manage. Linkage is already there, and not to be introduced by conscious policy-making. Détente is simultaneously the perfection of superpower diplomacy in the twentieth century and the symbol for its decline: such diplomacy can no longer encompass international politics.

Besides the increasing fragmentation of diplomatic fields, Kissinger's fail- ure testifies to the eluding control of foreign policy élites on crucial issues. This is in fact a greater problem for anyone who wants to base Western diplomacy on an increasing accountability of foreign policy to domestic constituencies. Transnational relations have driven a rift between demo- cratic principles, where delegate power in turn for control over a territory, and global politics, which are outside the reach of domestic constituencies (Kaiser 1969, 1971). Transnational relations undermine the political and social contracts which are underpinning the international order of the great powers. Seen from the canon of International Relations as a discipline, Kissinger's heroic failure prompts a redefinition of diplomacy and politics alike.

As mentioned above, Kissinger notes that power is increasingly divorced from influence and from politics. If the causal relationship between power and influence (over outcomes) no longer applies (if it ever did), then realism needs to revise its explanatory theory. If power is not directly related to politics, then realism is no longer the self-evident culture for diplomatic behaviour. We are looking for a new paradigm for understanding, and making, international politics.

8　International Relations in disarray: the inter-paradigm debate

Kuhn (1970a: 180) states that a paradigm governs, in the first instance, not a subject, but a group of practitioners; therefore any research on paradigms should try to locate that group. Applying Kuhn to the discipline of International Relations means locating the scientific community for which realism became the defining paradigm. As this book claims, the search for the substantial core, and for the institutional independence, of the discipline became inextricably linked with the discussions about the relevance of realism, in both directions. For this reason, many attacks of realism have often been targeting not the content but the (narrow) scope of the discipline for which realism stood. Similarly, many substantial criticisms of realism have been misunderstood, and accordingly answered, as undermining the boundaries of the institutional independence.

The endemic identity crisis of the discipline had found in realism its temporary answer. Consequently, the crisis of realism triggered debates about the discipline's own self-conception. At the beginning of the seventies, International Relations faced an increasing fragmentation of research and ever widening boundaries of legitimate scholarship; its underlying identity problem, covered by realism for several decades, resurfaced. With a certain delay, however, the discipline came to describe itself in a new way. Relying on research in the sociology of knowledge, and in particular Kuhn's studies, the discipline was no longer defined by one single subject-matter, or a single school, but, more abstractly, by debates between mutually irreducible schools of thought. Realism was relegated to the status of one of three schools, although it was clearly the one commanding the widest audience.

This chapter will first offer a sketch of the fragmented state of International Relations research at the beginning of the seventies when the state of the discipline resembled a global web. Then, it will take up the introductory remarks on Kuhn (see Chapter 1) in an attempt to criticize the partial, and at times internally inconsistent, use made by International Relations scholars when they presented the discipline as an inter-paradigm debate (a phrase coined by Michael Banks). The argument made here is that the inter-paradigm debate did not discover unbridgeable theoretical differences. Rather, its main effect was to freeze one historical moment in the development of the discipline into allegedly immutable categories. Although initially this move legitimated new approaches in the discipline, it quickly turned into a protective buffer for academic spheres of influence (for this point and the chapter in general, see Guzzini 1988).

After presenting the main argument of the inter-paradigm debate and its self-indulgent use of the concepts of paradigm and incommensurability, this chapter lays the foundation for the underlying claim of Part II: after the decline of realism and the concomitant extension of significant variables and subfields, international theory has been marked by an ongoing debate over the limits of the field of inquiry. As could be expected from a Kuhnian approach, a discipline which has lost its paradigm, is looking for self-defining and legitimating boundaries.

THE FRAGMENTATION OF INTERNATIONAL RELATIONS: THE GLOBAL WEB

In the seventies, the realist paradigm got into a real crisis (see in particular Alker and Biersteker 1984; Banks 1984). During the long years of legitimated puzzle-solving, realism was confronted with a number of problems, such as the different level of analysis (Singer 1961), the fiction of a monolithic state (Marxist and pluralist critiques), and the discussion of the concept of rationality and the significance of bureaucratic and cognitive factors (see Chapter 5). Yet only in the aftermath of the behaviouralist revolution did these puzzles become anomalies, that is, potential threats to the validity of realism.

There has been a great deal written about the illusion of a traditionalist–behaviouralist debate, or the Bull–Kaplan debate. Since behaviouralism criticized the normative bias and the traditionalist, more historical methodology prevalent in the discipline, the dispute was not primarily about content, but about methods. One can be a realist and a behaviouralist at the same time, as John Vasquez (1983) cogently argued.

Nevertheless, behaviouralism did eventually weaken the dominance of realism, because it thwarted one crucial paradigmatic function: by presupposing a common methodology for domestic and foreign policy research, it justified the intrusion of sociological concepts, approaches and standards into International Relations. It undermined the internal/external distinction upon which the realist paradigm relies. It undermined the paradigm's claim that the international realm is qualitatively different from all other social systems and requires therefore different research, in fact a different discipline. In other words, behaviouralism destroyed the distinctiveness of International Relations. As Rob Walker (1980: 14–15) notes, what universalist idealism in the first debate, and general behaviouralism in the second, had in common was that they challenged the specificity of International Relations.

As the boundaries of International Relations were softened, the anomalies became legitimate areas of research. The focus on the domestic system made it possible to analyse transnational actors and bureaucratic decision-making, for instance. Interdependence and transnationalism became new keywords. For some, borders became the organizing point for setting International Relations apart: it became a world of flows, passing through borders, states, and other actors. The definition of international actors expanded accordingly. In a rather representative way, Marcel Merle (1982: 90) defined them as structures able to influence transborder flows. They operate in an international environment which is no more defined as only that which exists 'above' states, but including all domestic realms.

Linkage might symbolize more than anything else this stage where the picture of International Relations relentlessly expanded. Nixon and Kissinger embarked on a policy of geopolitical linkage which consciously connected strategic interests around the world with bipolar competition, and a policy of diplomatic linkage which used different resources as leeway for connecting policy fields, whether economic, financial, military or other (see Chapter 7). At the same time, researchers explored the diffusion of political authority which made such linkages possible. Here, linkage meant the interaction of different levels of the external and internal realms of world politics.

This chapter proposes to picture the fragmented research programmes as a global 'web' (see Fig. 8.1). To put the different strings of research together I have deliberately chosen an Eastonian input-output model. The central stage of the discipline remained the explanation of foreign policy state behaviour. But the significant causal variables have been expanded on the international, governmental and transnational level.

Assuming a security dilemma in international anarchy, earlier realist thinkers deemed that knowledge of the international distribution of power was sufficient to explain state behaviour (for this and the following, see Chapter 3). The international realm was subsequently qualified as an anarchical society, or different contexts delimited as in Wolfers' poles of power and poles of indifference. The black box of governmental decision-making was opened by foreign-policy analysis (Chapter 5). Linkage approaches worked on transnational relations both of economic and non-economic actors. The only remaining black box was now the domestic system. Of course, its input into the decision-making process was acknowledged. But the study of social relations or domestic political dynamics was left to sociology or political science proper. The International Relations scholar would draw on the results of research done in other disciplines to the extent they affected foreign policy behaviour. Similarly, domestic state actions, if not caused by transnational or international factors, was not part of International Relations proper.

For the illustration of the causal factors on the international level, I have used Keohane and Nye's (1977) influential reworking of these debates where

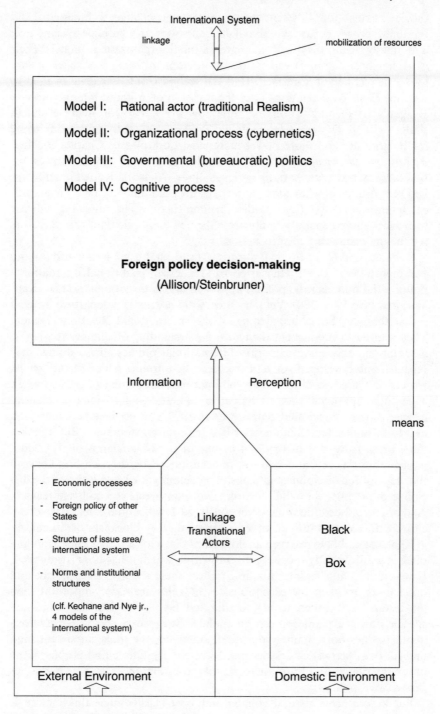

Figure 8.1 The global 'web' (Guzzini)

they distinguish four different sources of systemic change: technological and economic processes, an overall balance of power and an issue-specific one, and finally what they call the international organization model. Their work has been the most representative attempt to frame this wider picture into a new coherent approach. Had the second Cold War (a term used to describe East–West relations after the invasion of Afghanistan and Ronald Reagan's 're-ideologization' of superpower rivalry) not made Kenneth Waltz's (1979) *Theory of International Politics* apparently more convincing for its grimmer and more power-materialist outlook (see Chapter 9), their *Power and Interdependence* (1977) would have stood good chances for becoming a text with paradigmatic qualities. At least, Keohane and Nye laid the grounds of what today is perhaps the predominant theory in empirical International Relations studies, regime theory. The following will use their work more generally to illustrate the new multiplicity of causal factors for the understanding of state action.

Keohane and Nye's original purpose was to establish a new world politics paradigm (1972: xxiv). They tried to synthesize 'traditional international politics, the bureaucratic politics approach and transnational actors' (Keohane and Nye 1972: 380). Yet their theory did *not* imply a departure from all realist thought, but a broadening of the International Relations agenda. They wanted to supplement the realist understanding of change, and realist assumptions about contemporary international politics. In so doing, they repeated and developed some of the basic dichotomies which former realist writers had used to differentiate the international system (see Chapter 3). That their approach was often read as a damaging critique of realism, despite their own repeated claims even in 1977, can perhaps be understood as a form of academic blindness or bad faith in our discipline. But it makes more sense to read it in the light of one of the basic claims of this book, namely that theoretical debates have been moved by the tacit link between the scope of the discipline and realism: by defining the boundaries of the discipline differently, they did, according to many realists, challenge realism. And so their book became, erroneously as I will argue later, part of an entirely different paradigm, called interchangeably pluralism or liberalism.

Keohane and Nye reserved an important place for a realist understanding of change, for exactly those conditions within which it has been formulated. If we are in a non-regime situation, 'where there are no agreed norms and procedures or when the exceptions to the rules are more important than the instances of adherence' (Keohane and Nye 1977: 20), then an issue-specific power explanation can be applied. In this case realist assumptions about politics hold, namely that first, states are the most important (and unified, or coherent) actors; second, force is a legitimate and usable means of foreign policy; and third, there is a hierarchy among issues ('high' politics versus 'low' politics).

But at the same time, Keohane and Nye insisted that this picture is becoming an increasingly smaller part of world politics at least in certain times and parts of the world. Several issue areas display features of what they call regimes, defined as 'networks of rules, norms, and procedures that regularize behaviour and control its effects' and also as 'governing arrangements that affect relationships of interdependence' (Keohane and Nye 1977: 19). This environment is better qualified as 'complex interdependence' in which first there exist multiple channels connecting societies: inter-state relations, transgovernmental, and transnational relations; second, the usability of military force varies between the issue areas; and finally there is no hierarchy among issues. Under these conditions international relations work differently. This has consequences both for research and for the understanding of world politics.

On the theoretical level, any analysis of international change must deal with regimes, because 'a set of networks, norms, and institutions, once established will be difficult either to eradicate or dramatically to rearrange' (Keohane and Nye 1977: 55). This is what Keohane and Nye called the international organizational model. Also the understanding of politics changes. Linkage strategies between the different issue areas which try to exploit concessions in other issues (e.g. in high politics) become possible. The lack of clear hierarchy among multiple issues 'leads us to expect that the politics of *agenda formulation and control* will become more important' (Keohane and Nye 1977: 32). Finally, transnational and transgovernmental relations will further blur the distinction between domestic and international politics, in which international organizations play a role distinct from the balance of power which underlay them.

The distinction between realism and complex interdependence has many similarities with Aron's distinction between homogeneous and hetero-geneous systems (Aron 1962: 108–9). Complex interdependence elaborates the homogeneous system, and its codes of conduct, by integrating trans-national and transgovernmental relations to a much greater extent. Keohane and Nye's establishment of issue structures within which conventional realist might apply, stressed the lack of fungibility across issue structures, rather than within it. This was an attempt to rescue the central explanatory value of the concept of power – by limiting (and defining *a priori*) the scope in issue structures.

The final reason why this approach is not a rejection, but just a supplement of realism lies in the relation between realism and complex interdependence: the latter pertains only to the exceptional case when realist assumptions do not hold. An incremental regime change would be characterized by moderation, the non-usability of military forces in all issues and the developing of a diplomacy of agenda-setting and linkage. Yet, Keohane and Nye attached many conditions to incremental regime change, the most important being that it required a general consensus on the usefulness of a predictable, stable international order (which might be morally repulsive) as at least a second-best solution. Consequently, regimes are at the mercy of its most uncompromising actors (Keohane and Nye 1977: 24, 57–8).

This argument has an important research implication. The respective logic of state behaviour, whether according to realism or complex inter-dependence, depends on the conditions of the specific case under scrutiny. Unfortunately, this is not necessarily known beforehand. When Robert Keohane (1980) applied this twofold approach to what has come to be called hegemonic stability theory (see Chapter 10), he reaches the conclusion that in some issue areas realist explanations prevail, and in others those of complex interdependence. Thus, Keohane can prove the analytical value of the IOM only *ex post facto* with historical analysis.

In summary, Keohane and Nye acknowledged a crucial, although limited value for realism, but included it into a wider picture whose basic causal determination could no longer be attributed to any level in particular, be it bureaucratic, transnational, or international. In a sense, their work illustrated, succinctly synthesized, but could not contain, the exploding research programme of the global 'web'.

THE INTER-PARADIGM DEBATE

With the crisis of realism, the self-descriptions of the discipline in the seven-ties and eighties proposed not to subsume this fragmented picture under one single theoretical approach. Instead, it was as if the perception literature of foreign policy analysis was applied to the discipline itself (Wæver 1996: 159). Also Allison's models exemplified how our interpretation of historical events was theory-laden. And so was also our definition of the subject matter of International Relations. As there were paradigms for the inter-pretation of events, there were 'three models of the future' (Gilpin 1975) in International Relations.

The concept of paradigm appealed widely to International Relations scholars. The persistent and unsuccessful attempts to replace the declining realist school, despite its widely known internal insufficiencies as an explana-tory theory, and the unsuccessful reaction of realism against these attacks let some scholars believe in the idea that some schools of thought could logically not be subsumed under one more general theory.

It is not too surprising that scholars thought to have found in Kuhn's history of science an adequate description of their situation. Kuhn speaks of a paradigm-debate in times of crises which is characterized by a prolifera-tion of competing theories, the willingness to try out anything, the expres-sion of explicit discontent, the recourse to philosophy, and the debate about fundamentals.

Despite Kuhn's own doubts (see Chapter 12), his ideas have, in many ways been applied to social sciences. As mentioned in Chapter 1, part of the literature focused on the first concept of the paradigm as a normal science, that is, as a legitimated and dominating theoretical source for puzzle-solving (Mansbach and Vasquez 1981; Vasquez 1983). Others ques-tioned the validity of Kuhn's revolution. Lakatos' more cumulative (albeit also not teleological) view of scientific progress as superseding research pro-grammes, was said to fit the history of particular sciences better than a gestalt-switch (Blaug 1975; Keohane 1983). Finally, a last group of scholars discussed the notion of incommensurability and the inter-paradigm debate. Let us turn to the latter who have produced the by now widely used text-book triads of international theories (for long lists of these, see Rittberger and Hummel 1990: 23; Wæver 1996: 153).

The obsession with triads

K. J. Holsti (1985: 11) sees the following 'sufficient, and probably necessary, criteria to distinguish between genuine paradigms in our field' (see Table 8.1). Curiosly enough, when he introduced his first criterion, the central problematique, he did so in terms of one particular paradigm, the classical tradition. (Holsti is close to this tradition.) This slip produced some confusion when, for instance, the neo-Marxist paradigm is said to refer to question of war and peace as only of peripheral interest. This three-fold view of International Relations/International Political Economy is, however, not limited to traditional realists. Michael Banks (1985), disciple of John Burton's 'world society' approach, established a similar triptych (see Table 8.2). He gave different names and included regime analysis out of the interdependence tradition within the global society which he called pluralism.

Table 8.1 Holsti's *Divided Discipline*

| | Paradigms | | |
Criteria	Classical tradition	Global society	Neo-Marxism
(1) Causes of war and conditions of peace society/order; 'an essential subsidiary problem is the nature of power'	= central problematique	conditions for global community	inequality/ exploitation
(2) The essential actors and/or units of analysis	diplomatic-military behaviour of states	web of transborder interactions	class/ social groups
(3) Images of the world/ system/society of states	anarchy	world society in a global economy	core– periphery

Table 8.2 Michael Banks' three paradigms

	Paradigms		
Criteria	*Realism*	*Pluralism*	*Structuralism*
Basic image	'billiard-ball'	'cobweb'	'multiheaded octopus'
Actors	states	states and others	classes
Dynamics	force	complex social movements	economics
Dependent variables	explain what states do	explain all major world events	explain inequality and poverty
Scope of the study of International Relations	interstate relations	relations between all actors and market and nationalism	International Relations = surface phenomena of the totality of social relations and modes of production

Out of this apparent irreducibility of theories, Holsti and Banks derived far-reaching conclusions about the possible evolution of International Relations. While both agreed that the quest for a single paradigm could only remain elusive and that the debate was not between, but within schools of thought (see also McKinlay and Little 1986: 266–73), they pursued different objectives. From the paradigmatic nature of theories in International Relations, Holsti could deduce that chances to synthesize theories, in particular Marxism and realism, were slim. Banks, on his side, tried to make sure that these schools were there for good. This was meant to avoid a kind of vacuum effect, where realism would swallow everything valuable stemming from other paradigms, a strategy he called 'realism-plus-grafted-on-components' (Banks 1984: 18).

Colour it Kuhn

The Kuhnian concept of paradigm in its sense of *Weltanschauung* (understanding of the world) is central for the claims of the inter-paradigm debate. Kuhn argued that paradigms have a logic of their own. Since there is no neutral ground to compare paradigms, they are therefore incommensurable. One paradigm cannot judge the other. To prefer one paradigm instead of another cannot be rationalized by any non-circular argument (Barnes 1982: 65). In the understanding of the inter-paradigm debate, this feature provided an extraordinary protective belt for any school of thought. 'Don't criticise me, we speak different languages'. Unfortunately, scholars in

International Relations have surrendered to this marvellous invitation in a way which hopelessly trivialized Kuhn's important insights.

Holsti, for example, conceptualized paradigms rightly with a criterion for 'images of the world'. Yet he sincerely admitted in a footnote that:

> There are numerous definitions of paradigms, but for our purpose the notion of their function is most important. They are basically selecting devices which impose some sort of order and coherence on an infinite universe of facts and data which, by themselves, have no meaning. . . . I realize that this use of the term paradigm is somewhat narrower than the meaning developed by Thomas Kuhn . . . To him, paradigms are rooted not just in rationally analyzable differences, but in trans-rational perceptions, or gestalts.
>
> (Holsti 1985: 14, fn. 6)

In the first part he referred to the phenomenon that data cannot speak for itself, that is, there is no knowable fact without an underlying theory which gives meaning to it. Consequently, he very correctly conceived of theories as the very condition of knowledge. This is a faithful interpretation of Kuhn and can be called epistemological constructivism. Yet the latter part of Holsti's quote claimed that the differences between paradigms are rationally analysable, and not a question of gestalt. But if paradigm should be something more than simply another word for theory, it requires that the logic of the different paradigms only partially meet. Meaning is given within the paradigm; it travels only through translations. As usual in language translations, part of the ontological context is lost on the way. Expressed in meta-theoretical terms, Kuhn's theory of meaning is holistic: the whole (i.e. the paradigm) gives meaning to its parts. If Holsti excludes such an understanding of paradigm he cannot simultaneously hold the position that paradigms are incommensurable, or derive the limited contact of theories in International Relations, because for Kuhn it is precisely the holistic theory of meaning that excludes a common ground for inter-theoretical comparison.

Consequently Holsti's argument for an impossible synthesis between realism and Marxism is weakened. In making his point he first relied on factual reasons, or rationally analysable differences, namely his criteria. Classical writers are interested in war, peace and order whereas neo-Marxists are interested in exploitation and inequality; for Holsti, they also differed concerning the units of analysis and the key actors. Recent research suggests, however, that this is a distorting presentation. In a literature which is considered part of the structuralist/neo-Marxist paradigm, the state is reintroduced as an autonomous actor and as a unit of analysis (for early statements, see Evans 1979). As Halliday (1987: 219) rightly points out, the fact that a common concept is used, does not imply that it is used in the same way. On the other hand, many of these writers are self-proclaimed Weberians – as are many realists. It seems that a more profound difference lies within the 'classical tradition' between those who open up the black box of the state, often using sociological approaches (as the Weberian Aron, for instance) and systemic or structural realists à la Waltz, for whom the domestic politics is an exogenous variable for explaining international politics (see Chapter 9).

With regard to core interests, Holsti admitted that:

> Obviously the traditional paradigm has to be expanded to account for and measure the influence of new types of core objectives of states. Many have noted recently that traditional power-territorial issues have been supplemented by welfare goals.
>
> (Holsti 1985: 140)

Robert Gilpin has been one of those pointing to the relation between wealth and power and who Holsti included in the classical paradigm without further discussion. Gilpin does, however, define this relation between power and wealth in a way not dissimilar to neo-Marxist writers. His synthesis is, as we will see later (Chapter 11), certainly much further away from the polarity debate, as from some neo-Marxist writers (Cardoso, for instance).

This is no plea for a possible synthesis between these two frameworks of analysis although recent research in International Political Economy does suggest that there are some points of encounter and mutual criticism (see Chapter 11). It is just meant to show that once the concept of paradigm is stripped of its characteristics, it cannot explain the assumed futility of debates in International Relations, let alone fulfil the protective function that Holsti assigned to it.

If incommensurability is not the reason for the seemingly irreducible debate, the question of what is the reason remains. Holsti showed in some parts of his book why these frameworks might indeed be incompatible. The impossible synthesis is not a question of gestalts, but, more traditionally, of values. 'The debates which have been summarised in this volume have a largely hidden dimension of value preferences ... The real difficulty ... is that the value premises of the paradigms are often incompatible' (Holsti 1985: 132). He also questioned the desirability 'of a synthesis between world views which have diametrically opposed normative claims and ideals' (Holsti 1985: 77).

Value incompatibility might not exactly be the rationally analysable differences he started out by showing us. Certainly, it has little to do with Kuhn's approach. But the reference to incompatible values explains why the triads had known such an incredible success. The cohesion of our triptychs relies upon a rationalization of three main political ideologies, as they appear naturally to the Anglo-American core of International Relations: conservatism, liberalism (in its US sense) and radicalism. Hence it seems self-evident to Michael Banks to mix such heterogeneous approaches as that of Beitz (1979), a normative theorist much inspired by John Rawls, Keohane and Nye (1977), namely interdependence, with the world society paradigm to which Banks himself subscribes. The simple reason is that in one of its multiple meanings, all these approaches can be called liberal. But such a mix can hardly convince as a single type of explanatory theory in International Relations.

Why value-incompatibility should exclude a rational debate, or the *rapprochement* of writers of different ideology, is never discussed. There is no explicit argument as to why some values are automatically tied to specific frameworks of explanation. Value-incompatibility becomes the taken-for-granted justification for the limited usefulness of theoretical debates between schools of thought. The basic problematique remains unsolved: the question to what extent different variables, methodologies, and epistemological assumptions are inherently and exclusively linked to one ideology. As long as this explanation is not supplied, there is no *a priori* reason to infer from value incompatibility a case for paradigm incommensurability, although incommensurability might well exist on another, the epistemological level (Neufeld 1993; see also Chapter 12).

The banalization of paradigm incommensurability

In many crucial ways, the inter-paradigm debate does no justice to Kuhn's concept of paradigm and of incommensurability. First, it reduces paradigms to simple theories because it banalizes the relationship between a paradigm and its practitioners in their self-definition:

> If, as in the case of the social sciences, we can identify paradigms only in terms of their super-theoretical content, there will be an unlimited variety of ways of dividing a discipline into paradigms. For any interrelated set of beliefs, values and methods, that have been held by a fairly substantial number of practitioners can be justly dubbed paradigms in this sense . . .
> It is only in consideration of the function of a paradigm in generating consensus in a discipline that allows us to decide among the wide variety of ways of dividing the discipline.
>
> (Gutting 1980: 14–15)

Second, it waters down the meaning of incommensurability. Instead of relying on a holistic theory of meaning, which acknowledges the social construction of knowledge, it generally rests upon the different normative projects of scholars. This is the reason why many of the debates are coming up with triads which nicely fit the main Anglo–American way of distinguishing the political ideologies of conservatism, liberalism, and radicalism. Clearly, different values can make a difference in seeing the world, but it is not impossible that scholars can make mutually acceptable, or translatable, sense of the same world and still judge it differently.

Third, despite the aforementioned point, the inter-paradigm debate in fact seeks to, and indeed does, mobilize a strong meaning of incommensurability which suggests that there are epistemological reasons why debates across schools of thought are inconclusive. This is close to a version of relativism. But Kuhn's position is conventionalist. It is not relativist because scientific progress is decided by the informed judgement of the scientific community. It is not abstractly rationalist either, because the rationality of beliefs depends itself on social factors:

> What Kuhn still doubts is only whether progress in puzzle-solving, or rather problem-solving, ability constitutes 'progress towards the truth' . . . Thus Kuhn sharply separates the empirical success of a theory from the verisimilitude or truthfulness of its ontology.
>
> (Musgrave 1980: 49)

Lastly, the inter-paradigm debate used Kuhn's concept of paradigm not in order to shed light on the nature of theoretical discussions in the social sciences, which must always imply an idea of a hermeneutical translation, but as an argument to show the futility of such debates. This assumes that either one has a common language, say mathematics, and then there is debate, or if not, then tough luck. This is in fact a positivist assumption (for this argument, see Bernstein 1983). But, of course, debate and critique can happen also among contradicting social theories. Interpretation and deliberation have an 'essential role in paradigm switches. [Kuhn] says only that they do not *terminate* a crisis; i.e. they by themselves are not sufficient to effect the transition from one paradigm to another' (Gutting 1980: 6).

CONCLUSION

In the 1970s, realism had lost its control over the discipline and the scope of International Relations expanded. The discipline described itself in the form of an inter-paradigm debate where generally three different schools of thought were said to propose incommensurable theories. As argued above, this does no justice to Kuhn's concept of paradigm. According to the general thrust of this book, the inter-paradigm debate is best understood as a particular historical stage in the debates between International Relations theories when the discipline was faced with the decline of its paradigm.

Scholars made sense of the increasing, and apparently irreducible, fragmentation of the discipline by referring to incompatible values. This legitimated established research programmes, and avoided the more fundamental challenge to the empiricist assumptions in International Relations/International Political Economy, namely that the elusive quest for a single accepted paradigm in International Relations is not just the product of different political ideologies, but of the theory-dependence of all facts. Not the incompatible values of researchers, but the constructed nature of all knowledge might result in profoundly different interpretations. It also blinds us from a more hermeneutic understanding of theoretical debates.

The meta-theoretical debate has been reduced from the construction of knowledge via Weltanschauung to the old established value-fact distinction of empiricist research (George 1993: 202 ff.). As a result, a predefined theoretical pluralism allowed academic business-as-usual. If at the start the inter-paradigm debate protected challengers of realism from being swept away, over time it became a welcomed barrier against any criticism and a good legitimation for academic routine. A policy of academic spheres of influence became wrapped up in a somewhat scientific Kuhnian blanket (see also Kratochwil 1993: 68).

This evolution exemplified how in a paradigmatic crisis, the discipline started to argue about its foundations, and allowed for research at the fringes of the established canon (Kuhn 1970a: 91). It epitomized further-more that a discipline threatened in its identity, might welcome barriers of any kind to legitimate an independent status. Not the phoney war between ideologies, but the debate about the boundaries of the discipline, or the borders of the 'international' unknown, characterized the debate from the 1970s onwards.

In this volume, Part II does not discuss all reactions to the realist crisis. Given the focus of this study, it deals only with those responses which were inspired by realism. It will show that realist-inspired debates in Inter-national Relations (and International Political Economy) can be fruitfully understood in two interrelated ways. They are all reactions which have to come to grips with the puzzles with which Kissinger was confronted. If the link between power and politics is loosened, realist explanatory theory needs to react. It cannot give up the central place of power and politics as such in its explanations. Power materialism is the hard core of realism. But there are different solutions to this puzzle. Waltz's neorealism (Chap-ter 9) proposed the most restricted version of international politics, mainly concentrating on what states do, taking us back to before Kissinger. It also proposed a diminished scope of International Relations explanations, so that realist theory does not need to claim it can predict particular out-comes from power distributions. Hegemonic stability theory (Chapter 10) took issue with the wider political concerns of the international order at the end of the twentieth century. International politics is characterized by functional differentiation, in particular in its political economy. Most visibly in its regime version, hegemonic stability theory lent a stronger causal weight to the distribution of power, but only within well defined issue-areas. Finally, realist theories which met with structuralist political economy (Chapter 11) pushed the redefinition of politics and power further. In a way back to early realists, the domestic-foreign distinction of politics was again removed. The concept of power was redefined, mainly as structural power.

The second, and interrelated, way to understand realist responses to the global 'web' is by focusing on the academic community and its self-definition. With the traditional boundaries of the discipline shattered by the decline of the realist paradigm, all realists, some consciously, some not, attempted to draw new borders of the discipline and legitimate research. Waltz's neorealism proposed the most exclusive and therefore strongest identity of a special sphere in the social world which functions following different rules, and which therefore allows for a well demarcated discipline. The different realist versions of International Political Economy cannot offer this. They must, and many are happy to, open up the discipline. Indeed, some want to see International Relations supplanted by International Political Economy, a move which is understandably not greeted with much enthusiasm from within the discipline.

Part II

Realist responses to the crisis of realism

9 Systemic neorealism: Kenneth Waltz's *Theory of International Politics*

If any book can be compared to Morgenthau's *Politics Among Nations* for its paradigmatic function in the discipline of International Relations, showing a model to follow and clustering central debates, then it is Kenneth Waltz's *Theory of International Politics* (Waltz 1979). Therefore, as in Part I with Morgenthau, the opening chapter on a new round in realist theorizing refers mainly to this single work and the debate it spurred.

Morgenthau was paradigmatic for the establishment of an independent discipline of International Relations. Waltz has become so for defending its independence which had been threatened by the potential demise of its boundaries and explosion of its research programmes. He articulated the most restricted response to the global 'web' of ever-expanding research issues in International Relations (see Chapter 8). Thus, a prominent reason for Waltz's success is, I will claim, linked to one of the central theses of this volume, namely the confusion of realism as a theory with the boundaries and identity of International Relations. The discipline, suffering from a permanent identity crisis, exacerbated in the sixties and seventies, found in Waltz's approach a welcome relief.

Waltz defines an exclusive terrain for the international specialist by setting international politics apart from any other topic in the social sciences. Moreover, by relying on an analogy with microeconomics, his book secures a long-contested scientific legitimacy for the discipline and its practitioners. Faced since the second debate with the critique of scarce methodological expertise, the imitation of the deductive methodology and the market assumptions of neoclassical economics proved fertile for theoretical debates, but also invaluable for the academic prestige of International Relations. In other words, by setting a demarcation and by imitating a respected method, the discipline and its independence was both identified and legitimated.

At the present time, coming to grips with the content of the *Theory of International Politics*, is a more formidable task than with *Politics Among Nations*. An objective evaluation is more complicated with a paradigmatic text whose role is still debated: one is asked to take sides, whether one likes it or not. Any reference to Waltz defines scholarly families. Indeed, looking at the wealth of articles which take issue with him, one is led to believe that if Waltz's *Theory of International Politics* had not existed, the discipline would have had to invent it.

More than with its analysis of Morgenthau, the following account differs at some points from the usual interpretations. Although Waltz's text has been both acclaimed as parsimonious and disparaged as simplistic, I think that at its core the text is at best multifaceted, if not ambivalent. Waltz does not resolve any of the tensions of central realist concepts, such as anarchy, power, or the balance of power. His theory is based on a series of dichotomies, reminiscent of the realist–idealist debate, which Waltz does not fully substantiate. Indeed, the problem with Waltz's book, soon referred to as the paradigmatic text of neorealism is not only that it consists mainly of old ideas wrapped up in a more fashionable blanket, as some critics contend, but that it allows – sometimes even seems to encourage – many contradictory readings. This is one of the reasons for the never ending debates around the book. Clearly, there was no grand conspiratorial design; but the ambiguity of the book allows Waltz and his defenders to respond to their critics by moving the goalposts. When critics have more or less carefully targeted weaknesses, Waltz's recurring response is that they missed the point (for another version of this critique, see Mouritzen 1997). I will argue that in many places this is not due to any analytical deficiencies in Waltz's opponents, but to the inherent ambiguities of his approach.

This chapter concentrates entirely on those critical points where Waltz's theory shows internal weaknesses. It does not claim to be a comprehensive assessment, nor does it do justice to the work as a whole. It is applied with the hindsight expressed in the remaining chapters in Part II, which attempt to answer some of these weaknesses. After a short introduction into the general explanatory scheme of the *Theory of International Politics*, a discussion of several of these internal ambiguities show how Waltz could conceivably move these goalposts. The chapter claims that although Waltz does his best to revise, and to belittle, those realists who keep their theorizing close to the maxims of diplomatic practice, such as Aron, Hoffmann, and Kissinger, his own self-defined scientific approach does not resolve the puzzles that Kissinger met. His ambition was to replace realist thought by neorealist theory (Waltz 1990). Yet neither his concept of power, nor his conception of politics, so this chapter claims, can solve the basic problems of realism as an explanatory theory.

THE SCIENTIFIC THIRD IMAGE

The continuity of several themes in Waltz's thought is conspicuous. In 1959, he presented the classic three images for understanding the origins of war: war originated either from human nature, the type of state regimes, or the characteristics of the international system. He favoured the international, or third image and in 1979, he came back to this account. The basic features of the theory are presented briefly here.

The discipline had got rid of the first image, where human nature is the root of war (see Chapter 3). Such an approach would have tied it down to philosophical discussion rather than empirical theory. Waltz therefore concentrates his attacks on those theories of International Relations which rest on the second image, that is, those that ground the understanding of the causes of war, and more generally of international events, on state attributes. He contends that since different states tend to act alike when put into similar (power) positions, there must be structural causes for state behaviour. The result is a classic balance-of-power theory.

Waltz defines a structure by three parameters. The first characteristic is the organizing principle of a system. For Waltz, this is either anarchy or hierarchy. Hence, what paradigmatically distinguishes the international system from other systems, and what gives this international structure its causal force, is its anarchical character: 'None is entitled to command, none is required to obey' (Waltz 1979: 88). The second characteristic is the specification of functions of differentiated units. Since the international system is anarchical, every state has to take care itself of all the essential functions: there is no division of labour within a world-wide system of governance. In other words, functions are differentiated only within hierarchical systems, such as states, but not across the international system. 'Hierarchic systems change if functions are differently defined and allotted. For anarchic systems, the criterion of systems change derived from the second part of the definition drops out since the system is composed of like-units' (Waltz 1979: 101). Third, and most consequential for actual international analysis, a structure is defined by the distribution of capabilities across units. Hence, systems are to be differentiated according to the number of power poles within which international competition takes place. Kenneth Waltz remains extremely constant in this matter. Already more than a decade before, he (Waltz 1969 [1967]: 312, fn. 18) referred to structures as the 'pattern according to which power is distributed'.

With this anarchical definition of the international structure, Waltz can develop a straightforward and classic balance of power theory. This theory openly assumes very little. Its most basic assumption is that, although states might want a lot of different things, fundamentally they all want to survive. The theory furthermore assumes that given the anarchical character of the international realm, the drive for survival will result in a security dilemma, and be expressed in a general system of self-help. Although such a system will not necessarily preserve all given distributions of power, the structure will influence state behaviour in such a way that the system will inevitably tend to restore a disrupted balance of power as the best mechanism for survival (Waltz 1979: 128). That is all; there are no surprises for classical realists here, as Part I has shown.

What sets neorealism apart from realism is its methodology and scientific self-conception. Whereas in 1959, Waltz makes his points in a philosophical discussion, twenty years later, the same points are deduced from a definition of the international system modelled on the neoclassical understanding of the economic market. Again the third image turns self-consciously scientific this time with reference to the economics model; a shift which has both an epistemological and methodological facet.

At the epistemological level, Waltz's theory relies on a cushioned version of falsificationism. The aim of a science is to produce models from which one can deduce hypotheses and predictions which, in turn, can be tested with empirical data, and, if necessary, replaced by better models: the balance of power theory is such a model. It is important to note that such an approach is not naïvely empiricist. Waltz repeats again and again that models and their assumptions are not to be judged for their closeness to empirical truth, but for their usefulness in making predictions. They are axioms with which we can make sense of the world, nothing more. He does not need to say that there *is* anarchy 'out there', only that a theory based on the assumption of anarchy can help us to explain 'a small number of big and important things' (Waltz 1986: 329). Furthermore, Waltz (1979: 123) admits some of the basic difficulties for explanatory theories, such as the theory-dependence of facts, that is, the phenomenon that the understanding of what constitutes a fact is already theory-laden: 'Data never speak for themselves' (Waltz 1979: 4). For this and other reasons, he eventually admits that a strong version of falsificationism cannot be applied to International Relations and that the empirical test-ability of his own theory is limited. This point will be taken up later.

On the methodological level, Waltz's theory makes a choice between the two classical models of social science equilibrium theory on which balance of power theory has been traditionally based (see the discussion of Kaplan in Chapter 3). Instead of relying on the homeostatic equilibrium of cybernetic theory or structural functionalism, Waltz's theory opts for the market equilibrium of neoclassical economic theory. Both these equilibrium theories have in common that they do not see arrival at equilibrium as deriving from intention; it is not an actor's purposeful efforts to reach equilibrium that makes it happen. Both theories differ, however, as to what actually does cause equilibrium. Whereas structural functionalism and also cybernetic theories see the causes of equilibria in the structural pre-requisites for the reproduction and adaptation of such systems, the neoclass-ical economist's equilibria are the unintended result of value-maximizing agents in a market, that is, the consequence of the pursuit of wealth in a competitive but regulated environment. The first theory is structuralist, whereas neoclassical market theory is individualist.

Since this last point has raised many confusions in International Relations literature, further clarification is perhaps warranted. The thorny question of whether Waltz's so-called structural neorealism is indeed linked to an individualist model has spurred a major debate (Ashley 1986 [1984]; Wendt 1987, 1991, 1992b; Hollis and Smith 1990, 1991, 1992). Hollis and Smith are right that neoclassical economic theory allows, indeed requires, a double causation at individual and market levels. Ashley and Wendt are right to argue that the structural explanation presupposes the existence and the constancy of the actor's preferences. Indeed, only by presupposing *homo economicus* (Kenneth Waltz's like-unit), who wants to survive (basic preference) and manages to do so by rationally calculating the costs and benefits of alternate actions, can market (anarchy) constraints be understood.

Economic theory is very powerful because it conceals and inextricably links these two levels. At the market level, dynamics are the result of individual utilitarian value maximizing behaviour. Here, individual preferences must be assumed and held constant. At the individual level, the so-called invisible working of the market must be taken for granted theoretically, and held constant, for explaining individual behaviour. In other words, utilitarian choices and a Waltzian market analysis are merely the two different levels of the same approach. If structuralism is defined at the level of causality, then the systemic part of neoclassical theory could be called structuralist, although the structure limits possible actions rather than directly causing behaviour. Yet the dynamic of this structure is the unintended result of individual actions not of systemic rules. After all, anarchy in Waltz's sense means precisely that there is nothing above actors or states:

> Balance of power theory is microtheory precisely in the economist's sense. The system, like a market in economics, is made by the actions and interactions of the units, and the theory is based on assumptions about their behavior.
>
> (Waltz 1979: 118)

Thus, the system is not necessarily more than the sum of its parts. In other words, by dropping the functionalist model for the market model of equilibrium, the theory is basically individualist, not holistic. Since structuralism and holism usually are used interchangeably, it is probably better to refer to Waltz as a systemic not a structural realist.

In brief, the systematic use of economics as a model of explanation for International Relations is the defining contribution of neorealism. This implies both Waltz's use of market theory and the rational actor model used in the game–theoretical approach and most of the regime literature. It is on the latter ground that insights from the traditional realist and liberal traditions have been integrated recently (Keohane and Nye 1987: 729; Nye 1988; Keohane 1989).

MOVING THE GOALPOSTS: WALTZ'S INTRACTABLE POSITION

Waltz's book is clustered with dichotomies, through which he distinguishes his theory from pre-scientific realists. He attacks realists in the tradition of historical sociology. A similar fate is reserved for inductive theorizing, which he seems to define as knowledge derived from empirical generalizations. He ridicules state-based explanations which he calls reductionist or, rather idiosyncratically, behaviouralist. Hence, by opposition, Waltz could be thought of as proposing deductivism, falsificationism, outside-in, or systemic, explanations. However, he does and he does not: as this section will argue, there are so many caveats, that at the end of the day he can no longer uphold the strong demarcation he needs for setting International Relations apart from other disciplines, such as political science, and for singling out the balance-of-power theory as its only real theory.

A weak version of falsificationism

As already mentioned, Waltz openly addresses the limits for falsifying theories generally in International Relations, and also his own in particular. This provides a good window through which his meta-theoretical stance can be seen more clearly. I will argue that Waltz, anticipating usual criticisms of balance of power theories, eventually relaxes his scientific assumptions so much as to realize the falsificationist nightmare: it can never be put to a disconfirming test (see also Keohane 1983: 172).

Waltz distinguishes between laws and theories. Laws are empirical correlations. They are true or not. But they do not explain. On sunny days on the streets of Budapest, one can see more people wearing clothes in bright colours. But this is just a correlation, although probably not a spurious one. It does not mean that sunny weather directly causes the choice of bright coloured clothes. Correlations do not explain why things happen, but theories do. Theories, in turn, are not true or wrong, but need to be judged for their usefulness in explanatory power (Waltz 1979: 1–9). Theories are built upon assumptions which, similarly, are not judged for being true or not, but for being useful and sensible. Usefulness 'depends on whether a theory based on the assumption can be contrived, a theory from which important consequences not otherwise obvious can be inferred' (Waltz 1979: 91). To return to our Budapest example, one could assume that the choice is linked to the fact that bright colours reflect sunlight and therefore people feel the heat of the sun less. Or, one could assume that the choice of cloth is dependent on the fashion available in the shops. On the basis of these assumptions, one could make small-scale explanations with changing usefulness for this or other similar cases.

A theoretical analysis starts by checking the logic, coherence, and plausibility of a theory. Empirical checks are only necessary when this first theoretical check has been passed (Waltz 1979: 16). The actual testing of theories 'always means inferring expectations, or hypotheses, from them and testing those expectations' (Waltz 1979: 123). Applied to Waltz's theory, there are central causal links from which he infers hypotheses. The theory assumes an anarchical structure at the systemic level, and the motive of survival on the actor level.

From these two assumptions, Waltz deduces two different sets of expectations, respectively at the level of collective and individual action. On the level of collective outcomes most generally the expectation is that, given these constraints, states will behave in a way which will tend to establish balances of power between them. Hence, 'balance of power theory claims to explain the result of state actions, under certain conditions' (Waltz 1979: 118). At the state level, however, the theory expects particular state actions: states will compete and be socialized into similar action patterns by emulating the most successful ones:

> Within a given arena and over a number of years, we should find the military power of weaker and smaller states or groupings of states growing more rapidly, or shrinking more slowly than that of stronger and larger ones. And we should find widespread imitation among competing states . . . The socialization of nonconformist states proceeds at a pace that is set by the extent of their involvement in the system.
>
> (Waltz 1979: 124, 128)

In other words, here the theory does not just explain the result of state action, which is said to be the balance of power, but particular types of state responses where 'a certain similarity of behavior is expected from similarly situated states' (Waltz 1979: 122). The international structure is the cause not of one, but of two varying effects.

Waltz's theory hence implies a double causation. First, international structure is said to operate as a cause (Waltz 1979: 89). Given its anarchical character and its particular distribution of power, states with similar power and in a similar position are expected to behave similarly, independent of their motives, traditions, and other reductionist attributes. Second, state behaviour is an intervening variable for explaining the inevitable formation of balances of power as the result of their action. Put in another way: given the distribution of power at time $t1$, states act in a certain way (first causality) which will tend to balance power distributions at time $t2$ (second causality).

By applying Waltz's own methodology, this explanatory scheme displays two main and interrelated problems. First, faced by critics, it can easily shift back and forth between the two possible dependent variables, namely patterns of state action, on the one hand, and their result, the balance of power, on the other. Second, it cannot be conclusively tested, even through the weaker tests offered by Waltz himself (for an excellent discussion of falsification and Waltz's theory, see Mouritzen 1997).

Waltz openly discusses why falsification might not work all that well for his theory. He gives two reasons. In a passage where he treats the collective result of actions as the dependent variable, he points to the difficult assessment of the distribution of power: 'Because only a loosely defined and inconstant condition of balance is predicted, it is difficult to say that any given distribution of power falsifies the theory' (Waltz 1979: 124). In other words, when state action does not seem to result in a balance of power, this can be attributed to the difficult comparison of power (loosely defined) or to the constant flux of power (inconstant condition). The second reason is that balance of power theory is self-avowedly only a partial theory. In a passage where Waltz uses again the result of state action as dependent variable, he writes that:

> What [the theory] does explain are the constraints that confine all states. The clear perception of constraints provides many clues to the expected reactions of states, but by itself the theory cannot explain those reactions. They depend not only on international constraints but also on the characteristics of states . . . The theory explains why a certain similarity of behavior is expected from similarly situated states . . . To explain the expected differences in national responses, a theory would have to show how the different internal structures of states affect their external policies and actions.
>
> (Waltz 1979: 122)

Hence, anticipating criticisms of his balance of power theory, Waltz refers to the need of unit-level theories. But their interaction rules falsification out again. 'System theory explains why different units behave similarly (given their different placement in the system). Unit level theory explains why different units behave dissimilarly, despite their similar placement' (Waltz 1979: 72). This puts unit-level theories at the level of a residual theory which is needed to explain away the anomalies of system theories. Thus, when Waltz's critics accuse him of being purely structural, he can rightly say that he is aware of the need of unit-level theories. But given the place he reserves for them, he, then, cannot uphold any empirical falsification of his system theory: theoretically speaking, there is no way to find an empirical incidence which could be used as a disconfirmation of the theory. If there were ever an exception which could not be talked away by the difficulties in assessing the distribution of power, it could still be handled by a unit-level theory, which Waltz generously leaves to others to develop. As Waltz himself writes:

> The failure of balances to form, and the failure of some states to conform to the successful practices of other states, can too easily be explained away by pointing to effects produced by forces that lie outside of the theory's purview.
>
> (Waltz 1979: 124–5)

Indeed; and this move is very consequential. Waltz criticizes Aron, Hoffmann, and Rosecrance and the school of historical sociology for being inductive (Waltz 1979: 44), whereas his approach is scientifically sound and deductive.[1] Yet, when Waltz is confronted with the choice to keep up either a version of testability, let alone falsificationism, or his balance of power theory, he chooses the latter. Consequently, he should not (though he does) use the scientific prestige of deductivism against his opponents.

Anti-reductionism, anti-behaviouralism or just power materialism?

Waltz is outspoken in his condemnation of those who want to derive international theory from state motives and attitudes, or the nature of regimes. He calls these theorists interchangeably reductionist, as opposed to structuralist, and behaviouralist, strangely defined as 'an explanation in terms of behaving units' (Waltz 1979: 64).[2] The following discussion will show that Waltz is pushed by his own logic to relax also his systemic assumption of anarchy. In the following reconstruction of Waltz's argument, what appears as his real target is not reductionism as such, but a theory which should not be driven by strictly power materialist factors.

According to Waltz, his theory makes a decisive step forward compared with both the modernists (scientists) and traditionalists of the second debate. Waltz holds that these two approaches, while differing in method, were united in methodology. They 'insist that theorist's categories be consonant with actors' motives and perceptions . . . [and that] explanations of international political outcomes can be drawn by examining the actions and interactions of nations and other actors' (Waltz 1979: 61–2). But, in fact Waltz's theory itself is also defined in this manner: 'The system, like a market in economics, is made by the actions and interactions of the units . . .' (Waltz 1979: 118). The difference cannot be that all these prescientific realists did not look at the system level. Balance-of-power theories were not exactly new for Morgenthau or Kaplan. Nor is the difference that all the other theoreticians can conceive of the international system only in terms which are consonant with actors motives and perceptions. Specific motives besides the drive for survival through security, which Waltz uses himself, do not play a central role in the security dilemma. This dilemma is exactly based on the idea of an unintended collective outcome of rational individual action (Chapter 3). Similarly, perceptions are also central in Waltz's theory. Balancing behaviour only happens when power differentials have been perceived by the units. The ranks of different powers must be known by the units if they are to trigger balancing power politics.

There must be another reason for Waltz' self-contradictory claim that his theory is different from reductionist theories, although it relies on similar assumptions. It seems that he often confuses the distinction between material and non-material causes, on the one hand, and the distinction between the systemic and unit-level, on the other. For him, system level and power material causes go together. He tries to create an international theory

---

[1] It is very debatable if the Weberian Aron would accept a purely inductive theory of knowledge. Weber had a neo-Kantian theory of knowledge. Weberians are perfectly aware of the construction of knowledge (through meaning-giving), that is, of the Kantian idea of categories as prerequisite for the possibility of knowledge. What the school of historical sociology does refuse, however, is the covering law approach of positivism.

[2] This definition of behaviouralism is bizarre. Usually behaviouralism is defined as a theory which aims at explaining behaviour, hence the dependent variable, in terms of a stimulus-response scheme, such as, for instance, the different psychological tests based on animals (Skinner) or human beings.

which is entirely materialist. His target is not unit-level reductionism, it is the reference to any purpose, ideas, intentions, norms, in short any non-material causal factor. Hence, the balance of power must be the result of purely material causes, not of intent or of shared rules.

But reserving materialist causes to the systemic level produces contradictions in his system versus unit-level distinction. There are two examples of this contradiction. First, he discusses Aron's distinction between homogeneous and heterogeneous systems (see Chapter 3) as unit-level attributes (Waltz 1979: 45). But this will not do. When defining his structure, Waltz says that power is, of course, to be found at the unit-level, but that its distribution is part of the structure. A similar defence could be applied to Aron. When Aron distinguishes heterogeneity and homogeneity of international systems, it is not the domestic system as such, but the similarity of states across the system which interests him. The very concepts do not even make sense on the unit level. Similarly, Waltz dismisses Kaplan's balance of power theory because Kaplan 'smuggles in rules, which are unit-attributes, into his systemic theory'. But, for sure, rules are not unit-level attributes although their individual understanding might be. Rules are based on intersubjectively shared understandings. But Waltz has no category for intersubjectivity: either something is objective and material or, if it is not, it cannot be anything else than a unit-attribute.

This surprising contradiction seems to indicate that Waltz's main interest is not the systemic character of his theory. Again, as with deductive falsificationism, Waltz eventually fails to make a decisive argument against his realist opponents, such as the classical writers of the English school or the school of historical sociology (see Chapter 3). Several of their basic variables, although not strictly speaking material, are systemic attributes, such as the distribution of political regimes or shared norms. Furthermore his own theory, in good micro-economic fashion, eventually relies on units and their interactions. Though, should he be attacked on it, he would probably refer to all those passages where he proclaims the systemic character of his theory. He can always move the goalposts.

In the end, Waltz is not a fervent anti-reductionist or anti-inductivist. Relaxing the systemic and the deductive falsificationist assumptions, Waltz loses the two points on which he could set his theory of International Relations apart from the pre-scientific ones, namely the demarcation from unit-level theories and from historical sociology. The only point from which Waltz never seems to waver is the defence of a purely power driven character of international politics: the structure is defined by the distribution of power; actors react in conformity with their position therein; their action inevitably tend to restore a balance of power. This is, by all means, a classic behaviouralist theory, in which the stimulus of power differentials (input) triggers balancing responses (output). States are reduced to throughputs, occasionally investigated when their behaviour seems to conflict with the expectations of the theory. Waltz' theory is, furthermore, nothing new. It is the automatic version of balance of power theories already discussed in Chapter 3, although with a diminished explanatory range.

A THEORY OF POWER POLITICS WITH SHAKY CONCEPTS OF POWER AND POLITICS

Waltz suggests that by grounding his theory on a micro-economic analogy, he can overcome the problems of earlier automatic balance-of-power theories. This section will argue that he fails to do so. Waltz's economic analogy resurrects, and centrally needs, the money–power analogy already criticized by Raymond Aron (see Chapter 3), but without giving any new arguments in its favour. Similarly, Waltz's attempt to put a lid on the exploding research agendas in International Relations results in a conception of international politics whose narrowness is defended only through tacit assumptions.

A balance-of-power theory without a coherent concept of power

Waltz's *Theory of International Politics* is based on the analogy with microeconomics. This analogy implies two important conceptual translations. First, Waltz has to find an equivalent of the micro-foundations of markets in international relations. Second, he must conceptually translate survival into behaviourial patterns.

Waltz is very careful in stating that the primary goal of states is not to maximize power, but to achieve or maximize security (Waltz 1979: 126). Yet he writes:

> States, or those who act for them, try in more or less sensible ways to use the means available in order to achieve the ends in view. Those means fall into two categories: internal efforts (moves to increase economic capability, to increase military strength, to develop clever strategies) and external efforts (moves to strengthen or enlarge one's own alliance or to weaken and shrink an opposing one).
>
> (Waltz 1979: 118)

This means that improving one's power is indeed only a means to other ends, but it is an inescapable one. Indeed, it is the only one Waltz mentions when asked to specify how like-units behave to achieve security. His balance-of-power theory is derived from the assumed motivations (security) and actions (improvement of power position). The motivation of achieving or maximizing security is translated as improving the relative power position. Hence replacing security for power has not changed anything in Morgenthau's traditional analysis which centred on power as a necessary immediate, although not final, goal.

Waltz would probably insist that looking for a better relative power position does not mean power maximization. At some point he even writes that states seek just to maintain a position, and that they do not maximize but balance power (Waltz 1979: 126). This is a very interesting, but odd point for Waltz's economic analogy. Only the accepted players of the oligopoly, the concert, might want a *status quo*; others would not. Indeed, the dynamism of market economies partially derives from the drive to improve position and to reap, even if only temporarily, monopoly rents.

Maybe one can save some coherence by saying that states want, as a minimum requirement, to keep their position, but that their actions cannot be distinguished from those who want to improve their position. If everyone does so, the system would, in this reading, tend towards a balance of power. Since Waltz insists that this heavy assumption of a 'preference for power balancing' among the big has not much to do with motives, ideas, and so on, and that, furthermore, he needs no assumption of rationality (Waltz 1979: 118), the balance of power is assumed as a kind of automatic response to the system (in good behaviouralist fashion). It is very important to note, though, that in no way does Waltz's theory improve on the more 'scientific' balance-of-power concept that could be found in Morgenthau; it is but a repetition.

In the Morgenthau–Kaplan version, the market and its equilibrium correspond to the balance of power. The striving for utility maximization, which can be expressed and measured in terms of money, parallels the national interest (security) expressed in terms of power. In an anarchical context, without a central sanction mechanism, the impulse to survive pushes actors to maximize power at least as an intermediate goal. Therefore, so the story goes, power becomes comparable to money in neoclassical theory. The aggregation of the individual striving for power results in an international competitive order which, as market constraints in the economy, sets the external constraints on national actions. Inversely, once these constraints are known, actors can rationally decide for the optimum allocation of their resources (power) to achieve the highest possible utility (national interest or security).

Besides the behavioural automatism, the central problem of these theories is the underlying money–power analogy and the related issue of fungibility. In a late answer to Aron's criticism (see Chapter 3), Waltz (1990) writes that the problems in the money–power analogy are not qualitative, but just a question of measurement; power is difficult to measure, but can function as a medium of exchange. But this misses the point: money is not only a medium of exchange, but, and most importantly both for economic theory and for the practical establishment of modern markets, a standardized measure of economic value (for this critique of Waltz, see Baldwin 1993: 21–2). Yet political actors have no such integrated measure. Therefore, they cannot reduce the variety of their goals into a single concept of utility. Without a direct power-money analogy, there is no utility-National

Interest (security) analogy either (Guzzini 1993: 453). Whereas neoliberal economics and the market analogy presuppose money (market) economies, power relations are, at best, comparable to barter relations (Baldwin 1989: 125). In other words, the fact that international relations cannot imitate the neoclassical framework of analysis, lies in the conceptual problems which derive from the underdeveloped nature of International Relations as an exchange system as compared to economics – and not in the intellectual laziness or incoherence of its researchers.

A similar argument applies to the question of the limited fungibility of power: unlike money, power resources cannot be easily converted from one sector of the system to another. Consequently, it is difficult to assess the overall power of an actor. This is one of the reasons why many analysts prefer to study international relations in well circumscribed issue areas. Yet Waltz initially wrote that 'the economic, military, and other capabilities of nations cannot be sectored and separately weighed' (Waltz 1979: 131). Relying on Baldwin's studies, Keohane (1986 [1983]: 184–5) explicitly criticized him on these grounds. In his response, Waltz wrote:

> Obviously, power is not as fungible as money. Not much is. But power is much more fungible than Keohane allows. As ever, the distinction between strong and weak states is important. The stronger the state, the greater the variety of its capabilities. Power may be only slightly fungible for weak states, but it is highly so for strong ones.
>
> (Waltz 1986: 333)

This argument is, however, self-contradictory. If power is so highly fungible, that it can be assumed to be used in different scopes, then one does not need the variety-definition: economic capabilities can be used for producing political, ethical and other outcomes. If one assumes a great variety of capabilities, one implicitly assumes that the strong state is strong not because it has a lot of overall power, but because it possesses different capabilities in distinctive domains. Even though Waltz needs the high fungibility of capabilities to derive his systemic theory, his argumentation is based on high capabilities in different domains. In other words, he cannot argue his case for the fungibility assumption.

As a consequence of the limited fungibility of power, power analysis and comparison have to be limited either to circumscribed sectors (or regimes) as Keohane and Nye (1977) propose it (see Chapter 8), or to even more concrete and time-bound 'policy-contingency frameworks', as Baldwin (1989: 129–68) describes them. Both contradict Waltz's single systemic approach. Similarly, one can no longer objectively assess the overall-power of an actor: the weighing and adding of different resources is made impossible, because there is no common measure, comparable to money in economics. This means that there is no final measure for the establishment of the poles in the balance-of-power theory. Without the fungibility of power and, given the lacking power–money analogy, without a structure comparable to a monetized market, there is no equivalent to the firm's market control as expressed in percentages of market share. Contrary to Waltz, counting poles in international relations is not of the same kind as 'saying how many major firms populate an oligopolistic sector of an economy' (Waltz 1979: 131).

Waltz's neoclassical market analogy has not improved on the traditional problems of turning the study of realist practices into a scientific discourse and predictive theory. Indeed, the fundamental difference between economic and political exchange undermines the bases of his analogy, the basis of his neorealism.

A theory of international politics with little politics

Waltz's *Theory of International Politics* offered a much desired limitation of the exploding research agenda and a welcome legitimacy to the discipline of International Relations. As already seen, central to this paradigmatic effect was a recourse to falsificationism and the micro-economic analogy. Equally important was his explicit attempt to set international politics aside from other sectors of the international system. In this last section, I will argue that in so doing, Waltz defines politics in a very narrow way which cannot be defended conceptually. What is at stake for many of his critics, including realists or those who just want to supplement realism, is the repeated call for redefining the very content of international politics, its issues and actors.

Waltz has a state-centred definition of the international political system. 'International structures are defined in terms of their primary political units of an era, be they city states, empires or nations' (Waltz 1979: 91). Hence today, there is no primary (international) political unit outside of the state. Inversely, the structure of the international political system is defined by what states do (therefore war and diplomacy are the central manifestations of international politics). Although this seems quite obvious for many realists, this circular definition poses some tricky conceptual problems. In the following, I will argue that politics, also at the international level, can be much more easily conceived as involving more than state actions. Moreover, a different definition of politics immediately questions Waltz's characterization of the international structure as undifferentiated and basically unchanged over the millennia.

Waltz's first contention is that politics is what states (i.e. governments) do. In domestic affairs, it is certainly true to say that politics has to do with what governments do. But clearly, there are other phenomena which would be defined as part of politics. Acts by social movements, parties, firms, or other actors of the so-called civil society which are targeting state behaviour, are also considered political. Indeed, some would go as far as defining politics as everything which, whether intentionally or not, affects, expands or diminishes, the public sphere; this includes the very understanding of the dividing line between public and private spheres, problematized in many feminist writings.

Applied to the international realm, one would therefore first need to include all those actors who try to influence the behaviour of governments. This is usually recounted in textbooks with the obligatory chapters on IGOs, NGOs, MNCs, mass media and public opinion among others. But one would also need to think about all those actions that push states to enlarge or diminish their agenda, i.e. that redefine what are public matters and what are not. Indeed, classical diplomacy about questions of war and peace, is an increasingly smaller, although very important, part of statecraft. It is supplemented by, for instance, the bilateral and multilateral negotiation of trade barriers, currency convertibility, distribution of wealth (as requested in the ill-fated new international economic order), or the global management of information. If all this is part of diplomacy, and its management part of international politics, then the state is just one among other actors in making international politics. Civil society actors such as firms or NGOs have their own diplomatic corps. Many of them act on a transnational basis. Similarly, if the management of these issues is now considered high politics, then anything which affects the international sectors of trade, money, information, or any other, is part of international politics. This part of international politics is necessarily neglected when looking only at governments.

Waltz would probably react with at least two arguments. First, he argues explicitly that states are primary actors because their death rate is remarkably low (1979: 95). This is an odd argument. The birth-rate of firms is also much higher. The important point for his theory is not which individual unit survives, but which type of unit survives: and both firms and states do. He might as well argue that states are there since millennia, firms or other transnational actors are not. This is a consequential argument only if one assumes two things (which can also be circularly combined), namely first, the fundamental sameness of political organizations as states, and second, 'the sameness in the quality of international life through the millennia, a statement which will meet with wide assent' (Waltz 1979: 66). Wide assent or not, this is just an assumption. It is a very wide step from saying that the risk of war, that is violence between human collectivities, has been with us since millennia, to saying that this is all what characterizes international politics, as long as we do not move from anarchy to hierarchy, i.e., as long as we do not get a world empire or world government.

Second, Waltz could also reply that the above argument on the definition of politics is an unpermitted domestic analogy, that is, a transfer of thought from domestic structures which are hierarchical and role differentiated, to the international realm which is anarchical. But this contention is based on the hidden assumption that international relations is mainly about (military) security. In other areas, role differentiation is common currency in today's international system. Indeed, an entire debate about hegemonic stability theory, coming out of the realist school, has focused on the necessity of a hegemony to provide particular public goods within delimited issue areas (Chapter 10). If one accepts a non-circular definition of politics which is about something other than war and peace, and more than what governments do, then the international management of the Bretton-Woods system, and the role central banks played therein, is a clear case of differentiation: only the institutions of one country were issuing and managing the reserve currency (Chapter 12).

In a similar vein, this redefinition of international politics asks for a more historical differentiation of international systems. If political organizations are not assumed similar to states, then the internal organization, and the way it affects international politics must be studied. If politics is not just about (military) security, then the international provision of wealth, or of rights, whether done by states or other actors, comes back into the picture.

In a nutshell, Waltz's *Theory of International Politics* which provides a restriction of the subject matter in well-established fields of traditional security studies, ends up with a definition of politics whose narrowness cannot be defended. It is based upon circular assumptions about states, understood mainly as governments, and international structures; these make it blind to the understanding of changes in collective forms of human organization towards nation states, also towards welfare states, and the increasing list of governmental tasks which need to be pursued internationally. It cannot account for the enmeshment of states and other actors in the management of the international system. As we will see in the following chapters, for many realists, the underlying problem with Waltz's thesis, in fact, is not that it narrows International Relations down to international politics, but that politics is defined so narrowly.

CONCLUSION: REALIST CRITICS OF WALTZIAN NEOREALISM

Waltz's attempt to reduce the picture of the global 'web' (see Chapter 8) within the discipline of International Relations has been challenged by many, including realist scholars.

First, all variants of regime theory, although restricting the analysis to particular issue-areas, expanded the causal variables to include other than strictly materialist factors in the international structure. 'International regimes are defined as principles, norms, rules, and decision-making procedures around which actor expectations converge in a given issue-area' (Krasner 1982a: 185). In the original version in *Power and Interdependence*, Keohane and Nye (1977) attempted to integrate idealist and realist thought around a redefinition of power within an overall approach where bureaucratic politics and transnational actors are taken into account (see Chapter 8). In the more strictly realist version of regime theory, regimes are still ultimately a function of the distribution of power between states. Yet even then, Krasner notes that there need not always be congruity between power distribution, regimes and related behaviour or outcomes, especially because power distributions change much quicker than regimes once set up. Therefore, the lags and feedbacks between power base and regime are the basic puzzles of this approach (Krasner 1982b: 499, see also Krasner 1985).

But other realist approaches in International Political Economy (some of which would dispute that regime theory is part of International Political Economy), study the functional differentiation which exists (or, must exist) in a functioning international liberal economic order. This is the claim of hegemonic stability theory. Such and similar approaches take the underlying domestic analogy within the Waltzian market analogy very seriously: in an anarchical world without rules, no such a complex institution as a market could exist.

Waltz himself writes that firms are 'self-regarding units' (1979: 98). This means that the simple fact that units are self-regarding does not exclude them from being part of a hierarchical system. Also, self-regarding states can be part of a hierarchical international system. There is no market economy without a political order which has at least some features of hierarchy. This invites a domestic analogy, but one presented in terms of political economy.

As a result Waltz is caught in a dilemma. Either the market and the international system are structurally similar (Waltz 1979: 89), and then neorealism must think about the international equivalent to domestic hierarchy, as many International Political Economy theories do. Or they are not, and then, as Jones remarks, the economic approach and the market analogy is not applicable to the international system (Buzan, Jones, and Little 1993; see also Chapter 13). In both cases Waltz's theory does not hold.

The following chapters will turn to these realist approaches in International Political Economy which expanded the Waltzian picture again, and which can be understood in the context of a realist redefinition of international politics and power.

10 International Political Economy as an attempt to update realism: the end of the Bretton-Woods system and hegemonic stability theory

Kenneth Waltz attempted to save the overlap between realist theory and the boundaries of the discipline of International Relations. Other realists took a less academic path. They tried to rescue the overlap between the expanding agenda of international politics and a redefined realism. Whereas Kenneth Waltz's theory reacted to the turmoil of the discipline by restricting the global 'net' to its classical international component, other realists accepted the challenge and started to redefine central categories of their theory in order to match a wider part of the global agenda. It is perhaps not fortuitous that these realist theories became part of a different branch of International Relations, if not a different discipline, namely International Political Economy.

If International Political Economy has a birth date, then it was the 15 August 1971, when the Nixon Administration decided to suspend the Bretton-Woods monetary system. Not only did this unilateral decision change the way the international monetary system was run, but the US officially declared its power position as challenged. After the 1973 crisis, observers began to link the presumed erosion of US power with the recession and rising protectionism. US academics began for the first time to apply analyses of the decline of powers to their own country. The oil crisis and the accrued influence of economic weapons moved economic issues to the level of high politics, i.e. to questions of diplomacy and war.

The most prominent realist theory which developed in response to this new agenda was hegemonic stability theory. The debates around this theory epitomized again the close link between US foreign policy concerns and the research interests of the academia in International Relations. It is a theory which is similar to neorealism in so far as it relies on a single causal relationship where the distribution of power is the basic independent variable. But it is also a theory far wider than Waltz's neorealism, because it does not understand international anarchy as mere absence of government; rather, it applies ideas from the management of national economies to the international system. Its understanding of the international order is much more hierarchical.

This chapter will first discuss assumptions, theses and schools of hegemonic stability theory. Then, the main theses will be scrutinized both theoretically and empirically with reference to the international monetary system for which Kindleberger had initially developed the theory. Finally, the chapter will assess the contribution of hegemonic stability theory to realist thought. It will be argued that it is an amendment of realism. In one case this amendment is tinged with idealism: US policy concerns might have trapped Kindleberger to support idealist theses that contradict his basic realist tenets.

ASSUMPTIONS, THESES AND SCHOOLS OF HEGEMONIC STABILITY THEORY

The definition of hegemonic stability theory and its three theses

The standard definition has been given by Robert O. Keohane:

> Hegemonic structures of power, dominated by a single country, are most conducive to the development of strong international regimes whose rules are relatively precise and well obeyed . . . The decline of hegemonic structures of power can be expected to presage a decline in the strength of corresponding international economic regimes.
>
> (Keohane 1980: 132)

This definition fails, however, to highlight what can be considered the originality of the approach, namely the concept of public good and its provision by the hegemony:

> What is novel in the theory is not the claim that strong actors can impose regimes in international politics (which goes back at least as far as Thucydides) but the use of the collective action formulation and the implication that hegemony is more widely beneficial. Moreover, once the public goods formulation is invoked to explain the emergence of regimes under hegemony, the distributional argument follows as a logical conclusion. Indeed, the proposition . . . seems central to Keohane's *After Hegemony*, which poses as a fundamental question how the benefits of hegemonic cooperation (which are generalized beyond the hegemonic actor) can be maintained after the decline of hegemony.
>
> (Snidal 1985: 581)

Economic theory refers to public or collective goods as those which, although beneficial to the interests of market actors, would not be provided on the basis of individual cost-benefit analyses. This is because public goods are characterized by 'jointness' and non-exclusion: when different actors simultaneously consume the same good, we speak of jointness; non-exclusion is defined by the inability of actors to prevent non-contributors benefiting from the public good (so-called free-riders). A common example of a public good are sidewalks. If their construction were to result from individual investment decisions, where the incurred cost would reap no comparable benefit, sidewalks would not be constructed. Usual examples of public goods are found in the infrastructures necessary to run efficient markets. As such, collective good theory is closely linked to the analysis of governmental functions in an efficient market economy.

Flowing from its collective good formulation, hegemonic stability theory can be presented as proposing three hypotheses. First, the emergence of a hegemony is necessary for the provision of an international public good (the hegemony thesis). Second, the necessary existence of free-riders (and thus the unequal distribution of costs for the provision) and/or a loss of legitimacy will undermine the relative power position of the hegemonic state (for the entropy thesis, see Kindleberger 1976: 18, 24). Third, a declining hegemonic power presages a declining provision of the international public good (the decline thesis).

Three schools of thought

The different approaches within hegemonic stability theory can be distinguished by which particular public good each believes to be the product of the hegemonic system. In their chronological order in the debate, these goods are seen as a liberal international economy, international order, and international regimes.

In Charles Kindleberger's (1981, 1986) and Robert Gilpin's (1972, 1987) authoritative formulations, the international liberal economy is the public good. Both interpret the interwar period as one where one established leader (Gt Britain) lacked the strength, and one potential leader (the United States) the will to guarantee a liberal international order. Although for a while closer to the second school (see below), Gilpin recently has returned to this line of thought, and has proposed a long list of functions that a hegemony needs to provide for an international economic order to work (Gilpin 1987: 368). The following list relies on both Gilpin and Kindleberger. First, the hegemonic state has to stabilize monetary relations. It achieves monetary stabilization by providing the rediscount mechanism for insuring liquidity during international crises. When credit is internationally squeezed, the hegemonic state should accept the role of lender-of-last-resort. Similarly, the hegemonic state must assume the management of the international monetary system by maintaining a structure of exchange rates and by contributing to the coordination of macroeconomic policies. Second, the hegemonic state must also stabilize world trade. In times of crisis in particular sectors (such as the automotive industry), it must leave its respective markets open. When investment diminishes it should encourage a steady, if not countercyclical, flow of capital. Third, a liberal order relies on capital redistribution through foreign aid. Finally, the order, and in particular the hegemonic state, must have a sanction mechanism to address abusers of the system.

Another school sees international order/security itself (Gilpin 1981, Webb and Krasner 1989) as the public good. As alluded to above by Snidal, this school simply restates the traditional realist assumption that power differentials, and not the equal distribution of power, are conducive to stability. Bull uses this argument for describing the international realm as different from a Hobbesian state of nature and for deriving its anarchical society (see Chapter 3). It is most concisely put by Waltz (1969 [1967]: 312): 'Extreme equality is associated with extreme instability.'

Even though this school accepts the idea that some goods beneficial to many might not be provided by the international system, it puts a greater weight on the implications of international economic interactions for state power and national security. In an argument that echoes Carr's early critique of his British government (see Chapter 2), this second school distinguishes itself from the others by pointing to the fact that no generally beneficial effect is to be expected from the hegemon's provision of the public good. In other words, they deny the existence of a common interest in international economic liberalization and stability. But then indeed, this version provides little new compared to traditional realism. And Snidal's critique is not contradicted by Gilpin (1981: 184): 'the nature of international relations has not changed over the millennia . . . One must suspect that if somehow Thucydides were placed in our midst, he would . . . have little trouble in understanding the power struggle in our age'.

Finally, as in the definition mentioned initially, some versions of hegemonic stability theory define international regimes as the international public good (Keohane 1984). This school's most prominent representative, Robert Keohane, refuses to be likened to hegemonic stability theory. This is to a certain extent correct. He does not subscribe to thesis three: he argues that a declining hegemonic power might endanger the further provision of an international public good, but that cooperation can replace the hegemony. This takes up the critique of realism that he and Joseph Nye had already offered in *Power and Interdependence* (see Chapter 9), which is that realism is too power-deterministic: it tends to neglect that the ends for which power is sought might be affected by the norms of international society, or by regimes.

In Keohane's framework, regimes are in the last resort a function of the distribution of power and relations between states. Thus, he opts for regimes as intervening variables (Keohane 1984: 64). Applied to hegemonic stability theory, Keohane (1984: 49, 100) therefore argues that for 'the creation of international regime, hegemony often plays an important role, even a crucial one', but that the 'importance of transaction costs and uncertainty means that regimes are easier to maintain than they are to create'. He set himself the task of assessing under what conditions, realist (what he subsumes under a crude version of hegemonic stability theory) and liberal/institutionalist accounts on cooperation are more convincing. He pleads theoretically for a synthesis of realism and liberalism, and politically for the possibility of multilateral regime management.

A CRITIQUE OF THE THREE THESES

The following critique first concentrates on internal theoretical arguments, and then supplements them with an empirical critique of Kindleberger's initial application of hegemonic stability theory to the international monetary system.

The hegemony thesis: the role of US leadership

The first thesis of hegemonic stability theory argues that the existence of a (liberal) hegemonic state is a necessary element of, or conducive to, a stable international liberal order. Following Keohane's critique, this hegemony thesis has been qualified. First, hegemonic stability theory seems to imply that the existence of a single hegemonic state is a necessary condition for the provision of the public good. Strictly speaking, the theory of collective goods does not rule out the provision of a public good by more than one leader. Yet, the initial realist argument consists in claiming that the provision by one single leader is the most *likely* to occur. Kindleberger (1976: 26 ff., 38) made an extensive analysis of the different possibilities for the provision of the public good and discarded all of them except what he called leadership. His argument assumes that all management, whether by rule or institutions, is structurally dependent on governments and their interests. This excludes altruism because it will be overruled by self-interest. Nor does enlightened self-interest guarantee that an aggregation of enlightened self-interested actors will necessarily produce a generally beneficial outcome; there is also the free-rider problem. Finally, regional blocs are no solution either because they cannot function in an integrated economy. For him, there remains only leadership or benevolent despotism as a likely solution. Keohane challenged this thesis claiming that an international public good that can be managed through cooperation is theoretically possible. Similarly, Gilpin's (1987: ch. 10) proposal of a tripartite division of the world into an American, a Western European and a Japanese hegemony, as well as Krasner's (1985: 13, 30) argument of different systems of collective self-reliance actually plead for a regionalization of politics, big enough to allow the level of interdependence to subsist, but protected enough to fetter the negative impacts of it.

A second qualification of the hegemony thesis is again raised by Keohane. According to him, general clauses about a hegemonic state power do not necessarily tell much about its capacity to prevail in international finance or trade disputes, or its capacity to establish cooperative ventures in the management of vital resources, such as oil. In line with his previous writings about the issue area-specificity of power (see Chapter 9), he argues that the provision of a specific public good must be analysed by examining the power distribution within a specific issue-area. Here, the analyst can control for the issue-relevant power resources, and systematically (and selectively) include other non-state actors to the extent that they possess them.

Besides these qualifying critiques, there is also a more fundamental critique, indeed a realist critique of Kindleberger's hegemonic stability theory. This can be illustrated with Kindleberger's case, namely the international monetary system. The underlying logic of Kindleberger's argument is a Keynes-inspired domestic analogy. Markets are considered inherently unstable, and consequently in need of management. Applied to money matters, hegemonic stability theory develops from the idea that an economy increasingly based on credit needs to be managed by a public monetary authority (Walter 1993: 36). In no market economy is the management of money something which is left to the market or economic agents alone. A market economy presupposes rules, such as private and especially contract law for the development of stable labour relations and markets.[1] It rests upon a generally recognized currency that functions as a standard of value and which is usually issued by a public authority.

That a modern monetarized market economy is backed by a public authority does not mean that such an authority must be national. Indeed, there are examples of a multilateral management, such as Keynes' initial plan for the post-war system, which was not retained in the Bretton-Woods system, and the present plans to create a European monetary union which would replace the national management of a currency by a multilateral one (and a new common currency). Yet, these arrangements have seldom been manifest: monetary management is such an inherent feature of state sovereignty that those countries with relatively independent currencies jealously keep their right of seigneurage. For this reason, hegemonic stability theory assumes that an international monetary system which manages currencies and exchange rates, will work best if there is power-asymmetry in the system. A hegemony can best guarantee the enforcement of common rules and take over some of the functions of a central bank for the international monetary order. It is thus far a realist-sounding theory.

But it can be argued that the lack of any institutionalized constraint on the key currency country was an inherent and eventually fatal flaw in the Bretton-Woods system. This points to an internal contradiction in realist hegemonic stability theory of the Kindleberger version. On the one hand, if we follow the realist assumption that international rules follow power relations, the existence of a single major power, a hegemonic state, would logically lead us to expect an order biased in its favour. The resulting system is a function of the hegemonic state's will. On the other hand, it cannot be excluded that such an order will, sooner or later, put some

[1] This is one of the main initial insights of institutional economics. See, for example, S. Todd Lowry (1979), Oliver E. Williamson (1985); and Geoffrey M. Hodgson (1988).

external constraints on the international monetary manager. At this point, given the power differentials in a hegemonic system, realists would expect the system to break up when the hegemon perceives the system's utility inferior to an alternative system (or non-system). Making a system dependent on the whims and wills of a single country might help the system to be set up, but not necessarily increase its long-term prospects of stability: the hegemony can be as much an obstacle, as a condition to, a stable international monetary order (Walter 1993: 78–9). As a consequence, in order to defend the thesis that a hegemony is necessary and conducive to a stable liberal international order, Kindleberger needs the idealist leap about the hegemony's sacrifices for the international interest (see pages 157–59). That a dominant power would voluntarily and permanently relinquish control over main policy instruments even if a particular international order would be more costly for it, will hardly convince a realist. This approach cuts the realist link between an actor's power, interest and behaviour.

The entropy thesis: free-riders or insufficient rules?

The second thesis of hegemonic stability theory argues that hegemonic orders systematically tend to diffuse power and consequently end up undermining the position of the managing hegemony. Traditionally, hegemonic stability theory concentrated on the external reasons for entropy, such as the mounting resistance of the weaker states to the alleged or real abuse of hegemonic powers and/or by the dissemination of industrial centres through the export of capital and technology from the hegemon. Barry Buzan (1984: 621–2) has synthesized the main effects of hegemony on the hegemonic state itself:

> long-term economic self-weakening through the export of inflation, and the outflow of capital and technology; the growth of structural rigidities in the economy as a result of sociopolitical demands arising from the sustained experience of power and success; and the disproportionate costs, particularly military, that burden the hegemon's economy in relations to its rivals.
>
> (Buzan 1984: 621)

Crucial for this argument is the second characteristic of public goods, non-exclusion, and the phenomenon of free-riders in the system. Since the hegemon cannot exclude free-riders, so the argument goes, the latter will inevitably erode the hegemon's relative lead over crucial resources. Now obviously complete exclusion is hardly ever possible. The free-rider problem is hence always a relative one. No government can avoid its roads from being used by residents who evaded the taxes needed to build them. In practice, however, discriminations can be made and/or sometimes contributions can be enforced. For instance, persons resident in other countries (driving hence with a foreign number plate), paying income-tax abroad, can be asked to pay a special consumer tax employed to maintain or improve roads. Thus, although free-riders themselves might be inevitable, their presence does not necessarily undermine the power advantage of the hegemony which is always a relative phenomenon. Moreover, only if the benefits of free-riders are converted into an aggregate power that would march the power of the hegemon can one speak of entropy.

For this reason, some critics of hegemonic stability theory (and US foreign policy) argued that entropy arises out of the possible postponement of structural adjustments. This is similar to Karl Deutsch's influential definition of a power as the capacity of a person or organization to impose a projection of its inner structure on its environment. Whereas less powerful actors have to adapt their organization to that of the powerful, the latter can 'afford not to learn' (Deutsch 1966: Chapter 7). Entropy can result when the hegemonic state gets lulled into believing that all structural adjustments can be postponed indefinitely. Consequently, Strange and Calleo (1984: 108) turn this argument against those who see in the ending of the Bretton-Woods system a decline of US power. During the Vietnam War, so they claim, the US faced a trade-off between several of its commitments. It needed to spend increasing sums of money on the war (and on providing equal opportunities in President Johnson's 'great society') which conflicted with conservative monetary policies to back the Bretton-Woods system. The US could, of course, have adjusted domestically by changing its tax system. When it opted for inflationary policies, it understandably decided to keep the domestic social contract and shifted the adjustment abroad. The international monetary system had to give way (Calleo and Strange 1984: 108). In other words, if it is true that the hegemon keeps its position as long as it succeeds in making others adapt, the end of Bretton-Woods is an indication of US power, not decline.

Kindleberger's explanation of the break-up of the Bretton-Woods system as a consequence of entropy, has also been criticized by Strange (1976, 1986b). The main thrust of her argument is that although it is true that the system imploded, the reason was not increased free-riding but the insufficient instruments provided in the Bretton-Woods system for handling an international monetary system. To exclude other reasons for the system's instability, the entropy thesis must presuppose that the rules set up in 1944, if carefully applied, could have matched the demands for stability. The instruments of Bretton-Woods, however, were not able to confront several intrinsic problems. Besides the fact that there were no exact IMF criteria for the permission of credits which evolved only during the late fifties, the Bretton-Woods system failed to prepare the provision of liquidity. Likewise, it did not anticipate the crucial links between the gold market and the exchange market, and between both and the reserve currencies. On the one hand, the system relied on a single central bank for the provision of liquidity, which must produce a dollar overhang in the system. When the US no longer ran trade surpluses, the Bretton-Woods system became a strain on the US management of the dollar. But also the omission of the market links did their part in dooming the Bretton-Woods system. Indeed, its history can be read as the repeated attempt to remedy these initial omissions. Despite continuous savings of its reserve currencies, at some point the cost of these remedies became too high for the dollar: the US decided to unlink the gold from the reserve currency market.

The decline thesis: declining US power or shifting US interests?

This last critique leads directly to the qualifications of the decline thesis. Hegemonic stability theory was formulated after the equivalent of what many experienced as an economic Vietnam: the end of the Bretton-Woods system. Many assume a link between US power decline, as witnessed by the Vietnam quagmire, and the collapse of the core regime that provided the international monetary stability, a vital element of the liberal international economic system. But, so critics argue, this reasoning in fact proceeds from a reversal of the third thesis. Scholars do not first analyse the declining US monetary power, but deduce it from the declining provision of the public good. This reversal of thesis three is fallacious (Strange 1987; Keohane 1984: 196). The declining provision can perfectly correspond to a deliberate choice of the hegemonic state. 'For the US, increased discord was a precondition for cooperation on American terms' (Keohane 1984: 208). The following will assess this central question whether it was declining US power or shifting US interests which brought the Bretton-Woods era to an end.

For Kindleberger, the Bretton-Woods system was eventually undermined because some middle power countries refused to share the burdens of the system (France and Germany). The US was no longer strong enough to impose devaluations on other countries. Faced with an increasing balance of payment deficit, and resistance by other countries to change this situation, the US was left no other choice but to put an end to the gold exchange system.

This interpretation accepts a change in US interests, but claims that this change happened only because of its diminished power position. This argument has two weaknesses. First, it presupposes that US policies had been aimed at keeping the gold exchange system alive, if only the burden could have been shared differently. Second, it suggests that the US government had little power to enforce its preferred rules.

There were many pressures in the sixties to change the price of gold which the US government had always resisted. Not the least of the reasons for US refusal was that this idea had been continuously advanced by the French government, with whom the US administration was not exactly on the very best of terms. France, in its attempt to discipline the US and the dollar, had started to change massive amounts of dollars into gold, depleting US gold reserves and accumulating vast gold reserves itself. Hence, an increase in the gold rate would have had the politically controversial effect that countries whose reserves consisted mainly in gold, such as the US and later France, would see the value of their reserves increased at the expense of those countries who had been supportive to the dollar's role by not changing their dollar reserves back into gold (Germany).

There were also several indicators that from the mid-sixties, the US was resolved to remove the role of gold in the system and to convert to a paper dollar standard (Walter 1993: 189). Hence, the unilateral decision on 15 August 1971 did not come entirely as a surprise. The Nixon Administration suspended gold convertibility and imposed a 10 per cent surcharge on imports so as to force other countries to revalue. Furthermore, the US government requested to be given 80 per cent of the annual current account surplus of all OECD countries, that is, $9 billion out of a total of $11 billion. It asked other countries to accept a system in which the US was allowed to stand free from any responsibility for making domestic adjustments, and where it would get the major wealth created within the world of the OECD. In other words, put before the choice to keep a fixed gold exchange system but accepting some discipline on its monetary policies, or to let the dollar float and keep more monetary autonomy (at least this was the belief at the time), the US government rather consistently chose the latter. Floating exchange rates became increasingly the preferred US strategy. Given this, the outcome of the many negotiations during the early seventies actually show the success of US policies. For Walter (1993: 189–90), far from being weak, the US administration was strong enough to reshape the system to meet its own preferences.

This implies a critique of the link assumed by hegemonic stability theory where the change of interests is made dependent on a change in the relative power position of an actor. There are two logical ways out. First, we could relinquish the link altogether. It is perfectly possible that a government displays different interests and behaviour over time despite little difference in the overall power distribution. At the end of the Cold War, the USSR had a relative power position certainly not inferior to that of 1949, yet its definition of national interest and its behaviour was very different from then (Lebow 1994; Koslowski and Kratochwil 1994; see also the realist, but not neorealist, defence, by Wohlforth 1994/95). Similarly, one could imagine that a changed power position does not necessarily translate into changed foreign policy interests, as the evolution of post-war Germany from a defeated and ruined country to an economic superpower arguably bears witness. Second, the link between capabilities, interests and behaviour, could be upheld but reapplied with the inverse argument deducing the basic continuity of interests and relative power position from the continuity of behaviour, in this case the steady US efforts to shield the dollar management against external monetary discipline. If this escape is taken, the assumption of US relative power decline must be rejected. As one might expect, the more realist-inclined critics of hegemonic stability theory tend to employ this second way out.

Consequently, the decline thesis has provoked an important conceptual debate which, as usual with realist theories, concerns the correct definition and assessment of power. More precisely, the debate was prompted by the apparent contradiction between, on the one hand, a perception of diminished US control over world events, widely shared among US academics and politicians, and, on the other hand, the perception prevalent outside the US that the US had a continued unique capacity to impose unilateral decisions and to maintain its privileges within the new international order. The first linked the emerging disorder to an assumed decline of US power. Outside the US, the new order saw the US still as by far the most powerful player on the field, its relative advantage being unaltered.

The contradiction was resolved by a triple redefinition of power. First, and this is an echo of the interdependence literature, the sources of power in the international system have become more varied. If one takes trade figures (and gold reserves), then, indeed, the US has a less dominant position . today than forty years ago. Yet the picture changes if one leaves the focus on trade. Susan Strange (1987, 1988a) includes other major structures from which power in the international system derives, as for instance the military sector, the transnationalization of production, and, in particular, the control over knowledge and technology. Similarly, Joseph Nye's concept of 'soft power' (Nye 1990: 166–8) emphasized intangible resources, in which the US is very prominent, such as the bias of rules in regimes, and cultural and/or ideological attraction. Calculated in this way, the US might not have lost its overall hegemonic position, but its historically unique edge after the Second World War, an edge that the other liberal hegemonic state Great Britain never possessed (see also Russett 1985).

Second, the origins of authority have become more diffused. This resolves the contradiction between less US control and continuing US prevalence. The fact that the US has less control over world events, does not mean that it lost this control to other states: Strange has repeatedly argued that this lost power has devolved to non-state actors, and to markets. Finally, the effects of state actions have also become more diffused. Strange proposes a distinction between relational and structural power. Structural power refers to those effects, whether intentional or not, which can influence international politics and require other actors to adapt. This understanding of power looks backwards from the effects of actions and highlights those who can control the settings within which bargaining relations take place (see also Chapter 11).

The decline thesis has fallen prey to the often circular use of power; instead of assessing power independently of outcomes, outcomes are taken as indicators of changing power. The decline of the provision of some international functions is read as an indicator of diminishing US power, whereas a different analysis of power argues that the US power is not in decline, although today this does not mean that international state actors control as much of the economic sphere as they did after the Second World War.

HEGEMONIC STABILITY THEORY – AN INSUFFICIENT UPDATE OF REALISM

Until now, hegemonic stability theory has been understood as a realist theory of International Political Economy, a claim which is not uncontroversial, though a comparison both with classical and neorealism shows that the label is accurate. This notwithstanding, hegemonic stability theory has also produced the most unexpected idealistic leap by a realist writer. Kindleberger's attempt to blame European free-riders produced an internal contradiction in his theory; so here, the legitimate concern of US academics with US foreign policy played a trick on one theorist. Finally, although hegemonic stability theory is an attempt to match realism's classical theoretical body with the increasing international policy agenda, its update of realism appears insufficient.

Hegemonic stability theory: extension or critique of realism

Given the variety of subschools, the realist lineage is not always of the same sort. I will not touch upon the order or security version of hegemonic stability theory which is, in its own terms, only a replay of traditional realism. Instead, I will focus on Kindleberger's and Keohane's versions of the theory.

At first reading, Kindleberger's version seems strongly realist. He derives his outcomes from the distribution of power, and is therefore rather sceptical about the cooperative working of the international system. The system remains anarchical, because even though there are different states with different capabilities, there is no overarching and sanctioning government. The argument is largely zero-sum. What the hegemonic state loses, others gain. It remains basically state-centred. Not that other, particularly economic, actors are left out of the account. But the overall argument is concerned primarily with national power from which it derives its explanatory value. State-centering is also necessary for his historical comparisons with the inter-war system and the classical British-led gold standard. In its aim of differentiating international systems both historically and, in the present context, geographically, the theory does touch concerns of traditional realists, as for instance the English School (Bull and Watson 1984). Indeed, by arguing for the beneficial effects of power asymmetry and US leadership, Kindleberger rehearsed an earlier argument, advanced by a British Grotian realist, for similar beneficial effects of the British-led order. Martin Wight wrote:

We have seen that the international anarchy is restrained and to some extent systematized in practice by two opposing kinds of common interest, pulling alternatively to and fro. The first is the common interest of all powers in their freedom, of which they are faintly conscious in peace, and assert at the eleventh hour in war by an armed coalition against a common danger. The second is the kind of common interest represented by successive dominant powers. For their predominance has generally safeguarded real values, and offered real benefits for other nations, and sometimes they have wielded an international ideology as their most potent weapon – as the Habsburg powers were the protagonists of the Counter-Reformation, as Napoleonic France was the carrier of the French Revolution throughout feudal Europe, as Britain in the nineteenth century was the champion of liberalism.

(Wight 1979 [1946]: 289)

But the use of economics in International Relations introduces two important qualifications in regard to classical realism. First, modelling theories of International Relations according to positivist methodology implies the use of a single causal nexus. Kindleberger's book (1986) was that of an economic historian, not of a social 'scientist'. But later he accepted the remodelling of his major theses in such a way. Consequently, his approach can be seen as a special variant of Waltz's approach. For Waltz, the distribution of power in an anarchical system explains both the individual behaviour of states and the results of their action, i.e. is the tendency to restore a disrupted balance of power. Hegemonic stability theory assumes that the presence of a single major and liberal power is a necessary condition for the establishment of a liberal International Political Economy.

The second qualification is that by being derived from economic theory, hegemonic stability theory is based on a domestic analogy. The international liberal system is understood as analogous to a national liberal economic order. Since such an order presupposes a political orderer, hegemonic stability theory, although not openly challenging the assumption of anarchy, introduces elements of hierarchy into the understanding of the international system. Free markets can only function on the basis of private property rights, contract law, and central sanctioning mechanisms. By using such an analogy, scholars of the second school (Kindleberger and Gilpin) acknowledge the existence of role differentiation in the international system, the second tier which had dropped out of Waltz's international structure. Not all units have the same functions for the international system. To the extent that the assumption of like-units is central to neorealism, hegemonic stability theory is a critique of neorealism. And since hegemonic stability theory relies upon a domestic analogy, the deadly idealist sin once castigated by Bull (1966a), it might arguably be called antagonistic to traditional realism as well.

But this would overemphasize the restriction on domestic analogies in realism. Carr used domestic analogies when he compared international bargaining and conflict management to the labour–capital relationship. Similarly, Morgenthau's initial model for the balance of power was the checks-and-balances system of US democracy. In other words, realism does not exclude all analogical reasoning. Rather, it restricts the realm for such analogies. Those allowed are those where order is based merely on power in domestic politics. Not allowed are those who derive from the domestic legal-institutional setting, that is those where institutionalized norms solve conflicts (and even here the balance of power is a border case). Therefore, the second school of hegemonic stability theory can still be considered in the realist lineage.

Whereas Kindleberger refers to his approach as realist, Keohane understands his own approach as a critique of a strong (and realist) version of hegemonic stability theory. Yet he remains strongly attached to many core realist assumptions. Indeed, his approach both criticizes realist hegemonic stability theory from within and provides an alternative account which does not depart from more traditional realism.

Like Kindleberger's, his analysis starts from the idea of market failures, or more generally the suboptimal provision of specific goods in the international realm due to its anarchical character. His main attack on Kindleberger is that 'logically, hegemony should not be a necessary condition for the emergence of cooperation in an oligopolistic system' (Keohane 1984: 30). His study shows that cooperation and institutional rule can follow even from the core realist assumptions of egoistic self-interest and rational action. This is an interesting and consequential critique, which can be seen as having two implications. It could mean that realists overstate the conflictual nature of international relations, that is, that their approach constructs a bleaker picture of the world than it really is. This rejoins Bull's critique of a Hobbesian understanding of anarchy (see Chapter 3). But it might also follow the assumption of the conflictual nature of international relations, and then show that it cannot be derived from an egoistic rational action model under anarchical conditions. This would be a critique of Waltzian neorealism.

But does this correspond to a departure from *traditional* realism? The answer is negative with regard to the content of the theory. Keohane argues for a definition of cooperation, not as the absence of conflict, but 'as a process that involves the use of discord to stimulate mutual adjustment' (Keohane 1984: 46). This is very much a traditional argument for the balance of power. He maintains a realist, that is, instrumental view of the role of norms when he writes that

> norms and rules of regimes can exert an effect on behaviour even if they
> do not embody common ideals but are used by self-interested states and

corporations engaging in a process of mutual adjustment.

(Keohane 1984: 64)

Similarly, his vision of cooperation is instrumental:

Rational choice analysis is used in this book not to reinforce the conventional wisdom that cooperation must be rare in world politics, but to show that it can be pursued even by purely rational, narrowly self-interested governments, unmoved by idealistic concern for the common good or by ideological commitment to a certain pattern of international relations.

(Keohane 1984: 78)

For him, realist theories limit 'mutual interests in world politics . . . to interests in combining forces against adversaries' and thereby 'fail to take the role of institutions into account' (Keohane 1984: 62–3). Yet his ideas on the instrumental role of institutions are certainly taken into account – nearly all the classical Realist writers were after all international lawyers. He presents realism as implying 'the inevitability of either hegemony or conflict' (Keohane 1984: 84). This overstates the case; as discussed in Chapters 2 and especially 3 in this volume, there are many realist writers who believe in an alternative to those options, in the idea of a Concert.

With Keohane, there is no reference after these quotes, and no references throughout *After Hegemony*, to those realist writers who have theoretically developed the present-day adaptations of the diplomatic practices which characterized the European Concert: Aron, Bull, and Kissinger. He refers once to Stanley Hoffmann as an exception 'not representative of realism' (Keohane 1984: 8, fn. 1) and gives the impression that Wolfers' more subtle account of the concept of egoistic self-interest is exceptional. It is not that exceptional in the realist literature that Keohane does not quote, and which had been widely neglected, in particular after the different scientific versions of realism.

Therefore, where the content of his theory is concerned, Keohane sits squarely in the more sophisticated realist tradition. This is hardly surprising if the interpretation of Chapter 8 is correct, namely that his co-authored *Power and Interdependence* stays within this very classical tradition. Yet now he differs in his conception of a science. What distinguishes him from traditional realists is his research design which puts to test a single causal relationship between shifts in power distribution and international cooperation.

For this reason, and because the basic causal nexus leaves a central place to power differentials, as in balance of power theories, Kindleberger's and Keohane's version of hegemonic stability theory are but an amendment of realism. This does not mean that the theory is a simple rehashing of old ideas. Its attention to the international political economy is much more fundamental than that of traditional realism. It includes the economic system, and some economic institutions, within the core elements of the international system. It differs from neorealism also by taking more seriously the lack of fungibility in power resources; hence, its empirical analysis tends to be more carefully confined to a single issue area in which one state can be said to control the most effective means of influence. Compared with Waltz's neorealism, hegemonic stability theory clearly contributes to widening the scope of analysis and defines the boundaries of the discipline differently.

Kindleberger's idealist leap in defending US interests through hegemonic stability theory

By arguing that US leadership was generally beneficial to the international liberal order, Kindleberger was, of course, sure to provoke contradiction. After the Vietnam War, this kind of argument was certainly against the tide of world public opinion, and to some extent academic opinion. Since he argued that the Bretton-Woods system did not survive because it required a political discipline which the US was no longer strong enough to enforce on other countries, his theory had very strong political and ideological implications. Indeed, as with regime theory (Strange 1982a), Japan and European countries perceived it as a US attempt to blame them for the break-up of the Bretton-Woods system and to legitimate further US requests for burden-sharing.

Kindleberger's commitment perhaps explains the internal contradiction of his theory: to save his case for the US, his realist theory must rely on a central idealist assumption. The assumption became quite visible when he answered critiques of his theory. He wrote:

> I am a realist when it comes to regimes. It seems to me that the momentum set in motion by a hegemonic power . . . runs down pretty quickly unless it is sustained by powerful commitment . . . There needs to be positive leadership, backed by resources and a readiness to make some sacrifice in the international interest.
>
> (Kindleberger 1986b: 10)

It is curious to claim a realist lineage, if the argument is based on sacrifices made in the international interest. It makes only sense if these sacrifices have a bigger pay-off for the hegemony, now or later. Since hegemonic stability theory relies on a rational actor assumption of the collective good argument, the cost-benefit analysis must be positive, in particular for the hegemonic state which is to some extent a price-maker, not only a price-taker. Either his approach is no longer realist, because he contends that politics has been, and should be, shaped by concerns over the liberal nature of the international system, and, in particular, because he attributes altruistic motives to the hegemony. Or he remains a realist, and thus overstates his case in his quest to justify US policies.

Given Kindleberger's other writings, it seems more likely to assume that Kindleberger is driven by a political concern which muddles his theoretical assumptions. His use of the concept of public good is explicitly ideological. He refrains from using the word hegemony, because this would imply imposed rule. Instead, he prefers to 'think of leadership and responsibility' (Kindleberger 1986b: 10). He openly asserts that whenever a public good is not, or no longer, provided, the responsibility lies first with the free-riders, that is, potentially all actors except the responsible hegemony:

> The question is how to distinguish domination and exploitation from responsibility in the provision of cosmopolitan goods in the world economy, and whether there are not occasions when the world suffers from the underproduction of the public good of stability, not because of greedy vested interests and domination or exploitation but because of the principle of the free rider it is of some interest that on two occasions – in 1931 and again in 1971 – it was the small countries, more or less simultaneously and in pursuit of their private interests, that pushed Britain first, and then the United States, off the gold standard.
>
> (Kindleberger 1981: 247, 249)

Such a move has important political consequences. It opens the political debate around the more equal distribution of the burden and its provision, the never ending argument about burden-sharing. Susan Strange (1982) explicitly links the emergence of the regime literature to the US debate on burden-sharing. The implication of the argument is to shift the blame to the free-riders for the declining provision of a public good, whenever the hegemonic state is not able or no longer interested in providing the public good. With the empirical critique mentioned above, this blame would need more justification.

Expectedly, other realists in International Political Economy did not follow Kindleberger. It is exactly this claim of a universal interest provided with an international order that is beneficial to all (even in different degrees), which sets Gilpin and Krasner apart. They are, as one would expect from realists, on guard against the classical harmony of interests argument that was so forcefully attacked by E.H. Carr with regard to Britain (1946: 44, 46, 53; see also Chapter 2). For them, ideas derive from politics and power, and not *vice versa*. Consequently, claiming a harmony of interests is nothing more than the result of a specific configuration of power and the successful implementation of a particular interest so as to make it seem universal.

This last critique by Gilpin and Krasner resounds with dependency scholars. Hegemony is here considered as simple dominance, imposed by a hegemonic state seeking revenue. A public good is always and foremost a private good of the hegemonic state. Increased free-riding and the decline of power simply imposes higher costs on the hegemony for extracting benefits. This might reach a point where it becomes to the hegemony's relative disadvantage to provide the so-called public good. Yet, the resulting environment, far from removing the privileges in the system, might even further reduce the possibilities of weaker actors to benefit from the international order. According to this argument, if international regimes adapt, they do so to maintain the privileges of the stronger actors. To make the free rider responsible, assert Gilpin and Krasner, is to use a misplaced moralistic language, and, according to dependency scholars, obscures the order's systematically beneficial returns for the hegemon.

Hegemonic stability theory as an insufficient update of realism

This chapter has played out the realist critique of a realist theory of International Political Economy. If there was still need for it, it served to show the variety of realist thought. Kindleberger saw in the decline of US power the reason for the break-up of the Bretton-Woods system. Instead, a more consistent realist reading would have argued for the basic continuity of the US relative power position, and its steady attempt to remain untouched by international monetary discipline as initially agreed in the Bretton-Woods system. In such a system which expressed the underlying balance of bargaining power where the leader was neither confronted with a fixed set of rules for crucial adjustment processes, nor constrained by the existing principles to act in a self-enlightened manner, the tension between the national and international logic might not always be resolved in favour of the former. Yet whenever the leader does not adjust to the system, the system adjusts to, or breaks up for, the interests of the leader.

But also this more consistent realist reading of the Bretton-Woods system, is riddled with excessive statism. The 'US interest' simply does not exist, and is rather more a hindrance than a help to understanding International Relations. First, by focusing on the government, US government policies might appear costly to the collectivity of US citizens, but they have often important windfalls for private national and international actors. During decolonization, economic actors could open new markets and production sites, as well as cheap sources of raw material. Wars in the Third World might have been very costly for the state budget, but US-based multinational enterprises (as well as others) certainly did profit from the type of pacification: it created a relatively reliable legal framework for the working of the MNCs.

Echoing an argument made by Giovanni Arrighi, Bruce Russett says:

> Decolonization meant acceleration of the introduction of advanced capitalism into the Third World, and the United States was the most efficient capitalist. The postwar regimes in international trade and finance brought worldwide prosperity, not least to the United States.
>
> (Russett 1985: 218)

Second, taking the above-mentioned interpretation of the end of the Bretton-Woods system seriously, implies that the core of the explanation shifts from a relative power decline to a rigid state-society relation in the US. The more general point is that the historical evolution of states to modern welfare states demands a conceptualization of state policies which, increasingly, cannot be divorced from the understanding of the respective state-society relations. Today, it could be hypothesized that hegemonic states are structurally less able to manage an international monetary system, than liberal night-watch states. Yet, as with other attempts to apply realism, the underlying world-view of hegemonic stability theory turns back to the nineteenth century, where social contracts were less demanding, and foreign policies, including economic ones, more isolated. Although hegemonic stability theory seems to ask for such an inclusion of state-society relations into its analysis, it does not yet address the social contract, concentrating instead on governments and firms.

CONCLUSION

Hegemonic stability theory is undoubtedly a move away from Waltzian neorealism. The debate about US decline has shown a broader understanding of both international politics and of power. Moreover, the theory depicts an international system with hierarchical features. Indeed, although it respects the third tier of Waltz's definition of structure, i.e. the general causal relation between the distribution of power and international outcomes, it implicitly attacks the circular definitions of the first two tiers. For Waltz, anarchy implied the impossibility of functional differentiation. Hegemonic stability theory is built upon the idea that the hegemonic state, in a way not too different from domestic governments in the times of the liberal night-watch state, is functionally differentiated from other actors, and guarantees the order of the liberal global political economy. As a result, the first tier, the so-called deep structure of anarchy, increasingly appears as a hollow shell. It neither excludes rule without government, nor forms of hierarchy. This reappraisal of Waltz's second tier has been used both to criticize neorealism by showing its incapacity to understand major historical changes, such as the change from the medieval to the modern state system (Ruggie 1986 [1983]); and also as a way of developing neorealism further (Buzan, Jones and Little 1993). The following chapter shows how two realists within International Political Economy, Robert Gilpin and Susan Strange, in a reappraisal of international politics and of the concept of power, are stretching the boundaries of realism – and of the discipline – even further.

11 International Political Economy at the convergence of realism and structuralism

> On the question of power, however, opportunities of collaboration [between realism and structuralism], at least, do exist.
>
> (K.J. Holsti, *The Dividing Discipline*, p. 80)

International Political Economy not only provided a redefinition of neo-realism, but also set the stage for a *rapprochement* of two materialist positions – the power materialism of realism and the economic materialism of dependency theorists. International Political Economy focuses here on the interplay between the power and wealth motive (micro-level), or between international capitalism and its political organization (macro-level). The *rapprochement* was possible because some neo-Marxists conceptualize an autonomous political sphere and because some realists accepted a structuralist framework (not to be confused with Waltz's systemic approach).

The convergence of realist and structuralist thinking takes place mainly around the concept of power. Neomercantilists like Gilpin try to understand questions about the dynamics of power, that is, which factors historically define power and why great powers rise and decline. Dependency scholars argued for a structural concept of power, focusing on the bias or the social construction of options in the global political economy which systematically privileges some actors (following the old saying that 'everybody is free to eat at the Ritz and to sleep under the bridge'). Susan Strange uses such an approach for four structures, namely the military, as traditional realists do, production as Marxists stress, a knowledge structure similar to that in Gramscian theories, and particularly finance which she sees as being scandalously neglected in other theories.

Gilpin's and Strange's approaches are realist responses to the crisis of realism as a diplomatic practice and as an explanatory theory. But this is not the only way to read them. Indeed, although both have repeatedly called themselves realists, both have been most critical about several aspects of realist International Relations. For Gilpin, security can only be grasped by abandoning the ill-conceived focus on the military balance of power. Susan Strange castigates the territorial world-view of realism and

the blindness about the 'new diplomacy' in which states, for the very survival of their domestic legitimacy, must bargain with firms. By taking
seriously some realist assumptions like scepticism, and some realist concepts
like power, they argue in favour of research projects, which in practice
often come closer to neo-Marxist or Gramscian political economy, than
to Waltzian neorealism.

This chapter will first show the shifts in some dependency approaches to
concepts of structural power before examining Gilpin's and Strange's realist
International Political Economy.

POWER AND DEPENDENCY

The intellectual roots of dependency theories

Two important intellectual roots can be discerned in the development of
dependency theories: Western Marxist theories of imperialism, and structuralist critiques of liberal theories of international trade.

Post-war Western Marxist theories of imperialism were not mainly interested in the intra-bourgeois struggle among industrialized countries, as their
classical predecessors had been (see Chapter 6). Theories of surplus absorption tried to understand how capitalist classes in the core countries under-
develop the South, and how core states and multinational corporations
control periphery countries by means of (economic) exploitation (see
Fig. 11.1).

Compared with classical imperialism, post-1945 Marxism in the West (for
instance Baran and Sweezy) stressed three new phenomena. First, a new
kind of monopoly explains both underconsumption and imperialist expansion. In a situation of monopoly capitalism, price competition is eliminated,
thus prices are downwardly rigid. Yet non-price competition (product differentiation, advertising, cost-reducing innovations) is heightened and gener-
ates a tendency of falling costs. Rigid prices and falling costs combine to
the new absolute law of monopoly capitalism, namely the 'tendency of the
absolute surplus to rise', which replaces Marx's tendency for the profit to
fall. This is a considerable break. Since this surplus, despite public spending,
both civilian and military spending cannot be absorbed in developed
societies for reasons similar to the ones given by Rosa Luxemburg (see
Chapter 6), underconsumption follows. New markets have to be found, in
a changed historical situation where socialism might bar open access to
many areas (the theories date from before 1989).

Second, although writers disagree on their exact relationship, multinational corporations become more important transmission vehicles for
the expansion of international capitalism than states, with the result that:

> global foreign policy corresponds to the interests and perspective of the
> multinational corporation . . . The multinational corporation has become

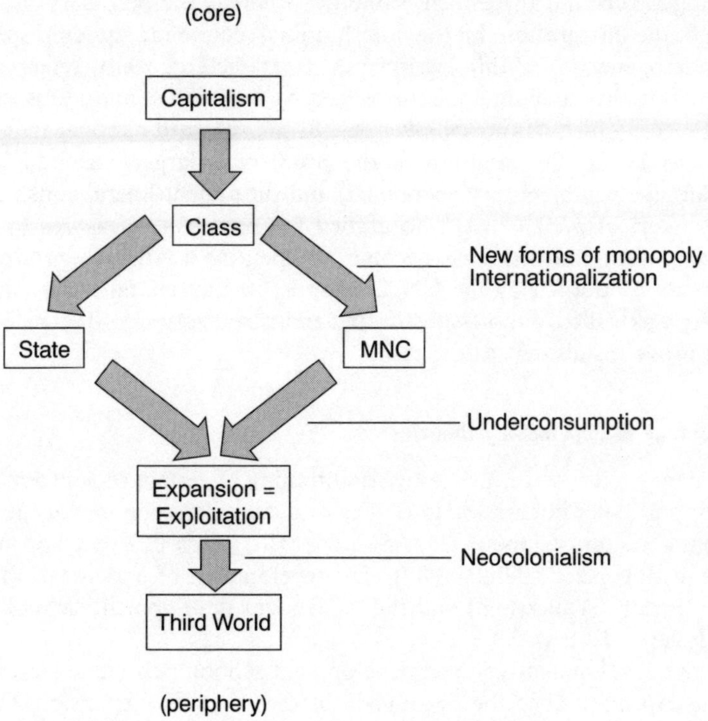

(core)

```
          ┌────────────┐
          │ Capitalism │
          └────────────┘
                │
                ▼
          ┌────────────┐
          │   Class    │──────────── New forms of monopoly
          └────────────┘              Internationalization
          ↙            ↘
  ┌─────────┐      ┌─────────┐
  │  State  │      │   MNC   │
  └─────────┘      └─────────┘
          ↘            ↙
          ┌────────────┐
          │ Expansion =│──────────── Underconsumption
          │Exploitation│
          └────────────┘
                │
                ▼
          ┌────────────┐
          │Third World │──────────── Neocolonialism
          └────────────┘
```

(periphery)

Figure 11.1 Theories of surplus absorption (Baran and Sweezy)

the instrument for the creation and consolidation of an international ruling class, the only hope for reconciling the antagonisms between national and international interests.

(O'Connor 1970: 150)

Third, it is economic and not necessarily military means that guarantee control, such as access to foreign exchange assets; the means of private direct investment; the control of local savings (either via International Monetary Fund and the World Bank, or via the MNCs in less developed countries); the control of mineral, agricultural, manufacturing and other real assets; and, finally, the organization and management of trade by foreign corporations.

The second theoretical input in dependency theories is the structuralist critique of the liberal theory of international trade. Whereas liberal theories understand development through specialization according to comparative advantage (Ricardo) or factor-endowment (Heckscher-Ohlin-Samuelson), Raúl Prebisch and others argued that such an international division of labour systematically favours the centre over the periphery. This is due to each area's substantially different structures of production. The centre has a homogeneous and diversified economy, whereas the periphery becomes, through the integration in the international economic system, specified and heterogeneous. Within peripheral states, heterogeneity refers to the nature of dualist economies characterized by a capitalist and industrialized export sector which has no spillover benefit to backward national economies (Senghaas 1982). The solution of the problem is largely inspired by the German nineteenth century economist, and prominent liberal constitutionalist thinker, Friedrich List, who argued for protective measures to allow German infant industries to become competitive to British production. The solution adopted by the UN Economic Committee on Latin America (ECLA) was called import-substituting industrialization (ISI) which soon would prove insufficient to the task.

The content of dependency theories

Dependency refers to the domestic conditioning of certain social formations by their particular integration into the world capitalist economy or the international division of labour (Dos Santos 1970). Two different approaches can be distinguished (Palma 1980), the 'development of underdevelopment' school (Frank, Wallerstein) and the 'dependent development' school (Cardoso, Faletto, Evans).

For the development-of-underdevelopment school, peripheral states have become capitalist since the beginnings of the capitalist expansion, that is, since colonialism (Frank 1966). The capitalist world system itself is best described as a chain of surplus extraction, in which the surplus generated at each stage, starting from the domestic class relations in the periphery, is successively drawn off towards the centre. As opposed to the traditional structuralist view, this implies, that peripheral societies are not dualist. The underdeveloped sector is an integral and necessary part of the developed one. It is not 'because sectors remain underdeveloped that the country does not overcome its dependence', but 'since some sectors are developed, others must remain underdeveloped'.

Immanuel Wallerstein (1979 [1974], 1984: 1–96) introduces some conceptual refinements to this (see Fig. 11.2). Most prominently he adds the category of semi-periphery which is constituted both by rising peripheral countries and core countries in decline. They function as a transmission belt, fettering the demands of the periphery and replacing direct control of the core. This dynamic element is compounded by a cyclical view of the world political economy. For Wallerstein, a hegemonic leader is necessary to sustain the world capitalist system. Following Kondratieff's cycles, he understands the 'Great Wars' as a struggle for hegemony. Thus, two 30-year wars, 1618–48 and 1914–45, can be understood as the violent rearrangement of international leadership. In the first of these hegemonic wars, Great Britain replaced the Dutch, before being, in the second, superseded by the US. Until the end of the Cold War, the present situation was,

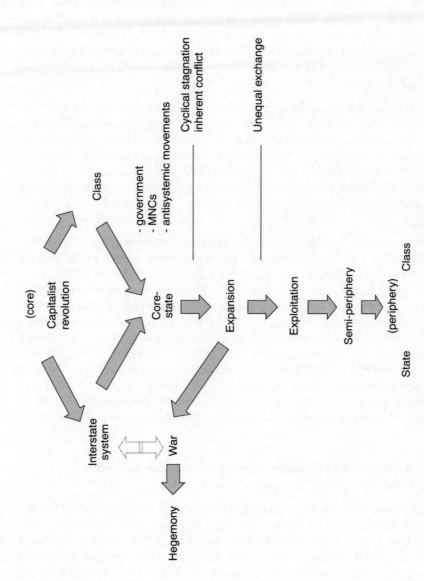

Figure 11.2 The world system, after Wallerstein

for Wallerstein, characterized by a declining hegemonic state and rising challenges from anti-systemic movements within (e.g. pacifism) and without the system (the socialist bloc).

The school of associated-dependent development focuses on the non-mechanical and non-determinist interplay of external and internal forces in the political and economic development of LDCs (Cardoso 1977: 22). A central concept in this approach is the phenomenon of crippled economies in late industrializing countries, a concept first developed by Friedrich List (Senghaas 1982):

> capitalist accumulation in dependent economies does not complete its cycle. Lacking autonomous technology – as vulgar parlance has it – and compelled therefore to utilize imported technology, dependent capitalism is crippled . . . It is crippled because it lacks a fully developed capital-goods sector. The accumulation, expansion, and self-realization of local capital requires and depends on a dynamic complement outside itself: it must insert itself into the circuit of international capitalism.
>
> (Cardoso 1973: 163)

The stress is laid on the domestic political and economic structure for the explanation how actually policies are made, applied, and which chances there are for a country to overcome its backwardness (Evans 1979).

In general, the recommendations are, if any, of a neomercantilist type, where one tries to selectively use the necessary foreign input without becoming in the same time overexposed to its competitive influences (Senghaas 1988: 142). Yet, this approach does not come up with a clear-cut theory of the way underdevelopment occurs or how, for any country, one can change this fact. It is closer to a historical-sociological method of trying to understand the ways semi-peripheral and peripheral countries work in a global economy, so as to understand the specific internal–external articulation of domestic systems and the world political economy (Palma 1980).

The politicization of dependency: power relations and international capitalism

André Gunter Frank has become a *bête noire* (and also a strawman) for different Marxist writers.[1] Their criticism was prompted by Frank's neo-Smithian definition of capitalism (Brenner 1977), which, based on exchange and the profit motive, would imply that 'from the neolithic revolution onwards, there has never been anything, but capitalism' (Laclau 1979: 23). Similarly, Frank's and Wallerstein's outside–in vision turned Marxist class analysis upside-down by making class relations (in the periphery) not the

[1] For a comprehensive critique of Wallerstein where the writers extend behind the rather simple sphere of exchange – sphere of production controversy, see Foster-Carter 1978, Skocpol 1977, and Brewer 1990.

origin, but the result of exchange relations (for a reassessment of the Brenner–Wallerstein debate, see Denemark and Thomas 1988). Neither Laclau, nor Brenner however, tackle the more historicist (and much less determinist) approach of Cardoso, nor the empirical content of Frank's thesis i.e. underdevelopment.

In this section I will argue that an important part of the critiques of dependency, by Marxists and non-Marxists alike, emphasized not only economic dynamics (of capitalism), but also their relationship with a more autonomous international political structure. As a corollary the dependency tradition contributed to a redefinition of the concept of power, so central also to realists.

A first step of this politicization of dependency approaches consisted in distinguishing between the power structures of the international system and the economic dynamics of capitalism. When Laclau compared the mercantilistic and the present epochs, he asserted that the development of the dominant economic structures could generate underdevelopment through the monopoly pricing of the core and for 'extra-economic coercion which retarded any process of social differentiation and diminished the size of their internal markets' (Laclau 1979: 37). He is hence describing power relations within the sphere of exchange (monopoly) and within the political system (extra-economic coercion). Similarly, Bill Warren (1980) re-established the autonomy of politics, rejecting the economic determinism that looms in certain dependency writings. For him, the (Leninist) equation of imperialism with the extension of the world market resulted in confounding the negative effects of the growth of capital, which should be seen as an economic phenomenon, and the impact of advanced capitalist countries, which is political.

If capitalism, as in orthodox Marxism, is progressive, then underdevelopment must be explained elsewhere, either by deferring positive effects to a future time (as Marx did), or by leaving a stronger causal determination to political relations. Such a stress on extra-economic causes for the analysis of imperialism can be found with Laclau who defined economic dependence as 'the constant absorption by one region of the economic surplus of another region' (Laclau 1979: 36), a purely descriptive definition which would hardly embarrass a mercantilist. But non-Marxist development economists have been going further down the road. Sanjaya Lall denied that external influence and conditioning were 'something peculiar in their occurrence in LDCs, which can be said to constitute dependence'. These characteristics were not exclusive to LDCs, but – and here Lall's position resembles Warren's – to capitalist development in general. Instead of deriving dependence from economic factors, Lall proposed a political conceptualization of different levels of dependence: 'a pyramidal structure of socio-political dominance . . . in the capitalist world with the top (hegemonic) position held by the most powerful capitalist country and the bottom by the smallest and poorest ones' (Lall 1975: 803, 808; for a similar line, see Cohen 1973).

Yet to replace dependence by dominance or power is not a considerable advance in explanatory value, if one cannot specify the content of the concept. What appears from this critique is therefore the question whether the understanding of power can be separated from the motion of the international economic system.

Dependency scholars gave a negative answer. James Caporaso agreed to the critique that political or power factors played a more important role for understanding dependency, but only if power was redefined. He deemed that bargaining power in asymmetrical interdependence, prominently represented by Keohane and Nye, was insufficient to apprehend power relations in the world political economy. Yet he also stated that:

> to focus exclusively on the concrete bargaining among actors and the various ways in which actors effectively exert their wills over others is to ignore the fact that the social structuring of agendas might systematically favour certain parties.
>
> (Caporaso 1978: 33)

This move rescues a concept of dependency very similar to that of Cardoso. 'Dependency focuses on the absence of actor autonomy . . . Actor autonomy is limited by *internal* fragmentation and the reliance on *external* agencies for the completion of basic economic activities' (Caporaso 1978: 18, 23). Caporaso defines structural power as follows:

> This kind of power is a higher-order power because it involves the ability to manipulate the choices, capabilities, alliance opportunities, and pay-offs that actors may utilize . . . We say this is a higher order form of power because it is a power to govern the rules which shape bargaining power. It is this type of power, structural power, which is crucial to the understanding of dependency.
>
> (Caporaso 1978: 4)

The following two sections will show how Gilpin and Strange include structuralist ideas for the understanding of power into their realist International Political Economy theories.

ROBERT GILPIN: THE THREE DIALOGUES OF NEOMERCANTILISM AND NEO-MARXISM

Robert Gilpin's research programme is an attempt to understand the historically changing nature of power and the rise and decline of great powers. In other words, it is about the dynamics of power. For Gilpin, two historical shifts are central for answering these concerns at the end of the twentieth century: the increasing prominence of technological and economic resources of power, and the qualitative change of states to welfare states. Gilpin concentrates both on the increasingly strenuous domestic adjustment processes of welfare states, prone to export their problems, and on the international accommodation of power shifts, especially of great power decline, where competition risks degeneration into technological or other wars (for a longer analysis of Gilpin's methodological assumptions and empirical analyses, see Guzzini 1997a). The result is a global, or national and transnational, 'struggle for efficiency' which makes the narrow, mainly diplomatic-strategic understanding of security obsolete (Gilpin 1987: xii). For historical reasons, Gilpin sees power and security as fundamentally linked to economic dynamics. He seeks to influence both the analysis and disciplinary boundaries of International Relations so as to take this into account.

Realist International Relations as necessarily neomercantilist International Political Economy

Gilpin proposes an academic project which tries to overcome the military emphasis of international studies, and which redefines the disciplinary borders of international politics. Particularly different from Waltz's form of neorealism is his sensitivity to historical changes in the form of inter-group conflicts. For him, with the evolution of groups' *internal* organization, also the nature of conflicts between groups change. The advent of the nation-state and market economy make a difference to realist theory: they require realist theory to become political economy. The advent of the welfare state in the twentieth century leads him to plead for a study of International Political Economy based around a *rapprochement* of neo-mercantilist and Marxist concerns.

The changed modern international political economy

Ever since his initial studies of technology and industrial policy, Gilpin believes that with the rise of the nation-state and market economy, power cannot be understood independently from the economic base. This basic insight of mercantilists and Marxists alike is the driving force of his theorizing: wealth and power, and the agent's pursuit of these, are inextricably linked. Based on this assumption, Gilpin provides a historical picture of today's global political economy.

Gilpin believes that the rise of an international market economy had a major impact on state security. It constituted a more or less autonomous sphere within and across borders, due to its independent dynamic and its aims which were separate from the state or society at large (for this and the following argument, see Gilpin 1977: 21 ff.). This extraordinary development was possible for three reasons: the invention of a monetarized economy, the rise of a merchant middle class, and the avoidance (or postponement) of a unifying empire in Europe. The European balance of power allowed the merchant class to develop its strength in an environment where competition for wealth and power was pushing societies to adopt the modern state organization. Since the modern nation-state had an unchallenged fiscal and war-making capacity, from then on it became the major group organization whose expansion has lasted until today (Gilpin 1981: 123).

From the advent of the European state system (that is starting from the Italian city-states) until the *Pax Britannica* is the phase of mercantilism; the first attempt of the modern world to organize a market economy on a global scale. Technological and organizational innovations in warfare bolstered the rise of mercantilism – as a form of political economy and concomitantly as a theory. Both the production of gunpowder and the rise of professional armies depended on the merchant trading system (to assure the provision of powder) and wealth (to pay the armies). In return, the sovereign guaranteed property rights.

It was Britain's victory in the Napoleonic wars, the industrial revolution, and new means of communication which brought together all the conditions necessary to create an interdependent world. The nineteenth century balance of power (balance for the continent and power for Britain) allowed the competitive leader to manage the international economy financially and commercially. Britain's comparative advantage and national security interest demanded a liberal approach based on an open market strategy. In short, the *Pax Britannica* provided the political framework for the emergence of a liberal international economy and concomitantly for (economic) liberalism as a doctrine. This doctrine was soon criticized by economic nationalists like Hamilton or List who argued for a dynamic theory of comparative advantage where endowments might be created by conscious policies and must be protected in their infant phase, and later by socialists and in Lenin's theory of imperialism.

For Gilpin, World War I was the test for the shift in power that occurred with Britain's decline and the rise of Germany and the US. The absence of strong leadership in the inter-war period produced the breakdown of the system. Only with the *Pax Americana* after 1945 could a new liberal international order be established.

Gilpin generalizes from this historical account the factors that affect the incentive structure of actors and thus the stability of an international system. In his utilitarian theory of war, instability arises whenever a state calculates that this will be rewarding. This calculus is affected by changes in transport and communication, in military technology, and by demographic and economic factors that distinguish our period from the pre-mercantilist ones (see Gilpin 1981: 55–84). Thus, although neorealist theory might refer to the eternal return of power politics, Gilpin's 'necessary' mercantilist approach introduces as endogenous factors many otherwise neglected features. The causal chain of his approach starts with (organizational and technical) technology and economic change, often induced by the international competition of states. This affects the distribution of power in the system, and the incentives for agents to change their behaviour.

Actual policies finally determine the specific international system (whether liberal or not).

Finally, Gilpin places today's global political economy in the context of an international system which does not start in 1648 with the Westphalian Treaties, but which has existed only since 1815 with the advent of a British-led international liberal order. 'First in the European system and then on a global scale, successive political and economic hegemonies have supplanted the pattern of successive empires as the fundamental ordering principle of international relations' (1981: 144).

If neorealism has been criticized for not being able to differentiate the change from the medieval to the modern system (Ruggie 1986 [1983]), Gilpin's historic and more dynamic account cannot be attacked on this charge. A neomercantilist realist finds the major ordering principle of international relations in the hegemonic governance of the international political economy, whether liberal or not.

Definition and ideologies of International Political Economy

The historical development of the international political economy in the last few centuries also informs Gilpin's (1975) typology of approaches to International Political Economy: economic nationalism (or neomercantilism), liberalism (called, with reference to Raymond Vernon, the sovereignty-at-bay model) and neo-Marxism (or dependency). Later the same models, initially created for the understanding of foreign direct investment, have been expanded into three ideologies of International Political Economy in general (Gilpin 1987: Chapter 2; see also Choucri 1980; Barry Jones 1981, 1982; Gill and Law 1988).

Since he repeats this threefold distinction at a time when the components have become commonly acknowledged in International Relations, Gilpin gives the impression that he wants to conceive International Political Economy as a sister discipline of International Relations, something like the 'economic approaches of realism, pluralism, Marxism'. Yet his view of International Political Economy *de facto* attempts to overcome the limits of International Relations by a wider approach essentially based on the integration of ideas derived from neomercantilism and neo-Marxism. If, for historical reasons, it is impossible to preserve a purely political understanding of the state in realist theory, realism must, according to Gilpin, be based on an approach which integrates the realm of politics and economics on the same footing. Similarly, the discipline of International Relations should become International Political Economy.

Together with the threefold typology, Gilpin provides a rather succinct focus of the subject-matter that International Political Economy is supposed to cover (and that defines its scientific research programme). His definition of International Political Economy is: 'the reciprocal and dynamic interaction in international relations of the pursuit of wealth and the pursuit of power' (Gilpin 1975: 40). It became a standard reference (Staniland 1985). This definition claims to be broad enough to integrate the three models of the future into one discipline. This is also what he attempts in the later textbook.

Yet the three ideologies do not seem to be internally coherent. The difficulty lies in the liberal model. There is, at least, a tension in the solution he provides us. In his book on multinational corporations, the liberal model is subsumed under the interdependence literature. The essential claim of this literature was that increasing economic interdependence and technological advances in communication and transportation are making the nation state an anachronism and shifting the control of world affairs to transnational actors and structures (e.g. the Eurodollar market). To this framework he adds a world-view of voluntary and cooperative relations among interdependent economies, whose goals consist in accelerating economic growth and all-round welfare by means of the multinational corporation as a transmission belt of capital, ideas, and growth. This presentation superposes insights from the interdependence literature on the liberal economists' or neofunctionalist credo. In other words, Gilpin links the transnationalist framework of analysis, which privileges non-state actors and dynamics, with the old established, and simplified, idealist creed, which says that more commerce breeds harmony. By fusing these two ideas, his category of liberal school bridges from transnational politics to the idealism of economic liberalism. As a result, Gilpin runs into a problem for his general definition of International Political Economy. For political economy, political or power-analysis is an endogenous variable of the explanation. Liberal international economics, however, treats power as exogenous. By the force of his definition (where power and wealth are integrated), Gilpin seems pushed to exclude liberal international economics from the body of his theory.

This tension may be why he adjusts the definition in the 1987 textbook to what seems to be the present orthodoxy for the definition of International Political Economy, the 'state–market nexus' (Gilpin 1987: 8, 11). This definition allows an integration of liberal economic theory as the model for the study of markets – even if power is treated as an exogenous variable. Nevertheless, he cannot avoid later admitting that therefore 'liberalism lacks a true political economy' (Gilpin 1987: 45). This squaring of the circle leaves one rather perplexed.

The stress on political economy (as in his first definition) was a reaction against the compartmentalization of the subject-matter into two different disciplines which often treat the other as exogenous to the subject. Gilpin found the field of economics unsatisfactory because it did not integrate power analysis in its explanatory models. In turn, he finds political science lacking because it often treats economics as exogenous to, or sometimes only dependent on, the political setting: the autonomy of market forces is missing. Yet, to alter the definition which stresses the organization of the pursuit of power and wealth, rather than the objective of this activity

(Gilpin 1987: 11), as Gilpin does, is to fall back on a conceptual and disciplinary split that political economy was supposed to overcome.

Dynamizing neomercantilism: three dialogues

In coherence with his earlier view, Gilpin in fact tries to overcome this split by elaborating an approach which is a *rapprochement* of the two 'real' theories of political economy: mercantilism and Marxism. Although he goes into some detail why he thinks the two cannot be mixed, his reasons do not forestall his *rapprochement*.

He admits that Hegelian–Marxist approaches in general, and Lenin's law of uneven development in particular are of heuristic value, but are too deterministic and ahistorical (Gilpin 1981: 48–9). Yet, neo-Marxist writers in the dependency tradition of Cardoso or stemming from a critical theory see themselves similarly as part of a 'historicist Marxism that rejects the notion of objective laws of history' (Cox 1981: 248). Gilpin does sometimes acknowledge the similarities of realism and Marxism in their perspectives on the nature and dynamics of International Relations. They differ essentially, according to him, with respect to the 'underlying dynamic: realism stresses the power struggle between states, and marxism stresses the profit motive of capitalist societies' (Gilpin 1981: 94). But for himself (and also for Marxists) 'the struggle for power and the desire for economic gains are ultimately and inextricably joined' (Gilpin 1981: 46). In his later work, he again discusses the difference between these two ideologies as being essentially two respective concepts of human nature. Marxism affirms the malleability of man and in the withering away of imperialism, war and the state after a communist revolution (Gilpin 1987: 43). Here, Gilpin touches upon a profound point. Realism is based on philosophical scepticism as to the potential of human nature, to an extent to which Marxism, child of the Enlightenment, is not. It points, like the values in Holsti's case, to a philosophical or ethical level where indeed incompatibility exists. Nevertheless, Gilpin proceeds to attempt a *rapprochement*. It will be articulated here in the form of three dialogues.

State dynamics: the dialogue between Lenin and Clausewitz

An economic approach whose basic unit is the state necessarily requires a theory of the state. Gilpin offers one that can accommodate both Marxists and the élitist theorists of the state (thus, also realists). The state is an 'organization that provides protection and [welfare] . . . in return for revenue' (Gilpin 1981: 15). This corresponds to the above-mentioned historical bargain between the political system and the rising middle-class when the nation-state developed in parallel with the (global) market economy. The primary function of states is to provide protection/security against foreign threats, establish property rights, and distribute wealth domestically.

Aware of the long-lasting problem of assuming a national interest, he states that, of course, no such thing exists, and that strictly speaking only individuals have interests. Hence, Gilpin refers to the national interest as determined 'primarily by the interests of [the states'] dominant members or ruling coalitions' (Gilpin 1981: 19). Yet when he goes on discussing the so-called national or foreign policy interests, he falls back on a universalist position, where the interests are security and welfare, and which are logical consequences of permanent interests at the individual level. Thus, he remains undecided as to whom to side with in what Raymond Aron has called the 'dialogue between Clausewitz and Lenin':

> [Clausewitz] did not question the notion of the common good (or the national interest, in today's vocabulary) . . . Lenin answered to Clause-witz, whom he admired, that in a class society, there could be no common good. The foreign actions of states would express the interests of one class or another. It seems to me that the events since the 1917 revolution refute the extreme versions of both theories.
>
> (Aron 1984: 30, author's translation)

If for the external function of the state there has been little change, at least on the domestic side, Gilpin sees in the type of social formations (the concept is taken from the neo-Marxist Samir Amin) a major source of international change. Social formations determine how the economic surplus is generated, transferred and distributed both within and among societies. The change from one social formation to another determines the change from one international system to another:

> The distinguishing feature of premodern and modern international relations are in large measure due to significant differences in characteristic social formations. The displacement of empires and imperial-command economies by nation-states and a world market economy as the principal forms of political and economic organization can be understood only as a development associated with the change from an agricultural formation to industrial formation.
>
> (Gilpin 1981: 110)

It is important to note here that for Gilpin the former socialist countries and the Western liberal countries have, of course, many differences, but share the aspect that the economic surplus is generated by industrial production and this affects their foreign behaviour. It is, however, probably not only the similar industrial social formation, but its insertion into a common international market system that creates pressure for similar behaviour. If for a Waltzian neorealist, states in a self-help system behave similarly, independent of their political system, neomercantilism redefines both the unit and the system level, as well as their effect on the behaviour of states. The historical shift to welfare states implies a redefinition of the self of the state; a new identity which needs to be protected and for which states compete. The

International Political Economy, which also results from the character of the political economy of individual social formations, means that the international system is not just a configuration of power, and that states have to find means to conform to the pressures of a world market economy.

Socioeconomic dynamics: the dialogue between Marx and Keynes

More recently Gilpin has come to specify a change that might in fact correspond to another major historical shift, although he does not characterize it as such. As Gilpin describes the global political economy after 1945, it is characterized by a hegemonic liberal international order, the *Pax Americana*. Yet this hegemony is different from the British one. The key to the difference lies precisely in the link between the social formations and the international system they create. The change that has occurred and that has been institutionalized after World War I, is the change to mass societies in which legitimacy derives from a regimes' capacity to enrich its people and to do it on a more equal basis. The *Pax Americana* is based on a special kind of the liberal state, the welfare state, which under US leadership collaborates in an international system of 'embedded liberalism' (Ruggie 1982).

Gilpin (1987: 59) analyses the Keynesian revolution as a response to the inherent problems of nineteenth century capitalism that Marx had more or less correctly identified. Yet capitalism is intrinsically expansionist. With the end of the territorial imperialism and consequently the diminished capacity to export the burden of capitalist adjustments, the contradictions of capitalism ricochet back on the leading economies. As the world has been recognized as finite since the end of the nineteenth century, capitalism becomes inherently conflictual on the international level. Whereas capitalism can be supplemented by a welfare state to overcome its contradictions on the domestic level, the question arises if it can work on the international level where no world welfare state exists. Gilpin believes that:

> the logic of the market economy as an inherently expanding global system collides with the logic of the modern welfare state. While solving the problem of a closed economy, the welfare state has only transferred the fundamental problem of the market economy and its survivability to the international level.
>
> (Gilpin 1987: 63)

The result is a system where states compete over the international division of economic activities, by using and creating comparative advantages, and by attracting production into their countries. The domestic welfare legitimacy makes states more nationalist than before. For Gilpin, only a hegemonic state can impose a liberal order in this competitive environment. Only the hegemonic state can provide the necessary public goods to allow the compromise of embedded liberalism, i.e. to run a multilateral system by allowing autonomous national economic policies.

International political economy dynamics: the dialogue between Lenin and Kautsky

If the present international system has been the second in a series of liberal hegemonies (and not just empires), then the rise and decline of hegemons are the major research focus at the international level. The research is part of hegemonic stability theory. As mentioned in Chapter 10, Gilpin does not subscribe to the idealist turn which speaks of the US sacrifice for a liberal order. He states explicitly that the hegemony must perceive it in its own (perhaps long-term, or enlightened) interest to provide the public good. Only this is consistent with the underlying economic approach of rational value-maximization (Gilpin 1984: 311–12). He does subscribe to the domestic analogy that the hegemon takes over the same functions in the international society that the government has in domestic society, namely providing the public goods of security and protection of property rights in exchange for revenue (Gilpin 1981: 145). He accepts Keohane's (1984) argument that regimes (Keohane's public good) once established can take on a dynamic of their own and subsist, although the hegemon that issued the system may decline in power. In that respect, Gilpin translates the common norms that realists have found necessary for the functioning of a (political) concert system into International Political Economy. The concert has to be run not just by the major powers, but, in order to allow a liberal order to function, by all the major *liberal* powers, their common code integrating domestic political and international economic issues.

This said, Gilpin believes that the decline of the hegemonic state definitely weakens the political foundations of such an international liberal order, which are: a dominant liberal hegemonic power or powers able to manage and enforce the rules; a set of common economic, political, and security interests that binds them together; and a shared ideological commitment to liberal values. Here, he refers explicitly to the classical socialist debate between Lenin and Kautsky on whether or not liberal capitalist states will find ways to avoid fighting each other (Gilpin 1987: 38–40; see also page 86 of this volume). Consequently, Gilpin's empirical questions, and his political, as well as moral, concerns, are not just about shifts in the balance of power, but about the future of the liberal order after the decline of the *Pax Americana*.

STRANGE'S STRUCTURAL POWER THEORY[2]

While Gilpin meets structuralist political economy for his study of the dynamics of power, Strange meets dependency approaches for her structural understanding of power (Strange 1984: 191). Like that of Gilpin, her move to International Political Economy is provoked by the historical changes the

[2] This section is co-authored with Anna Leander. Much of it is excerpted from Guzzini, Leander, Lorentzen, and Morgan (1993).

international system has experienced. Even more strongly than Gilpin, she conceives International Political Economy as including International Relations, whose established borders are thus decisively threatened.

Her explicit aim is to clarify what determines, and who bears responsibility for (if not what can be done to improve) the fundamental mix of values such as security, wealth, freedom to choose, and justice in society. Changes in the global political economy matter through their impact on this fundamental mix of values. They create winners and losers. Her key question is 'who benefits?'.

To answer this question, Strange holds that it is necessary to be a realist in the sense of maintaining close contact with the actual situation and its feasible remedies – politics as the art of the possible (Strange 1984: 184). Academics should not draft blueprints or prescribe remedies which are known to be unattainable. On the other hand, and reminiscent of Carr (see Chapter 2), Strange cautions against a rhetoric of reason and reality used as a conservative defence. A government official losing out on a proposed change might argue that it is not realistically feasible, whether or not that is true. But such conservative restriction might also result from a purely cognitive source; established theories bias the possibilities of choice. The question of who benefits should be continuously used as a safeguard against the apparent innocence of theories. Strange in particular criticizes approaches that present situations as inevitable and hence surrender to fatalism. To recognize that people and countries have differing chances from the outset, should never become an excuse for taking the easy way out – declaring the impossibility of change. Rather, this very condition should be an incentive to attempt change. The aim is to 'interpose policy between change and its victims' (Strange 1982b: 20).

Susan Strange pursues a critique of mainstream International Political Economy as represented by regime theory and hegemonic stability theory (see Chapter 10). She argues for a structural approach which wants to integrate the Marxist concern with production and the realist concern with security into a wider analysis of the world political economy around a concept of structural power.

Structural changes in the global political economy

The way to find the necessary and difficult balance between realism and the capacity for imagining change is to clarify where power is located, and how it restricts the art of the possible. For Strange, power entails the capacity to decide on the four basic societal needs in the modern world economy: security, knowledge, the production of goods and services, and the provision of credit and money (Strange 1989: 165). Most observers in the past, and many in the present, think of the provision of these basic functions as a domestic concern. One of the leading themes of Strange's work has been to show that such an analysis is misleading. The increasingly globalized political economy requires a wider understanding of how and by whom the provision of these basic needs is undertaken.

The international financial system has moved from being one where states (or a leading state) set up an international system regulating the international provision of credit and the relations between exchange rates, as in the Gold Standard and the Bretton-Woods system (Strange 1971, 1976), to one where states have to a large extent lost control over the provision of credit to the markets: the world delineated in *Casino Capitalism* (Strange 1986b). The link between the national economic basis and the strength of its currency has all but disappeared, though this does not prevent countries from over-valuing their currency for reasons of pride, prestige or other ill-conceived notions of economic well-being. Similarly, the sheer volume of liquidity available for speculation and the possibility of shifting information, thus exorbitant amounts of money, within seconds from one part of the globe to another has made autonomy on the part of governments and central banks akin to an illusion.

Due to the changes in the provision of finance, in communication systems, and the development of technologies, also production has been globalized. By the mid-eighties, international production was for the first time greater than international trade. Many firms are not only multinational, they are truly global. Nationality and loyalty to a state matters little. The scope of thinking, planning and acting is global. This has created an interdependence between firms that can shift their activities and hide their tax-base, and governments worried about employment, national income and fiscal receipts. The global competition depicted in *Rival States and Rival Firms* (Stopford and Strange 1991) makes the entrance of newcomers on the market increasingly difficult and accentuates the gap between countries. Finally, trade appears subsidiary to production and finance. The stress on trade and the now so popular idea of trade blocs becomes an anachronism (Strange 1989: 258). Intra-firm trade and international sourcing make protectionism costly for local firms. Likewise the strategic alliances between firms reduce the likelihood of trade wars.

The problem of market entrance is increased by the fact that a small group of people controls the necessary know-how and technology: the 'international business civilization' with scientists as priests and efficiency as the religion (Strange 1990a: 263). The access to this civilization which preaches social openness, is not equal. American black women stand a smaller chance than American white men, but a greater chance than Eritreans or Japanese of Korean origin. The point is that knowledge possessed and produced by the members of this group possess and produce is not tied to national borders. Again the nation-state as the reference frame has to be reconsidered.

Finally and consequently, Strange argues that the security of people and enterprises has become transnationalized. Economic security has lost its national character – international firms and markets are as influential as national governments. Solidarities that move groups to engage in civil wars cut across borders as the Mafia, Islamic movements, the church, or the pan-Turkish and pan-Slavic movements clearly show (1986a: 296).

These changes have altered the way that credit, production, knowledge and security are provided. In turn this has modified the way that justice, liberty, wealth and order are distributed both within and among countries. This is of course the main reason why Susan Strange has pushed for a better understanding of these changes. Globalization has made it more difficult for workers in any country to bargain with employers for better conditions. The threat not only of a relocation of the production of the specific firm, but the spectre of firms hesitating to make future investments at all looms in the background. Likewise globalization has penalized the weakest countries because of their incapacity to gain the confidence of international financial circles and the partnership of transnational firms:

> It is not enough to say, as successive reports from the IMF or the World Bank have tended to do, that it all depends on governments . . . That is to beg the question of why any particular government was able to act or was constrained from acting in an economically optimal way. The political economist has to look behind policy choices to the structural context of international relations.
>
> (Stopford and Strange 1991: 57)

Bias and limits of traditional theories

The starting point for Strange's theoretical work is the mismatch between, on the one hand, the increasingly global problems and their bitterly needed solutions, and on the other, the incapacity of both academics and politicians to understand and live up to this challenge. Theory is conceived as a necessary bridge between the understanding of the real world and the possibility of changing it.

This theoretical enterprise has two main targets. The first is the disciplinary divide of International Relations and International Economics, which systematically rules out the full understanding of power in international affairs (Strange 1970). The division results in theories that are out of touch with global changes. The realism-idealism debate in International Relations remains excessively state-centred and excessively biased in favour of order, and in fact leaves out the crucial power of markets and extra-governmental rule-making. International Economics in its neo-classical version is also no solution. It only allows for the market power of cartels and monopolies. This is hardly enough to understand the new diplomacy between multi-national corporations and governments or the way domestic decisions of dominant economies can, even unintentionally, affect the global political economy (Strange 1975: 211). 'Add politics to International Economics and stir', as her privileged target, mainstream 'Politics of International Economic Relations' (PIER) does, falls short of an integrated understanding of international dynamics and constraints (Strange 1982b: 17), that is of the possibilities and limits of choice. Thus International Political Economy is conceived as a renewed discipline of International Relations, integrating and superseding it.

Strange's second target includes all theories that misdirected possible choices, that is, theories that either deny or take for granted elements of choice in the management of the global political economy, or absolve actors from blame or responsibility (1985: 3, 7, 39). This is an exercise in continuous demystification. Of the two determinist theories she was criticizing, Marxism and the so-called hegemonic decline school, the latter especially is reprimanded. Since the end of the Bretton-Woods system, Strange has continuously repeated that the global economic disorder was not caused by the declining power of the US, but by a lack of US will to use its power. It was the unwillingness to tax US citizens for the Vietnam War, the unchecked domestic credit creation, and the refusal to devalue against gold that were responsible for the breaking up of the system (Strange 1985: 11–12). There was no change in the world's finance and monetary system in the 1970s that was not initiated or supported by the US (Strange 1986b: 38). Other choices, which were possible, would have made a difference to that system (Strange 1987, 1988b).

Strange refers to a large variety of theories that more or less complacently misdirect the agenda of choices and consequently of the responsibility for outcomes. International Economics, for instance, shows a bias toward issues of trade (and protectionism) when describing the situation after the oil shocks, ignoring the importance of money and finance. One reason is the underlying neoclassical ideology, which supports unchecked financial markets, even if they allocate resources quite inefficiently (Strange 1986b: 12 ff.), but rejects curbs on trade, even though such curbs might be necessary for cushioning the lows of cyclical demand.

She has gently, or not so gently, ridiculed the assumption that, since markets always tend towards equilibrium, markets are always right. If something goes wrong, this flawed thinking holds, it must be politics (Strange 1985: 17 ff.). Having absolved the economic system, International Economics in fact supports US government policies. By avoiding arguments about money, where the US authorities undoubtedly have most power and responsibility, the stress on trade and the widely spread new protectionism makes responsibility shared and detracts attention from US financial mismanagement (Strange 1985: 6). Yet, both the great depression of the 1930s and the stagflation period in the 1970s and 1980s were caused primarily by the mismanagement of credit provision and distribution together with monetary uncertainty, not by protectionism (1986b). More generally, Strange attacks the tendency of US academics to put blame abroad: if something went wrong, it was because of Vietnam, US government generosity toward its allies, the liquidity need of the Bretton-Woods system, the oil shocks, and so on. 'American theorising has thus become an elaborate ideology to resist sharing American monetary power' (Calleo and Strange 1984: 114). To round up, she attacks regime theory as a powerful fad, which still directs too much attention to intergovernmental relations and is thus biased in favour of the rich and powerful and their agenda (Strange 1982b: 17). It is the ideology of non-territorial imperialism (Strange 1982a: 482).

Taken together, the message is clear: mainstream theorizing in International Relations and International Economics either presents the international system as 'ordained by God or History' (Strange 1975: 215), or narrows the agenda down toward issues in the interests of the rich and powerful, the corporate managers, international bankers, public officials, and the élites in the developing world. Therefore, the real power, and thus the underlying dynamic of the system, goes unnoticed. Without this understanding, however, the theories cannot show where action is possible. Strange proposes a theory of International Political Economy based on a reconceptualization of power.

Structural power and the transnational empire

Strange calls the traditional concept of power relational power. It is the capacity to make someone else do what one would not otherwise have done. Yet, this concept of power cannot account for the power or dependencies that derive from the capacity to provide the societal needs of a global economy. For this, Strange introduces the concept of structural power (for a more general conceptual analysis of structural power, see Guzzini 1993, 1994b).

The term structural is used to refer to a diffusion of power, both in its origins and effects. Power is diffused in its effects, because globalization entails the linkage of actors and societies throughout the world. Power is diffused in its origins, because the state is no longer the single holder of international power. It is not the single mechanism through which security, production, credit and knowledge are distributed internationally. Quite the opposite, one must imagine the provision of these societal needs on a global scale as the result of decisions and non-decisions, made by governments and other actors, *whether intentionally or not* (Strange 1990b: 267).

This non-intentional power derived from the systematic bias of the international system is close to dependency approaches and uses a concept of power recalling François Perroux's 'dominance'. As much as Caporaso's redefinition of power, it departs from the mainstream realist International Political Economy. Klaus Knorr (1973: 77–8) has, for instance, criticized Perroux's concept and neglects it since these systematic effects were only incidental. Strange looks at the problem from the viewpoint of those who have to bear the burden of these power effects.

This form of power is non-territorial, 'exercised directly on people – not on land' (Strange 1989: 170). The actors most empowered are those in the international business civilization, constituted by public officials of some states, corporate managers, scientists, bankers and market players. Their headquarters are not in Washington, but in New York, Chicago and Los Angeles (Strange 1990a: 262–5). This transnational class constitutes the base for a 'non-territorial empire' (Strange 1988b: 7).

Strange argues that one must assess the power of states with regard to their position in this empire. Not the national figures on trade, but the transnational capacity to influence and benefit from the provision of societal needs is the prime criterion for the government authority in the global political economy. And here, international actors are structurally dependent on US government military decisions, US production decisions, because the biggest share of world output is still under the control of the executives of US companies; the US dollar; the US market and its tide whose stabilization attracts resources needed to balance the budget deficit; and finally on US scientific and artistic production and communication – the lingua franca is English (which, of course, is not a feature only of the US).

Consequently, US actors, whether public authorities or private actors, remain the biggest player in the game. Strange is not driven by prejudices against the US, nor by the illusion that any other state would have behaved in a more enlightened manner. The acute awareness of the location of power inspires Strange's repeated call to US responsibility. She would, unlikely as it might seem, agree with Waltz (1979: 210) when he writes that 'the leading power does not lead, the others cannot follow. All nations might be in the same leaky world boat, but one of them wields the biggest dipper'. In her increasing pessimism about the state's power, if anything (and this condition has become stronger in her latest writings) only US leadership can turn the international ship around to solve the remaining problems. Yet this cannot be done by means of traditional intergovernmental diplomacy. The game will be played with all actors of the transnational empire. Governance in the global political economy will have to be achieved through a new diplomacy where firms and banks play as important a role as states (Strange 1992).

CONCLUSION: INTERNATIONAL POLITICAL ECONOMY AS A REALIST CRITIQUE OF NEOREALISM

If Waltz's and Strange's structural analysis can both be called realist, is this not a conceptual overstretch? This book is based on a definition of realism as a paradigm. Morgenthau's *Politics Among Nations* had been widely received as such a model. It spurred debates which refined and rejected some of its assumptions, concepts, and explanations. The problem with realism is that thinkers who adhere to only some aspects of the theory, are also called realists. A balance-of-power theorist, like Waltz, is a realist.

A realist is also a power materialist who assumes that institutions, ideas, complex interdependence, and regimes can have an autonomous effect, but are ultimately prone to revert to power politics. Both Gilpin and Strange would subscribe to this position with the small, but important, proviso that power politics be redefined. Competition for technological innovation, for jobs and market shares does not need to be added to classical power politics: it has already become part of it. The classical diplomatic realm exists, but is just one among others. The international environment is not anarchical in any sense which would have significant theoretical consequences, but a political economic order in which basic functions, as for instance the seigneurage of the world currency, and of basic resources, as food and drinking water, are unequally shared and distributed.

If neorealism wanted to demarcate International Relations clearly from other disciplines, then realist International Political Economy again challenges the neorealist demarcation. Waltz harked back to the unity of realism with the boundaries of the discipline by distancing the academic discourse of realism from the ongoing restructuring of international politics. Gilpin and Strange strive for the lost unity of realism with the art of the possible by redefining both the concept and the dynamics of power, as well as the sphere of international politics. Academic divisions are, if anything, a hindrance to such an enterprise.

Curiously perhaps, both Gilpin's and Strange's research programmes take up Kissinger's frustrations with the loosened link between power and politics most thoroughly. It is this condition which undermined realism as an explanatory theory, and as a self-evident culture for diplomatic behaviour. Gilpin and Strange can be understood as saying that only by reaching a new understanding of this link, can the attempt to build a working diplomacy be successful.

Conclusion
The fragmentation of realism

INTRODUCTION

This book argues that realist theorizing in the discipline of International Relations can be understood as an ongoing, and repeatedly failed, attempt to translate the maxims of the European international society to the different context of the twentieth century. This translation of the sceptic and power-materialist world-view within which European diplomats used to be socialized had two main facets. First, realist theorists wanted to contain the practical idealist conceptions of international politics, prominent in the inter-war period but present also later, in particular in the US, the country which had to take on international leadership. Realism used the vehicle of 'scientific' presentation to persuade the new international diplomatic élite of the US. Second, since the academic discipline developed predominantly in the US, the academic group, in turn, needed to be isolated from those dispositions, typical of US empirical social sciences, which would water down the particularity of international politics. The independence of international expertise and the struggle against idealism, later against behaviouralism, are hence but two sides of the same endeavour.

But these two facets, the struggle in favour both of academic uniqueness and of realist assumptions of politics, do not fit together easily. On the theoretical level, there is perhaps only one way to combine the realist assumption that all politics is power politics with the claim that international politics is qualitatively distinct from other forms; one must posit that changing the social environment of politics – from domestic sovereignty to international anarchy – makes a qualitative difference. The criticism on this internal tension has, however, repeatedly threatened the translation of the practical knowledge of European diplomatic culture into a science.

In crossing the Atlantic, realism became exposed to a political culture which was much less accepting of the categorical distinction between the internal and the external aspects of politics, let alone of *das Primat der Außenpolitik*. Indeed, the foreign policy of the US not seldom aimed as a matter of course to remain apart (and aloof) of the petty power struggles which seemed to plague Europe. The Wilsonian approach, which struck a chord with some European politicians in the inter-war period, was an outright attack on the traditional way of running international affairs. The tenets of Wilson's diplomacy diametrically opposed those of nineteenth century European diplomacy: public diplomacy over secret treaties, multilateral institutions of collective security over bilateralism and competitive alliances, and – at the heart of the matter – a progressive view of human nature as rational with potentially common interests over the assumption of eternal wickedness and selfishness.

Morgenthau tried his best to convince his adopted country men and women that such a world-view was not only helpless in front of the disaster that had shattered the world in the midst of this century. Worse, such naïvety was responsible for the calamity. His approach combined the outlook of aristocratic European diplomacy with the new challenges that arose as societies became more tightly integrated and mobilized, and as legitimacy and domestic sovereignty became increasingly bound to broad popular consent. For him, the move to mass societies raised the level of violence inherent in international politics.

International Relations would be the academic support for the diffusion of the practical knowledge shared by the former European Concert. Though the diplomatic culture could no longer be reproduced by a transnational and often aristocratic élite, science was there to help the new élites to come to grips with the nature of international politics as conceived by realists. It is at this point that the evolution of realism, of US foreign policy, and of the discipline of International Relations became inextricably linked. To enable the preeminent international power to fulfil its responsibilities, Morgenthau packaged the practical realist maxims of scepticism and policy prescriptions into a rational and scientific approach.

Morgenthau helped to save the US from idealism. But as realism became the paradigm of the new discipline, the academic criteria of American social sciences increasingly undermined many of its assumptions. Idealists might be appalled by what realism did to the discipline of International Relations, but some realists, too, became distressed at how International Relations disciplined realism. The anthropological foundation of realism, uncomfortable bedfellow of empirical science, was removed in turning to the security dilemma as basic starting point. In the new formulation, violence was not deduced from human nature, but from the context of human action in international affairs – from anarchy. Realist analysts no longer derived behaviour from innate human drive for power, but rather from the socializing pressure of the international sphere. Empirical correlations supplanted human psyches as the building blocks of realist theory.

But turning realism into an empirical science stripped it of its particular view of politics, that is, of the indeterminacy of politics, and of politics as a practical art and not an abstract model. Hence, during the second debate, not only two different versions of the scientific enterprise, but also two different versions of realism clashed (see Walker 1987). For the followers of the 'continental finesse' and shrewdness of Niccolò Machiavelli, realism derived from practical knowledge and utilitarian reason. For others, more inspired by the allegedly mechanic world-view of Thomas Hobbes (see Vincent 1981; Bartelson 1996; but see also Navari 1982), realism had to be understood in terms of a testable science. The social engineer so despised by Morgenthau (1944) came back with a vengeance. And through the effect of his own writings on the nature of world politics, and the (one) rational national interest, he had done much to make such a comeback possible. Morgenthau faced a dilemma. If realism is practical knowledge, then it can be said to exist because it is shared by a diplomatic community; it is real and does not need explicit justification. Yet, if the same realist maxims are no longer or not necessarily shared, and need justification in our democratic times, this foundation cannot simply rely on tradition; instead it must argue with scientific evidence. To defend realism Morgenthau was forced to take the second road, although he believed in the first. His own ambiguity is shown in his treatment of the balance of power: on the one hand, Morgenthau viewed the balance of power as a contingent institution – it only works if its rules are shared and followed; on the other hand, this balance was also inevitable, even when the rules were *not* followed. From this contradiction, the two strands of realism depart.

When the realist discipline was engulfed in one of its deepest identity crises (and one of its richest theoretical discussions), the neorealism of Kenneth Waltz launched a second prominent attempt to combine realist scepticism and scientific criteria. This approach aimed at saving a commitment to power-materialism (see Chapter 9) as a much reduced form of the practical knowledge of Realpolitik. Waltz derived the necessity of realism from the qualitative difference between the international realm and domestic politics. Since the behavioural laws of the international sphere are irreducible to state policies, according to him, an international, called structural, determinism must exist. He combined this with an economic and scientifically acceptable approach based on the concept of anarchy and the market-analogy. Yet as neoinstitutionalists were quick to point out, anarchy alone does not necessarily substantiate Waltz's materialism: anarchy does not determine whether cooperation or conflict will emerge (Axelrod and Keohane 1986; Milner 1992). By assuming the same theoretical premises as Waltz, they conclude that neorealist expectations are neither right, nor wrong: they are a special case, a box in a wider picture better understood within the framework of different institutionalist typologies.

Some realists think that this time the price realism paid for academic respectability and audience was even higher than in Morgenthau's attempt. Certainly, during the crisis of realism, Waltz came as a welcome boost to the realist camp; indeed, his book redefined the entire disciplinary debate. But neorealism favoured Hobbesian mechanics so much that Machiavellian practice could be dispensed of lightly. Politics itself seemed to have been stripped away in a move to a 'science of Realpolitik without politics' (Kratochwil 1993). If power–materialism is the defining part of realism, then Waltz's inside–outside distinction does not hold. If it is to retain a sense of political changes, it cannot abstract from domestic or transnational forces and dynamics. Indeed, realists with a more practical sense of their tradition, such as Pierre Hassner (1986a, 1986b, 1972), had long since concentrated on different analytical levels for understanding political change, including social forces. The analysis of European security and détente policy would be hardly possible otherwise. Others, such as Gilpin and Strange (see Chapter 11), take power–materialist analysis seriously and apply it to those actors, whether states or firms, (dis)empowered by the increasingly global political economy. Doing anything else would seem utterly unrealistic in their eyes.

By the end of the 1980s, realism had become enmeshed, and its practical version largely lost, in the meta-theoretical turmoil that raged throughout the discipline. Formerly, with the inter-paradigm debate, the discipline was ideologically divided, and neorealism provided a way to unite the majority of academics behind a scientifically more neutral façade. Now, with the increasing professionalization of International Relations, the discipline might be on the way to being methodologically united, but, as we will see in this concluding section, at the price of fragmenting realism. In particular, one of the central purposes of realism is breaking apart, that is, its attempt to bridge historical practice to the worldview of present day officials and academics. The discourses of the foreign policy establishment and International Relations theories are perhaps more divided than ever.

Although some might rejoice at this result, and there are some advantages to a more detached observer position, there is also much to regret in losing a hermeneutic sense of history and the normative purpose of practical knowledge (see also Elshtain 1987: 87), and in the decreasing dialogue between newer understandings of international politics and the political élite. After all, in combining and bridging these realms, realism fulfilled a crucial function, whether or not we agree with its moral commitments and analytical assumptions.

This concluding part of this volume will therefore comprise two quite heterogeneous chapters. The following chapter deals with the meta-theoretical debates of the last decade. The final chapter will try to spell out the fragmented state of realism in this theoretical turbulence.

12 Realism gets lost: the epistemological turn of the 1980s and 1990s

This chapter serves two purposes. On the one hand, it uses the recent debates in International Relations to introduce categories which have become commonplace in the theoretical literature. Although it cannot, of course, cover as much ground as did Hollis and Smith (1990), it seeks to raise the awareness about the significance of meta-theoretical debates. On the other hand, it confronts and discusses the merits and limits of different meta-theoretical typologies, such as the meta-theoretical matrix proposed by Onuf or Hollis and Smith, Keohane's distinction between rationalism and reflectivism, and the postivism versus post-positivism divide.

This chapter will make four claims. First, it takes up the interlude by arguing that the inter-paradigm debate, the first valuable attempt to raise the meta-theoretical awareness in International Relations, was, however, riddled with some conceptual difficulties. These would finally give sway to a new typology, called here the meta-theoretical matrix. This matrix combined two major debates of the social sciences, naturalism–interpretivism and agency–structure. Second, it argues that the indisputable improvement of this matrix, as compared to the inter-paradigm debate, comes at a high price: its coherence was made possible by concentrating only on epistemological and methodological issues, leaving the normative aspects of International Relations now entirely out of the picture. The exclusive focus on the matrix achieves the gradual neglect of normative debates – and, incidentally, of central (classical) realist concerns. Third, it will show that the most influential typology of schools which is compatible with this matrix, Keohane's rationalism versus reflectivism, is either misleading or ironic. Finally, it will eleaborate on the several similarities of the post-positivism debate and the *Positivismusstreit* (positivism dispute) waged in German social sciences in the 1960s and 1970s. The meta-theoretical consensus which emerged there is introduced to show how another typology might be used to complement the matrix. The German meta-theoretical triad indicates the evolution of the meta-theoretical debate, and avoids the evacuation of normative concerns.

THE DECLINE OF THE INTER-PARADIGM DEBATE

The inter-paradigm debate provided the opening round of meta-theoretical discussions within International Relations. This raised the self-consciousness of the discipline. It also certainly helped to legitimate research agendas that have been present in International Relations, but for some time neglected, such as development economics and transnational relations, conceptual analysis and normative theory.

The inter-paradigm debate, however, had two fundamental flaws (for the following, Guzzini 1988 and interlude). First, it misused Kuhn's concept of paradigm. Whether explicitly or not, it often tried to use a strong meaning of incommensurability, namely the lacking common measure and meanings across theories, so as to show the limited use of theoretical discussions across paradigms. This was clearly a welcome plea for theoretical pluralism and a reminder that theoretical critique has, at least to some extent, to be done from within the criticized approach. But once the inter-paradigm debate became an established category, it tempted scholars to rebuff criticism for the simple, and then simply assumed, reason that it came from another school of thought. The inter-paradigm debate, intended to open up debate, could deteriorate into a doctrine of spheres of influence which legitimated the breakdown of communication in-between. Yet Kuhn (1970b) had long stressed that incommensurability implied the possibility of translation between competing theories. What he denied was that the final preference for a theory was solely based on a test because this would presuppose the existence of a neutral meta-language.

The inter-paradigm debate fell also short of clarifying the meta-theoretical level on which this incommensurability of paradigms was to be found. When referring to Kuhn's concept of paradigm, Mastermann (1970) describes the here relevant meaning as *Weltanschauung*. The fact that this word is used in its German original is not fortuitous. In Mastermann's work it refers to both an ontological and normative level. *Weltanschauung*, literally the way one looks at the world, implies first a selection of those phenomena that are assumed to be the fundamentals of reality. When Margaret Thatcher is reported to have said, that there 'is no such thing as a society', but 'only individuals', then this is an ontological assumption. Of course, having such assumptions is not value-neutral. Hence, a second, normative, level comes into the concept of *Weltanschauung*. For Thatcher's liberalism, for instance, the ontological assumption might have implications on the justification of collective requirements over individual liberties, say taxes, or the very notion of collective rights.

What happened in the inter-paradigm debate is that these two components were erroneously brought together under the heading of ideology, and not only for Gilpin (1987) who describes them thus explicitly. Incommensurability was reduced to value-incompatibility, which, in turn, was reduced to the clash of value-packages, namely ideologies. In other words, the replacement of some major theories (now called paradigms), such as realism or Marxism, was deemed unfeasible because of the impossible separation of the analyst from its object of analysis, and the intruding values that render analysis mutually incompatible.

As already analysed in the interlude, this derivation of incommensurability from value-incompatibility seems to be more taken-for-granted than analysed. The most spectacular version of this confusion is possibly found in Ferguson's and Mansbach's *Elusive Quest* (1988). They derive from the unavoidable value content of social sciences the impossibility of cumulation. This statement which used to be erroneously attributed to Kuhn in the inter-paradigm debate, is now, even more erroneously, repeated as a critique of Kuhn who is supposed to have claimed that sciences can cumulate and are *not* influenced by their environment. Of course, there is some truth in this, in so far as Kuhn speaks of cumulation, when a scientific discipline has acquired a paradigm and researchers engage in puzzle-solving. Yet, had Kuhn just held the usual cumulative view of science, he would hardly deserve a mention in textbooks on the philosophy of science.

There are several drastic conditions attached to such a view of cumulation (see also Chapter 1). First, due to the constructed character of knowledge, cumulation occurs within the paradigm and only for that paradigm. The shift from one paradigm to another can only be described as process, not progress. Second, during a paradigmatic crisis, the sociological and normative environment will influence the choice of new paradigms. It was exactly this claim which attracted the criticism that Kuhn depicted science as mob-psychology. Third, as far as social sciences were concerned, Kuhn did not propose an ideal of a normal science at all. There, he thought, the debate about philosophical assumptions and the plurality of competing schools of thought are necessary conditions for scientific progress; a view he shared with Sir Karl Popper (1970) and also Paul Feyerabend (1970), on this point united, although the latter two would apply it not only to social, but all sciences. Hence, 'if some social scientists take from me the view that they can improve the status of their field by first legitimating agreement on fundamentals and then turning to puzzle solving, they are badly misconstruing my point' (Kuhn 1970b: 245). As the *Elusive Quest* shows, it seems that by the end of the 1980s, the reference to Kuhn in International Relations does no longer presuppose even a cursory understanding of his writings, let alone of his most famous book whose title already does not speak of scientific cumulation, but revolution.

Be that as it may, once incommensurability was reduced to ideology, the literature found inevitably three of them, because the Anglo-American world where International Relations as we know it is predominantly taught and researched, distinguishes between conservatism, liberalism, and radicalism. Yet superimposing this triad on meta-theoretical issues produces several internal contradictions.

The first problem starts with the heterogeneity of the boxes. In particular, the middle category, be it called liberalism, interdependence, pluralism or the Grotian school, conceals a variety of heterogeneous approaches that defy any use of a common meta-theoretical category. World society after John Burton, James Rosenau's and other linkage approaches, some behavioralist, some not; the English School of International Relations; regime theory; normative theories, as long as they are liberal (as, for instance, proposed by Charles Beitz in 1979) – you name it. In other words, liberalism is a residual category for all those theories that cannot be easily boxed into the other two.

But the more important problem comes with the supposed link between values or normative commitments and explanatory theories. That values affect the analysis in the social sciences is not exactly a hot issue. But this does not yet establish a necessary link to a particular methodology used by the researcher, the world view implied by it and the outcomes of the analysis. Keohane (1988: 10) is perfectly right when he claims himself to be a liberal, despite accepting parts of the realist agenda and world-view. And the argument works also the other way round. Only a very small faction of so-called realists fit the guts-conservative, anti-communist or geopolitical-military rhetoric of what has come to be decried as Cold-War Realpolitik. Indeed, many realists, I think correctly, would take issue with categorizing such a world-view as being realist at all. Kissinger repeatedly argued for the need to protect the diplomatic culture from both the democrat psychiatrist who believes that conflicts are just a matter of misunderstandings, and the republican missionary who is going to roll back the evil empire of the day. This is perhaps best exemplified by the repeated criticism with which some realists commented the tendency of US foreign policy makers to perceive the world in military terms, and to make the just cause win by military force. In more than one occasion, realists saw this tendency as an unwarranted, if not reactionary, form of conservative idealism. Examples abound: Kennan opposed the formation of NATO (see Chapter 5); Morgenthau (1965) disparaged the US involvement in the Vietnam War, Kennan (1985–6) subtly criticized Reagan's Manichaeism, or, most recently, when Tucker and Hendrickson (1992) castigated the Bush administration's military involvement of the US in the Second Gulf War.

ADVANTAGES AND LIMITS OF THE META-THEORETICAL MATRIX

At the end of the 1980s a solution emerged which was able to disentangle this confusion between schools of thought or paradigms in International Relations on the one hand, and Anglo-American ideologies on the other. In this solution, the normative component of *Weltanschauung* was removed. The remaining ontological assumptions about 'being' were linked to

epistemological questions on the nature of knowledge, as well as methodological issues about how to acquire knowledge. As we will see later, these
last two have been combined. This move accomplished the meta-theoretical
turn initiated by the inter-paradigm debate, insofar as it openly analysed the
most basic assumptions of the scientific enterprise. It further removed the
normative core of realism from academic debate. Indeed, realism as a
school of thought dropped out of the self-defining categories of the discipline.

The meta-theoretical matrix in the 1990s

The meta-theoretical debate focused on two main dichotomies that long
characterized the philosophy of social sciences: the *Verstehen–Erklären*
(explaining–understanding) debate of German sociology and the agent-
structure debate. These will provide four cardinal points for constructing
a meta-theoretical matrix.

The explaining–understanding debate has known several historical
rounds in social theory, in which the respective positions have been updated.
The story starts with the very origins of the discipline of sociology. In the
nineteenth century, Auguste Comte, but also to some extent Karl Marx
and Émile Durkheim, were proposing to explain events through social
laws comparable to natural laws: this was the hour of positivism. The contest opened when Wilhelm Dilthey proposed instead an approach based on
an empathetic understanding of human motives.

More consequential for the future of the debate was Max Weber's middle
position. He argued both against a merely subjective and empathetic knowledge in the humanities, and against the similarity between natural and social
sciences. For him, the sociologically significant understanding of phenomena had to refer to the way events were understood by the actor. Take
gestures of greeting. Lifting a hat can be described in purely physical
terms. But this, according to Weber, is insignificant for the social sciences
which concentrates on the study of meaningful action. Hence, a person in
whose culture there is no greeting by lifting a hat, will register some physical
moves, but miss the point, namely the meaning of this gesture. Social scientists work as translators and can tell that this gesture was meant to express a
greeting.

Were there no concept for greeting in the other culture at all, the translation would be even more complicated. Such interpretations apply as
much to initially unintelligible action as to actions which are misunderstood.
Persons socialized in societies where kissing on the cheeks is reserved for
greeting very close relatives, will misunderstand this gesture in societies
where no such rule exists. Here the act of greeting was perhaps understood,
but still the exact meaning of the social action was not: the latter is only
decipherable after interpreting the self-understandings and intentions of
individuals within their cultural environment. Therefore, one can argue,

this necessary reference to human motives and intentions, human understandings, is a qualitative difference between natural and social sciences. Weber did not, however, think that positivism was to be wholly rejected. He argued in favour of a role for causal laws, although not as an end, but just as a means in social sciences. Ideal types could be extrapolated which would suggest a causal framework for understanding particular historical events, both in their generally comparable and particular aspects.

The Weberian compromise was, however, to be split up again. Carl Hempel (1965) argued that there was no difference between Weberian ideal-types and the causal laws of the nomothetical–deductive covering law approach. A nomothetical (or nomological) approach is one in which the analyst extrapolates general laws from empirical regularities and particular events (see also Chapter 3). These covering laws are, in turn, put to test by deducing hypotheses and confronting them with other events comparable to those which have given rise to the laws. If the test is successful, then the event is explained through this subsumption under a covering law. If not, the law has to be adapted or, if this turns out to be impossible without affecting the logical coherence of the law, rejected. In the latter case, the law is said to have been falsified. Hence, one lineage of Weber gives rise to a naturalist approach which could, in shorthand, be called deductive falsificationism.

The other Weberian lineage is in the interpretive tradition. The study of humanities by definition always has to refer to the human mind in its analysis. For the understanding of the meaning of social action, the researcher must understand not only the psychological and individual components, but also the cultural and intersubjective components (as already alluded to in the above example). There can be no neutral test. This would not only presuppose direct access to an external (that is mind-independent) world, but also a shared language among the audience for which the test has been pursued. For the latter, different meta-theoretical commitments exclude a common language which would be neutral. The scientific project consists therefore in making sense (within intersubjectively shared meanings) of particular moments in history, a method sometimes called idiographic, or, following Clifford Geertz (1993 [1973]), a 'thick description'.[1]

To sum up, two ideal types can be extrapolated from this debate, an epistemology of naturalism and one of interpretivism. Naturalism has four basic characteristics (von Wright 1971: 4). It implies methodological monism, that is, the idea of the unity of scientific method amidst the diversity of subject matter of scientific investigation. It strives for mathematical ideals of perfection. Mathematics and physics set the standard of the development of a science, including the humanities. This entails the search for

---

[1] There exists, of course, also a more radical, often called post-Wittgensteinian position which claims that there is no neutral language, that explanations therefore cannot but express language-internal relations, and that this applies to all sciences. In other words, this position is methodologically monist, but otherwise radically anti-positivist.

general – although not necessarily universal – laws as the scientifically legitimate research program. Thirdly, naturalism holds a subsumption–theoretic
view of scientific explanation. From covering (generally causal) laws
hypotheses are deduced and particular cases subsumed and thereby
explained. Finally, it has falsification as the scientific demarcation criterion,
which separates science from other undertakings and scientific theory from
ideology.

Interpretive approaches towards science oppose these fundamental tenets
of naturalism. The starting point of the hermeneutical approach is the idea
that whereas in the natural sciences the researchers and their objects are
independent, humanities have to deal with an internal individual or intersubjective relation. Human beings cannot be subsumed under the category
of unanimated or unconscious objects. The validity of a hypothesis cannot
be tested against a mind-independent outside world. Indeed, a double hermeneutical translation is necessary because the observer interprets the interpretation of the actor. The validity of such interpretations is assessed by
the intersubjectively shared conventional criteria of the participants in a
specific (here scientific) discourse. It is not a question of 'anything goes'.
Apart from controls of empirical accuracy, two main areas of research and
criticism are necessary: the epistemologically informed interpretation of
history and the theoretical, conceptual and philosophical internal criticism
of the given interpretations.

Besides the naturalism–interpretivism dichotomy, the meta-theoretical
turn in the 1980s referred to another dichotomy, this time on the level
of ontology and methodology: the agent–structure debate (Wendt 1987,
Dessler 1989, Carlsnaes 1992). There have been some misunderstandings
about the stakes of this debate. As Wendt (1991, 1992b) rightly admonished,
it was often reduced to a discussion about levels of analysis. The significant
aspect of the debate is not that there are at least two levels, called agent and
structure, that have to be combined in an analysis. All social theories are
aware of these two levels and include them in their theoretical formulation.
The important aspect is where logical, and sometimes ontological, priority is
given for building up an explanation.

Take for example even a purely structuralist reading of Marxism. If structuralism were just defined by levels of analysis, it would imply that Marxism
had no concept of agency. But surely, Marxism is not only aware of an
agency level, normally referred to as social class, but makes its theory
heavily reliant on it. Without this, it would be difficult to see how Marxism
could make the link between its synchronistic understanding of the relations
of production and its theory of history which is driven by class struggles.
What makes Marxism a structuralist theory is that it gives a prior explanatory or causal weight to the relations of production. Of course, groups and
individuals count and are analysed, but their intentions and actions have to
be understood within their particular material setting. Even if the analysis

focuses on class formations and strategies, it must start from the materialist background, the structural prerequisites for explaining agency.

Inversely, a methodological individualist position is not blind for the structural level of analysis. It will understand it as the product of individual action, institutionally sedimented. It is perfectly possible to devise a theory of institutions, which is, in the last resort, methodologically individualist (North 1990). Also, individualism can perfectly incorporate unintended consequences of individual action (Elster 1989). Indeed, its research programme is very much geared towards the elaboration of ideal types or models (depending on the epistemological stance), which give an explanation of collective action outcomes that have been unintended. The prisoner dilemma, where individually rational actions produce a collective suboptimal choice, is only the most famous example.

The problem is not that there are different levels and that we all know we have to combine them. Even if we proclaim that both levels are mutually constitutive, certainly the obvious solution, this does not help us in the actual explanation of a particular event, where we have to attribute the weight of causality or determinacy. Expressed slightly differently, what is significant is the origin of the dynamic part of the theory; from the effects, whether intended or not, of individual action; or from the slowly evolving rules of the self-reproducing structure. One can restate, but not resolve the chicken and egg problem by saying that they are mutually constitutive.

In order to demarcate the agent–structure debate from the level of analysis debate, I will refer to the two positions in the former as individualism and holism. Individualism refers to the position that any explanation must, in the last instance, refer to individual action, although the outcome might not reflect individual intention. Holism must be distinguished from mere collective action by looking at the attribution of the underlying dynamic. Collective action is derived from individual action and intentionality, although it does not necessarily reflect the latter. In contrast, a holistic approach sees the dynamic of the whole as self-perpetuating. If these are objective laws from which one can derive the functioning of its parts, as the classical Marxist laws of capitalism, then the theory is part of naturalism. For hermeneutic holists, there can be no objectivized structures, but only intersubjective practices which for their reproduction must be enacted and understood by individual action.

These dichotomies have been crossed in a matrix to offer four main metatheoretical positions, a matrix which can be found both for the social sciences in general (Sparti 1992, Hollis 1994), and for International Relations (Onuf 1989, Hollis and Smith 1990). I have tried to illustrate this matrix with some theoretical examples in International Relations (see Fig. 12.1).

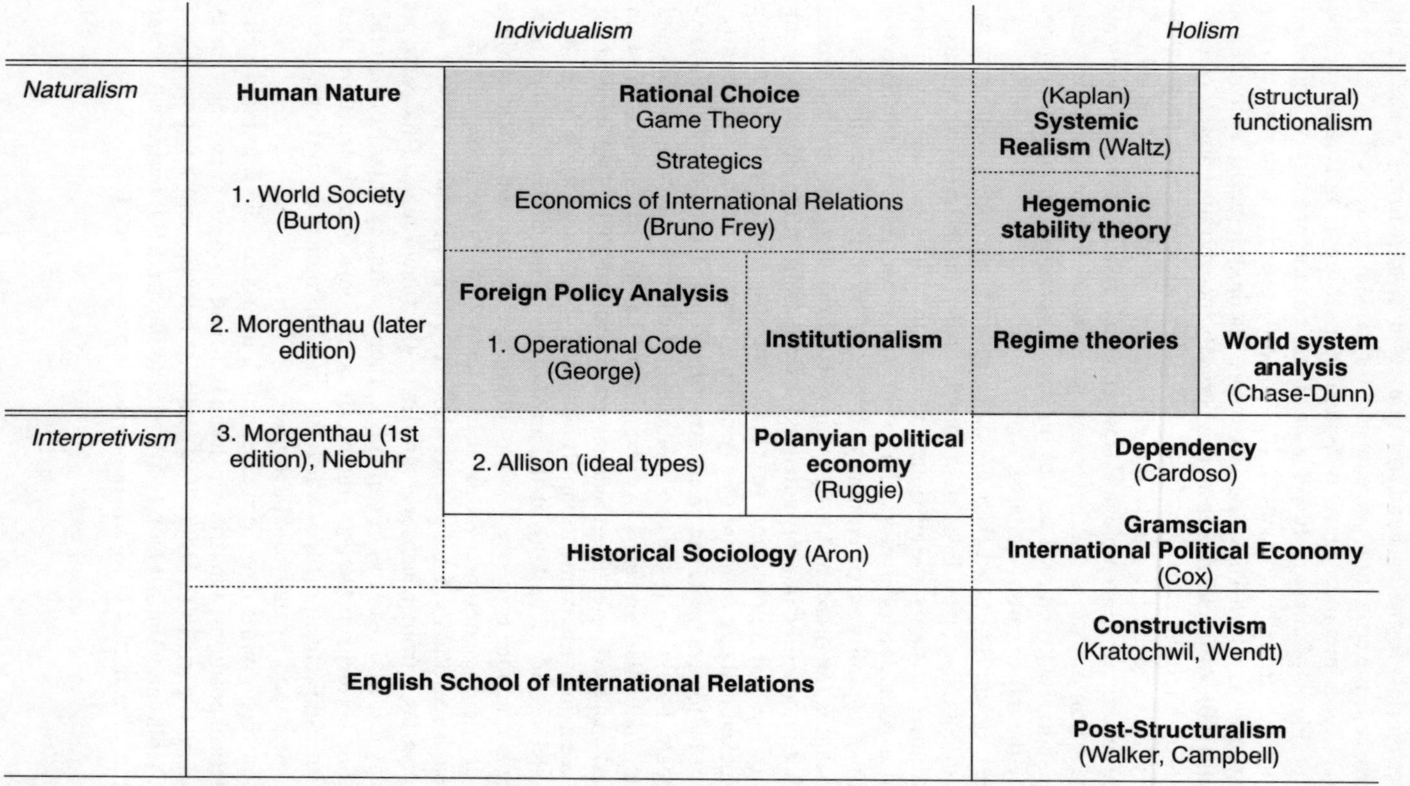

Naturalism

Individualism

Holism

Interpretivism

Human Nature

1. World Society (Burton)

2. Morgenthau (later edition)

3. Morgenthau (1st edition), Niebuhr

Rational Choice
Game Theory
Strategics
Economics of International Relations (Bruno Frey)

Foreign Policy Analysis

1. Operational Code (George)

2. Allison (ideal types)

Institutionalism

Polanyian political economy (Ruggie)

Historical Sociology (Aron)

(Kaplan)
Systemic Realism (Waltz)

Hegemonic stability theory

Regime theories

(structural) functionalism

World system analysis (Chase-Dunn)

Dependency (Cardoso)

Gramscian International Political Economy (Cox)

Constructivism (Kratochwil, Wendt)

Post-Structuralism (Walker, Campbell)

English School of International Relations

Figure 12.1 A map of selected theories in International Relations and International Political Economy at the beginning of the 1990s (Guzzini)

Advantages of viewing International Relations through the meta-theoretical matrix

This meta-theoretical matrix, as I will call it, continues to raise consciousness about metatheoretical assumptions in International Relations that was started with the inter-paradigm debate. At the same time, this new categorization can be seen as an attempt to break out of the previous epistemological orthodoxy of three ideologies. The matrix has at least two advantages: it sharpens theoretical critiques, and it shows theoretical *rapprochements* largely invisible to the inter-paradigm debate.

The use of meta-theoretical arguments for theoretical debate can maybe best be exemplified by 'Kratochwil's and Ruggie's (1986) critique of regime approaches. Their critique focuses at first sight on the underlying methodological individualism of regime approaches. But it does not just rehearse the usual shortcomings of this position. Indeed, Kratochwil and Ruggie criticize regime approaches from within their meta-theory. According to them, regime literature assumes the existence of norms and rules, which are neither a natural fact (objective), nor the offspring of some voluntaristic action or understanding (subjective), but intersubjectively constituted and reproduced. More consequentially, these norms have to be assumed prior to the expression of individual preferences and action. Yet, regime analysis proceeds generally out of the aggregation of already given individual preferences and actions. In other words, whereas the reference to rules calls regime theory to consider intersubjective units of analysis, its methodological individualism cannot do so: it must reduce the macro-level of the analysis to mere structural constraints. Kratochwil's and Ruggie's conclusion was a perfect and pure meta-theoretical critique: the individualist and positivist methodology of regime theory clashes with its intersubjective ontology. Oddly enough, this critique, although published in *International Organization*, has only very rarely been addressed since within the regime literature (for an exception, see Kohler-Koch 1989).

Besides helping to clarify the theoretical discussion, the meta-theoretical matrix can make use of the issue of incommensurability in a much more subtle way, so as to capture better the theoretical debates in International Relations. Its second major advantage is that it shows *rapprochements* and parallel research agendas where the rather static inter-paradigm debate would see only pillared paradigms (Guzzini 1988).

Some illustrations of these rapprochements will suffice. Since the early nineties, Ole Wæver (most recently 1996) has been describing two main *rapprochements* which make little sense in terms of incommensurable paradigms, but do appear in the meta-theoretical matrix (they can also be traced out of Alker and Biersteker 1984). The first *rapprochement* takes place in the grey area of the matrix, namely between neorealism and neoinstitutionalism which share a common rationalist ground (Keohane and Nye 1987; Nye 1988). Wæver calls it the neo-neo-synthesis.

The second *rapprochement* takes place in the interpretivist tradition. It is more multifaceted, but at least two important features harken back to Max Weber who has known a remarkable comeback in social science and International Relations. There is, on the one hand, the encounter between the classical realist historical sociology (see Chapter 3) and historical materialism when it comes in historicist or Gramscian forms. It epitomizes around topics like revolutions (Halliday 1990, who refers to the Weberian Rosecrance 1977 [1963]). In particular, the increasing internationalization of comparative political scientists and sociologists (Skočpol 1977, O'Donnell 1973, 1978; Giddens 1985; and Mann 1986) meets both dependency and classical English approaches in the conceptualization of the state and state-society relations (Evans, Rueschemeyer, and Skočpol 1985; Halliday 1987; Banks and Shaw 1991; Palan 1992, Navari 1991). Indeed, this Weberian battleground, where dependency and classical realism meet comparative sociology could be one way of defining a framework for International Political Economy, as witnessed by several contributions to the *Review of International Political Economy* launched in 1994.

The other Weberian encounter falls partly outside the matrix because it touches the renewed interest in normative theory. The Weberian heritage is the discussion around the 'ethics of responsibility' or any other form of practical ethics, as well as Weber's thoughts on relativism and rationality. It does link classical realists (Aron 1962; Hoffmann 1981; Hassner 1995) with the English School of International Relations (Bull 1977; Vincent 1974, 1986), critical theorists (Hoffman 1987, 1988; Linklater 1990; Brown 1992; Patomäki 1992, 1995) and poststructuralist theorists (Wæver 1989; Walker 1988–89, 1993a).

Limits of the metatheoretical matrix

The meta-theoretical matrix, as all typologies, has shortcomings. The limits apply both to the matrix as such, and to the epistemological and methodological focus that has accompanied it. First, some theories are not easy to box within the parameters of the matrix, although the latter offers at least a way to apprehend them. That the boxes are not necessarily mutually exclusive, however, is due to the subject-matter itself: the meaning of the categories is itself contested. Second, the focus on meta-theoretical issues contributes to obfuscate the ethical aspects of theoretical debates. Hence, the typology does not comprehend all theoretical assumptions. Indeed, realism, to the extent that it is mainly a sceptical attitude (Gilpin 1986 [1984]), is completely lost from the picture.

The contested boundaries of the matrix

The difficult boxing of some theories within the matrix can be illustrated by two examples which seem to criss-cross the matrix in both directions.

The first example was already mentioned in Chapter 9 by introducing the debate around Kenneth Waltz, namely whether his neorealism was structuralist (holist) or individualist. The answer was that it should be handled like the economic approach. The economic approach is, for sure, methodologically individualist: it starts from individual behaviour. It is, however, not obvious how this can be combined with the undoubtedly independent status of the macro-level of economic analysis, the market (and here applied to International Relations, the international anarchical system). In Chapter 9 it was argued that these are just two moments, and two different levels of analysis, of the same ultimately individualist approach. And indeed, applying the analogy of firms and markets to International Relations results in a behaviouralist explanation where in a world of anarchy (market structure), the distribution of state (firms) capabilities will define the particular system, e.g. bipolarity (duopoly) that, in turn, determines the actor's *behaviour* – but not, as a truly holistic approach would do, the *constitution of the structural elements themselves* (Wendt 1991: 389–90). Instead of explaining the powers and interests of agents in terms of irreducible properties of social structure, they are assumed as given. Economic theory might have an independent structural component, a constraint, but no structural dynamic. The two boxes of individualism and holism are at some pains to satisfactorily capture this distinction, as the debate between Wendt and Hollis and Smith also testifies.

The second example relates to the difficult distinction between naturalism and interpretivism when applied to rational action theories. The proposed matrix distinguishes between a more interpretivist and a naturalist version, the first being subsumed under a Weberian historical sociology, the other under rational choice. But this is not an obvious distinction. The tricky element is that even rational choice refers to intentional action: it refers to the individual's mind.

Confronted with this reference to mind and intentions, there have been two solutions which both end up conflating all rational action into one category. On the one hand, Davide Sparti (1992) unites both rational choice and a more hermeneutic Weberian action theory as intentional and meaningful action under the interpretivist label. When describing the naturalist individualist corner, he refers to approaches which deduce action from psychological drives. Analysis is thoroughly input–output based, reducing the actor to a mere throughput. Such an approach would, indeed, be different from rational choice proper, but then, it might seem curious not to see in rational choice a naturalist research programme, often explicitly based on falsificationist criteria. On the other hand, Mark Neufeld combines all rational action theories within the naturalist camp, although he carefully distinguishes between strict and meaning-oriented behaviouralism in a way similar to Sparti's distinction between purely psychologically determined and intentional action. As a result, however, interpretive theories are strictly speaking only available in the holist or intersubjective category (Neufeld 1993: 41–9).

But there are also good arguments for splitting different rational choice theories. Rational choice makes two main assumptions. First, actors are self-interested utility maximizers. Second, action is rational in the sense of consistency (that is, preferences are transitive) and completeness. Given these assumptions, the three variables of the analysis are desires, beliefs and behaviour:

> Desires motivate whilst beliefs channel the action. So an individual who desires z will do y because of her beliefs x. The three go together in a triangle of explanation and given any two of the triumvirate the third may be predicted and thereby explained . . . This is a behaviouralist theory of action, since it is studying the behaviour of individuals that allow us to understand their beliefs (by making assumptions about their desires), or their desires (by making assumptions about their beliefs). We may understand both by making assumptions about different aspects of each.
> (Dowding 1991: 23)

Whereas the quote starts in a meta-theoretically relatively open manner, the last part indicates an important distinction. Here beliefs and desires are deduced from behaviour. Moreover, the choice (behaviour) is given an external meaning by the analysts which allow them to reconstruct the actor's desires and beliefs. A more hermeneutic approach, although still based on the rationality assumption, will first try to understand desires and beliefs in terms of the actors themselves, before explaining rationally the action – first in terms of the actor, and then, if necessary, in terms of the audience for which this explanations occurs. In foreign-policy analysis, there are cognitive approaches sensitive to such individual choices (Jervis 1976). Similarly Alexander George (1979) proposes an approach of process-tracing instead of simply assuming the rationality of the choice from the behaviour. Finally some approaches to belief-systems (Little and Smith 1988) recreate entire world-views and fall hence outside behaviouralist action theory.

The evacuation of the normative debate

In the middle of the 1980s, Holsti (1985) deplored the lack of a normative core in International Political Economy. Although his own attempt to combine normative and explanatory criteria for distinguishing approaches in International Relations was not entirely coherent (see Chapter 8), he very correctly sensed that theorizing in International Relations was moving away from its normative roots. The inter-paradigm debate might have wrongly boxed different meta-theoretical criteria together, but it was not mistaken in its claim that normative concerns are vital in the theoretical debates of the social sciences.

The meta-theoretical move of the 1980s has a major consequence for realism: removing normative concerns, it further marginalizes a practically oriented and normative realism from the mainstream in International Relations. It is an irony of no small proportions, that Waltz's neorealism – so staunch in defending a materialist view of international politics, so confident that the anarchical fundament of scepticism is superior to any other – would ultimately undermine the realist world-view in International Relations. This is, of course, to a large extent the fault of the more general realist attempt to turn their world-view into a science; that is, of the hope that the best policy, one which was to be compatible with the maxims of nineteenth century diplomacy, could be derived from a general causal theory. Since the world is what it is, this is the best we can do: but, clearly, such a vision is not ethically neutral. Indeed, the realist attitude makes no sense without reference to its ethical assumptions.

The bottom-line of realism is a particular form of scepticism. This scepticism is derived either from human nature or from the particular context within which politics unfolds in the international sphere. For Morgenthau, defender of the first derivation, the state is the one exceptional institution that fettered the otherwise general human drive for power. For Herz and Waltz, international violence is not a human, but a social phenomenon to be explained by the particular anarchical environment.

If one defines scepticism as the opposition to all moral values, as Giesen (1992) does, one could distinguish between three different facets of realist ethics: scepticism, consequentialism, and empiricism. But then, the purely sceptic realist argument applies just to the international level and relies heavily on the unquestioned moral value of the state. If realists were thoroughly sceptical they would question the value of the state, a critique they are facing, among others, from cosmopolitan studies (Beitz 1979; Pogge 1994), feminist writers (Peterson 1992), and from poststructuralists (Connolly 1991; Walker 1990, 1991). They do not. Hence, their philosophy is based on the idealist defence of the nation state (my country right or wrong), following the analogy with organic self-interest and self-defence of an individual, as it developed out of German idealism in the nineteenth century (Palan and Blair 1994).

Their philosophy is moreover consequentialist, where international politics is in the last resort geared towards both protecting the national interest, and maintaining or striving for a legitimate international order, as Kissinger would put it, an order which enables diplomacy to work and which limits inevitable conflicts. More demanding ethical theories are said to be of no avail on the international level. Scepticism works here as a weakening condition for morality. The striving for a Concert system is the only check on the state that realists accept, because it is desirable to keep conflicts at the lowest possible level. For Bull this international society really exists, concerned about rules and common interests in defending these rules. This is the moral empiricist (and legal positivist) part. For Kissinger, it is less clear whether he assumes the constant existence of such a society of states, but certainly he thinks it should exist: it is the only available ideal – given the legitimated scepticism.

Destiny played a mean trick on Waltz, when his success launched a research programme which ultimately undermined scepticism, not because it gave arguments to idealists, but because it neglected ethical attitudes altogether. In the face of the interdependence literature, more idealistically inclined, his version of neorealism was meant to save a much reduced version of realist scepticism, namely its power materialism (for this and the following, see also Chapter 9). The scientific references replaced the traditional empiricist and historical justification for realism, which had a weakened standing within the academic community (although not among the foreign policy establishment). Yet the success of his text was more and more nurtured by the implicit and explicit legitimation of social science methods, even though his own version was rather cautious in this regard. Hence, the criteria for academic reputation set by this paradigmatic text, eventually derived not from the possible plausibility of his realism which would allow a better grasp on the nature of international politics, but from the neo-positivist means employed for this purpose.

Within this move, neorealism was increasingly captured in debates which reflect but a pale shadow of its former self. In its most restricted version, the basic neorealist input into the debate was now reserved to defend the position that under anarchy, states seek not absolute gains, but relative gains, such as to improve their relative power position compared to other actors (Grieco 1988, 1993). Keohane (1993), the neo-institutionalist opponent, again as in the co-authored *Power and Interdependence* (1977), coherently keeps up with the richer realist tradition (see Chapters 3 and 8), when he shows that this is sometimes, yet not necessarily the case (for the entire debate, see Baldwin 1993a).

With the removal of this last bastion, the ongoing theoretical debate developed with little connection to realism in its tradition of practical knowledge. The academic requirements eventually relegated writers inspired by classical realism into apparently less worthy disciplines. Neorealism, as a scientific approach, was part of the rationalist school, as Keohane named it; the rest found itself either among the 'reflectivists' or denied (social) scientific status like diplomatic history for those in International Relations, or economic history for realist International Political Economy. Realism is no longer a coherent category: it drops out of the main theoretical divides. The next sections can do without it.

THE FURTHER REDUCTION OF THEORETICAL DIVIDES: RATIONALISM VERSUS REFLECTIVISM

Many International Relations scholars, less concerned about knowing what they assume and how the assumptions of their explanations fit together, did not see the purpose of the meta-theoretical niceties developed in the previous sections. Increasingly a new typology boxed theoretical approaches more easily into just two categories, between proper theorizing and ultimately useless one. Seeing the boundaries of the discipline threatened, as well as the criteria of what is authorized good, and hence legitimated, research, the academic community reacted as usual: it defined the line which should not be crossed.

It is within this context that one can understand the success, but also the reciprocal animosity, of the temporarily most influential categorization of a new dividing line, Robert Keohane's (1988) distinction between rationalism versus reflectivism. The underlying issue is not only whether this distinction is correct, and we will see that it has some flaws, but also how, despite accepting a plurality of theories on *prima facie* equal standing, it employs theoretical commitments in order to distinguish the 'competent' scholar.

The starting point of Keohane's distinction is indeed at the roots of the meta-theoretical matrix just mentioned. Keohane, addressing the (US) International Studies Association (ISA) in 1988, as its president, tried to give a comprehensive, fair, and innovative picture of the discipline. He referred to two main camps. The one is the rationalist camp of the neorealist and neoinstitutionalist debate. The other he called reflectivists. There are two main flaws in this distinction.

The first problem with this categorization lies in the residual nature of the reflectivist category. It seems hardly useful to bring under one heading the variety of approaches which fall outside the grey shade of the matrix (see Fig. 12.1), just because they are less convinced about falsificationism in the social sciences, or are sceptical about (mainly single) causal analysis for establishing laws, or understand empirical research differently, or have other ontological assumptions (of structures or of intersubjective units), or do not share the same normative world view, if the latter is not blended out altogether. Hence, Keohane brought together critical hermeneutical approaches in historical sociology or historical materialism (Cardoso 1977; Cox 1986 [1982]), scientific realist epistemologies (MacLean 1981, 1988; Wendt 1987; Tooze 1988; Dessler 1989), constructivist epistemologies (Onuf 1989), and poststructuralism (Der Derian and Shapiro 1989). This is not the place to dwell on these differences, but, clearly, one is better advised to compare them (as did Hoffman 1991), than to collapse them.

The underlying logic of Keohane's distinction, whether intended or not, is to offer an ideal type of research, as represented by rationalists, which can fruitfully integrate ideas from the reflectivist side, but which should not lean too much toward the latter direction. Science is on the one side, mere good ideas on the other. The dichotomy tells a story of progress and its ideal. It also tells the academic community who are the right persons to whom one should listen. Hence, Keohane's widely-used dichotomy in fact mobilized a bias of closure, although, and this should be stressed, this dichotomy was certainly designed to open up debate. When Stephen Walt

(1991), a writer whose *Origins of Alliances* (1987) was rather appreciated by the other camp, similarly issued a warning against the sirens of post-structuralism, this bias for closure became more visible.

The second problem of the typology illustrates this closure despite the apparent recognition of equally valid theoretical approaches: it lies in the one-sided definition of major contested concepts in social science meta-theory, most visibly in the way Keohane defines the empirical. Keohane argues that reflectivists lack an empirical research programme and that until they develop one, they can in fact not really count as serious contenders to the rationalists (Keohane 1989 [1988]: 173).

This judgement relies upon an empiricist epistemology for understanding the empirical. Since there have been many misunderstandings of this point, it is worth recalling that it is not empirical research as such which makes the difference, but what is meant by it. The empiricist approach takes the real world as it is and tries to create either an intentional account or a causal construct between categories for its explanation. The correlation might then in turn be tested against an outside world, as positivist falsificationists would do, or be considered one particular way to reconstruct reality, as in traditional research in International Relations. Non-empiricist approaches problematize the relation between categories and the object of study, where the conceptualization of the research is not independent from its result. It does not first look at facts and then add theory to them, because theory informs our very selection and understanding of what a fact is (George 1994). Theory is hence not necessarily prior to facts as such, but without theory, and this is consequential, we are not able to distinguish facts from mere noise – or, in other words, we cannot give meaning to them. This entails that empirical research cannot be done without prior clarification of its meta-theoretical, but also philosophical commitments (for a similar response to Keohane, see Walker 1989: 178).

Given these different commitments, Keohane runs into troubles when attacking reflectivists for their apparently lacking empirical research programme (apart from the more visible empirical studies that were published later). Those who have been most criticized are poststructuralists. Their main empirical references are discursive practices. Indeed, constructivists and poststructuralists have concentrated for a long time on the study of how discourses in International Relations have embedded the way we conceive and debate our field and activity. This is obviously empirical. It is empirical to study what experts do. It is also empirical to study what ideas do to their understanding and behaviour. Were it not, we would commit the fallacy of reducing the empirical world only to its material part. Yet, as Pocock (1973: 38) put it, 'the paradigms which order "reality" are part of the reality they order . . . language is part of the social structure and not epiphenomenal to it . . .'.

As a consequence, Keohane's claim is either misleading or ironic. It is misleading, if the study of discourses which underlie the way International

Relations experts in academia or politics explain world events, which as such is also an event, is considered non-empirical. It is ironic, if what experts do is considered insignificant and therefore empirically negligible, because this relevance is the very justification for many rationalist studies.

POST-POSITIVISM OR THE *DÉJÀ VU* OF THE *POSITIVISMUSSTREIT* IN GERMAN SOCIOLOGY

This being said, Keohane's typology still informs the self-identification of many researchers both in the mainstream, and also those who pride themselves to be reflectivists. This happens despite the increasingly shared boredom about the tendency of the discipline to create ever new dichotomies: what might be called the iron law of the two trenches in International Relations.

Yet another version of this theme emerged with the claim that International Relations entered a post-positivist stage (Lapid 1989a, coined the term; see also Lapid 1989b; Smith 1995). Indeed, one might get this impression, in particular in Europe where theoretical research outside the mainstream gathers momentum in important departments, such as Aberystwyth, or around proliferating schools and journals, such as the Amsterdam School of International Political Economy (see, for instance, van der Pijl 1984), the Copenhagen School in security studies (see, for instance, Wæver *et al.* 1993), or constructivist debates in the newly launched *European Journal of International Relations* and *Zeitschrift für Internationale Beziehungen*. Yet it seems, to say the least, a little premature to talk of the stage of postpositivism for the discipline at large. It is unfortunately true, though, that the debate gets often stuck in friend–foe images along these lines which sometimes seem to have more to do with the contested academic identity of researchers (and the question of jobs and tenureship) than with meta-theoretical issues.

This very personalized, and often vitriolic, debate catches the eye of German observers as a *déjà vu* (Meyers 1994). Indeed, the two contenders seem to rehearse an updated form of the *Positivismusstreit* (the positivism-dispute) which raged in German sociology in the late 1960s and early 1970s, and included Theodor Adorno and Jürgen Habermas, as well as Ralf Dahrendorf and Karl Popper (Adorno *et el.* 1969). True, since then, the Cold War background has to a large extent vanished: there is understandably little reference to a comparison between US and Soviet policies, and neo-Marxist approaches are no longer prevalent as anti-positivist contenders. But the divide remains heavily politicized for academic and other matters.

Therefore, one could have thought of presenting meta-theoretical schools in International Relations according to the solution which reached a consensus in German social sciences. Indeed, that is exactly what was done in German International Relations in the 1980s (Haftendorn 1980; Wassmund 1982: 241–3). There, one distinguishes three major meta-theoretical positions (again, a triad).[2]

The three schools, as they historically appeared in the social sciences, are described as normative-ontological, empirical-analytical (neopositivist), and critical meta-theories. They can be easily illustrated with examples from International Relations. Indeed, depending on the individual calculus of the great debates in International Relations, and there is quite some difference, whether we are still in a third or already after the fourth debate (Wæver 1996), the historical emergence of meta-theoretical contenders coincides with the second and Yosef Lapid's (1989a) third debate.

A normative-ontological approach is normative, because it embeds its explanations explicitly within an ethical context. Indeed, anything else would appear as fruitless and absurd. It is ontological, because it defines the purpose of political science in working out the good order usually on the basis of a religious or humanist conception of human being. This meta-theory corresponds quite well to the first stage of International Relations, when the latter was established as an independent discipline. Idealists of the inter-war period (Chapter 2) pursued the purpose of international peace, and based their attempts on a particular vision of the human as rational being. In response, some early realists also referred to anthropological foundations, religious for Niebuhr (1941), psychological drives for Morgenthau, for establishing an opposite vision of what was feasible in world politics, a mere order of limited conflict. Hence, the first great debate took place within this meta-theoretical framework.

The second, neopositivist, approach is born out of the double refusal to embed empirical analysis within an ethical debate and to ground it on metaphysical foundations (although behaviouralism in International Relations more often than not has some utilitarian foundations). Here the second great debate in International Relations seems paradigmatic, when a naturalist contender was opposed by a defence of classical International Relations which both played down the possibility of finding empirical laws, and which wanted to keep International Relations embedded in more normative concerns (see Chapter 3). One can illustrate this debate within different types of realism. This book argues that realism can be understood as the attempt to update the European diplomatic culture of the last century. If we take the second debate, as represented by Morton Kaplan and Hedley Bull, there have been two realist solutions to this problem. On the one hand, a more positivist one tries to translate political maxims into social laws of more or less limited reach. The most rational policy is deduced from the knowl-

---

[2] Incidentally, this meta-theoretical triad is taught to political science students in Germany as part of the fundamentals of their discipline. In other words, they do not learn this after the facts, but in their first academic year. The following is hence taken from the introductory chapters of undergraduate text books (Berg-Schlosser, Maier, Stammen 1981: 43–86, Alemann and Forndran 1978: 41–65).

edge of these laws. On the other hand, the classical approach limits itself to the understanding of the historically evolved practical know-how for limiting conflicts. Here, it is important to grasp the evolution of the institutions which international society has given itself for this purpose, such as diplomacy, international law, the balance of power, and even (limited) war. Representatives of the first approach, speaking with a decisively US accent, will advise the prince in the manner of a social engineer. The other advisor, often British, propagates the practical knowledge of someone who has passed something like the rites of initiation into diplomatic culture.

The third meta-theory, critical theory, appears in the German textbooks mainly in its neo-Marxist form. As such it appeared also in International Relations during the first of the many third debates, the one between realism and globalism (Maghroori and Ramberg 1983). But also Lapid's (1989a) much later third debate could qualify. To keep track with the evolution of International Relations debates, one might now either add a fourth category for poststructuralist approaches, or subsume them under a more widely defined critical theory. But this is not important here.

What is important is that such a presentation captures better the evolution of meta-theoretical positions, not as a replacement of, but as a more dynamic complement to, the meta-theoretical matrix mentioned before. It can be used to show the same *rapprochements*, but does also problematize the relationship to normative aspects, in particular of the ontological and critical schools. Most importantly, it points to a theoretical and methodological pluralism within the discipline; a pluralism which should instill us scholars with a sense of limit and modesty of our particular claims, and invite us to more curiosity and careful listening across the alleged theoretical boundaries.

CONCLUSION

Epistemological turmoil swept through International Relations in the 1980s and 1990s. It improved on the meta-theoretical debates that were initiated by the inter-paradigm debate. Some might regret the loss of the protection that the inter-paradigm debate offered for those approaches that were marginal to the discipline. Indeed, the methodological and theoretical pluralism advocated here will not necessarily be welcomed by those scholars who have a very particular idea of what should be considered as standards for empirical research, or those whose approach by itself cannot accept pluralism as scientific (for the application of this argument applied see Meyers 1994: 128). By undermining the inter-paradigm debate in its legitimatory function for pluralism, the present argument, although aiming at pluralism, might in fact forestall it. This is not my intention. In any case, the inter-paradigm debate is a shrinking protective belt. In the long run, it does not make sense to rely on arguments one would be hard-pressed to defend.

Although the inter-paradigm debate was misleading in putting together particular value-systems with particular explanatory theories, it was very much to the point with regard to the centrality of values in theories of International Relations. Normative, even ideological commitments play a role and cannot entirely be filtered out of explanations. Not in all cases do they have to vitiate the scientific argument. The inter-paradigm debate registered the increased self-awareness of these value choices, an awareness which would make it easier to control this inherent bias.

The meta-theoretical debate of the last decade did, however, further remove normative thought from the criteria which characterize theoretical schools. This does not contradict that fact that normative theories have seen a remarkable comeback in recent years. But they appear in a different academic category altogether, which is something for specialists and their journals, but not for International Relations at large.

This fragmentation of disciplinary standards criss-crosses realism. Whereas during the inter-paradigm debate, realism was one (more or less) coherent contender, it splintered during the meta-theoretical turn. While realist ideas are still well alive and kicking, realism as a comprehensive approach has become lost.

13 Realism at a crossroads

The school of realism used to unite diverging research methods within one discipline. Now, in a similar way, the increasing professionalization of International Relations, in particular in some parts of the US PhD industry, may serve to unite the discipline on methodological grounds. Yet the result has been the fragmentation of realism in different research programmes. As a coherent category, still available even as late as during the inter-paradigm debate, realism dropped out of the picture in the meta-theoretical divides of the last decade. Not that there are no more realists around: they abound, but as curious one-dimensional figures: as pure materialists in Waltzian International Relations and anti-Waltzian International Political Economy; as game-theoreticians with utilitarian assumptions about relative gains, as sceptical normative theorists mainly in the English school (but see also Nardin 1983), or as diplomatic historians with a link to the foreign policy establishment.

Hence, Kenneth Waltz's attempt to rally the major part of International Relations behind a reformulated version of realism did not succeed. One could expect two realist reactions to this failure. One reaction would consist in a return to the roots of International Relations in an effort to expel all social scientific intrusions. This is, to use Roger Spegele's term, a return to an empirical common-sense realism (Spegele 1996: 17). The other reaction would try to invigorate the Waltzian approach in a further attempt to combine realism and science. Both try to recapture a lost unity: the first harks back to the unity of the language of International Relations and diplomatic culture; the second longs for the unity of realist assumptions within the discipline of International Relations as a social science. This chapter claims that both ways lead to dead-ends.

But, and this relates to a central point of the book, these two reactions feed into each other, producing a circular debate which has kept both realism and International Relations going. On the one hand, some realists insist on keeping realism out of a disciplinary straightjacket, of the unnecessary intrusion of alien scientific jargon into the cultural practice of foreign policy. On the other hand, as long as some realists continue to treat their theory as the way International Relations is, as traditional maxims and norms for the competent political and academic practitioner, the pressure of the discipline will push some others, including realists, to find scholarly more acceptable versions. As Chris Brown (1992: 90) very rightly pointed out, this pressure for a more scientific approach is, to some extent, pre-ordained by the realist world-view itself. Realism claims to refer to an unproblematic reality, a claim that must invite for more objectivist methods. Indeed, as Carr (1946) depicted realism, it is precisely the assumption of an empirical, and not normative, access to the lessons of history (that is, historical wisdom expressed in causal terms) which set realism apart from more idealist approaches. Both tracks, the return to a common-sense realism and an invigorated empirical theory of realism, seem to get trapped in exactly the same way as did previous unsuccessful attempts. Their story will continue as long as the shared knowledge of the traditional diplomatic practice and the requirements and legitimacy of a social science, in particular in the US, are institutionally reproduced.

Therefore, in a third step, this chapter also claims that it is impossible just to heap realism onto the dustbin of history and start anew. This is a non-option. Although realism as a strictly causal theory has been a disappointment, various realist assumptions are well alive in the minds of many practitioners and observers of international affairs. Although it does not correspond to a theory which helps us to understand a real world with objective laws, it is a world-view which suggests thoughts about it, and which permeates our daily language for making sense of it. Realism has been a rich, albeit very contestable, reservoir of lessons of the past, of metaphors and historical analogies, which, in the hands of its most gifted representatives, have been proposed, at times imposed, and reproduced as guides to a common understanding of international affairs. Realism is alive in the collective memory and self-understanding of our (i.e. Western) foreign policy élite and public, whether educated or not. Hence, we cannot but deal with it.

For this reason, forgetting realism is also questionable. Of course, academic observers should not bow to the whims of daily politics. But staying at distance, or being critical, does not mean that they should lose the capacity to understand the languages of those who make significant decisions, not only in government, but also in firms, NGOs, and other institutions. To the contrary, this understanding, as increasingly varied as it may be, is a prerequisite for their very profession. More particularly, it is a prerequisite for opposing the more irresponsible claims made in the name, although not always necessarily in the spirit, of realism.

NOSTALGIA FOR A NON-THEORETICAL REALISM

Great is the temptation just to say goodbye to science and to return to the undisturbed days when realism was the shared knowledge, or shared enemy, of a relatively coherent group of academic and political practitioners.

Despite the cosiness of some foreign services, these days are gone. The two worlds have changed. The change in academia should need no further discussion at this point of the book: the debates of the discipline have laid bare realism; the world-views of the classical scholars are no longer obvious, nor ethically self-evident. But, and this will be elaborated again, the world of international politics has also changed (see Chapter 11). It is no longer confined to the narrow definition of the diplomatic practice embodied in classical International Relations.

This last point can be exemplified by a closer look at the definition of international politics. As mentioned earlier (see Part II), some of the realist extensions into International Political Economy did not question the importance of politics in world affairs, but its narrow neorealist definition. This charge, although less strong, can be applied to classical realism as represented by the English School, too. In particular two of its basic concepts are in need of redefinition: the state and diplomacy.

The state is not the state: the necessary move to history and political economy

Realism has been often accused of looking at the state in unitary terms. Moreover, the state is seen as something essentially unchanged for centuries, a claim which has attracted the critique of realist ahistoricism (Ruggie 1993). Of course, realism is not entirely blind to the changes that have redefined the state's function. Morgenthau was well aware that the evolution towards mass societies and mass legitimation of regimes, sometimes misleadingly called democratization, has diminished the flexibility of foreign policy. This historical development introduced concepts and purposes, which were alien to the traditional diplomatic culture, as, for instance, the right of national self-determination. But Morgenthau still thought it possible to keep the statesman, the responsible one at least, aloof from these pressures.

It is not all that sure that such a division is indeed possible. The important historical change that came with the emergence of mass societies, at least in some parts of the world, is the increasing link between popular legitimacy and welfare provisions. The welfare state is not only a generous development of enlightened statesmen when their countries experienced booming decades. Several welfare states on the European continent developed out of the attempt to make industrialization possible without disrupting existing political orders. It did not always work. Bismarck was able both to coopt the working class while allowing a fairly mercantilist policy, by a policy of embedding Germany within a concert system where it would play a self-imposed limited role: unification for Germany, colonies for the others. But nationalism eventually got rid of him.

In the present this picture is further complicated. Welfare provisions have increasingly replaced other bases of (national) loyalty while meaningful ideologies have lost their appeal for rallying bodies and souls behind a common aim (Habermas 1976, 1985). This materialist solution to the latent legitimacy crisis of secularized societies should not come as a surprise to realists whose scepticism has done much to denounce the ultimate value of many of these ideologies. Indeed, the tragic ambiguity of an expanding rationalization in all spheres of life and a concomitant disenchantment has been a current theme of early realists since Weber. Nor should realists necessarily oppose the welfare compromise. Compared to irredentist nationalism, the welfare state has become a major stabilizing factor of mass societies. It is a necessary instrument for internal stability by compensating and redirecting those groups who are possible losers of the reduction of trade-barriers and the internationalization of production (Katzenstein 1985). But clearly if distributive policies are inherent features of a regime's legitimacy and stability, then the international competition of regimes will heighten whenever the cake from which every state cuts a piece seems to be shrinking. The recent globalization of the international political economy is putting severe constraints on welfare states, in particular of the corporatist Christian-democratic or the decommodifying social-democratic kind (for the distinctions, see Esping-Andersen 1990; van Kersbergen 1995).

Government functions and bases of legitimacy have changed and, hence, realism has to admit that international politics can no longer be understood without domestic and transnational dynamics, if it ever could have been. If power is a central concept of realism, if competition is the main feature of its international interaction, then surely, in the present global political economy, the macro–micro link of realism can no longer be limited to established great-power diplomacy (including military affairs), or to the isolated world of concert diplomacy and the institutions of international society. Of course, these features are still part of international politics, sometimes prominently so, but they do less than ever encompass it.

This point should not be confused with the classical question where transnational relations are superseding or replacing the state-system. In this debate stemming from the interdependence literature, realists have staunchly defended statism. Kenneth Waltz (1970) showed that interdependence in trade and investment has been already very high in the last decade of the nineteenth century. Therefore, being interdependent is not a new phenomena and cannot be taken to legitimate a paradigm shift away from a state-centred view. Similarly, Hedley Bull (1979) defended the centrality of the state and the state-system by showing its geographical and functional extensions. Both defences are correct in their terms. Indeed, Bull showed many of the new functions that have acquired prominence in the last decades. But the issue here is not whether other actors have become more important than the state, or should become so. The issue is that the historical entity and hence the meaning of the word state have changed. Both defences neglect the qualitative shift to mass societies and mass legitimation, that is, to different state–society relations. Indeed, they do not conceptualize these state-society relations which are essential *for the very understanding of*

the state. That the state as an autonomous actor is still important is not dis-
puted: but this means something else now, to before, for defining and understanding international politics.

More recently, realists have started to open up. Security studies have been
expanded to more and more security sectors: military, political, economic to
societal and environmental concerns are now included (Buzan 1991a, 1991b).
Still, there is some way to go in taking into account feminist perspectives
(see Tickner 1992) and more critical security studies (as, for instance
Krause and Williams 1997). Similarly, the Pandora's box of state theory
has been opened. But in realist hands, it remains a static view of the domestic environment. Krasner (1985), for instance, uses a weak/strong state distinction as one explanatory variable for development. This takes for granted
what should be explained: in the absence of an autarchic development in
world politics today, how can we understand why some states are staying
or becoming weak? Categorizing states as weak or strong is no answer,
this simply begs the question. Likewise, although correctly noting similarities of their argument with dependency writers, Mastanduno, Lake and
Ikenberry (1989) overlook first, that for Peter Evans (1979), whom they
mention, the actual articulation of local, state, and foreign capital is something that needs to be explained in the historical and societal setting; and
second, that the state is to be apprehended as something more than a top-
down machine for the mobilization of foreign policy tools.

Realism must revise its assumptions. State–society relations, including its
gender hierarchies, are no longer the implicit and constant foundations of an
international society of states, but the very ground on which international
relations take place (for the role of women in supporting classical diplomacy
see Enloe 1989: Chapter 5). International relations are not at the pinnacle of
societal relations, but the transborder processes that embrace them. It is
probably not fortuitous that writers in International Political Economy
have been particularly sensitive to these issues: since they tried to integrate
the working of the now global market (or capitalist) system into the analysis, the never innocent working of this transnational structure makes a view
that encompasses specific state-society-market articulations all the more
compelling. In other words, Gilpin and Strange have been taking realist concepts like power and competition seriously. One could imagine that they
further explore research on state-society relations, as, for instance, on
state theory (for instance: Jessop 1990; Evans 1995; Palan, 1989) and in
comparative political economy (for instance: Leander 1997; for my own
limited attempt, see Guzzini 1994a or 1995).

The communicative barriers of the new diplomacy

The shared language and codes of the traditional diplomatic culture do exist.
But diplomacy is no longer only made within this culture. The diplomatic

culture can no longer easily presuppose acceptance by other international actors, or impose it.

Kissinger was aware early on of the problems incurred when such a shared language can no longer be presupposed, for reasons of new state-society relations, universalistic ideologies, varying recruitment procedures, and differing socialization of diplomats; and also because in the nuclear age the meaning of basic concepts of the international society, such as security, order, power, and the balance of power, is not necessarily commonly shared. Likewise, the English school came to understand that the codes and norms of the European international society, which had expanded geographically over the centuries, could no longer be imposed on all states. In 'the revolt against the West', Hedley Bull (1984) noted that international law was not only made by the West, but also for the West. The implicit normative messages of the European international society, so common-sensical within this diplomatic culture, were exposed, and then its norms were opposed.

As a result, realists need to concentrate on area studies where different political cultures exist. A move to greater sensitivity in cultural area studies is, of course, not as far from the approach of classical realist political practitioners as some might think. Kissinger complained that the new foreign policy élite treated all nations similarly, ignoring their different histories. Kennan was an expert on Russian (and then Soviet) policy before becoming an international realist. Also, by cultural studies, I do not mean culture as the residual category when other explanations fail, or, worse even, the attempt to make cultural determinist explanations, again en vogue these days (Huntington 1993). Cultural studies refer here just to the greater hermeneutical sensitivity to the ways politics are done in different parts of the world. Here, the diplomatic culture is no longer the taken-for-granted background for diplomacy, but just one, although dominant, way of enframing it.[1]

Kissinger's puzzle has become more complicated by the presence of new influential international actors, other than states, whose world-view does not necessarily correspond to that of historically aware statesman. It is far from obvious that traditional diplomats, NGO activists and business managers speak the same language. Realists did take up this problem. Susan Strange analysed the world-view of what she called a global 'business civilization', since their understanding of the world will be crucial for decisions in that world. It is obvious that one cannot easily assume common interests and normative codes across the transnational political and economic élite. Starting again from Henry Kissinger's concerns for a viable diplomacy today, another interesting question might be to know whether the traditional diplomatic culture could coopt new élites, or inversely, how much

---

[1] Maybe this cultural sensibility is also the reason why theories inspired by poststructuralism or constructivism are so much interested in classical realism (Wæver 1992) and try to further develop them (see also Kratochwil and Lapid 1996).

managerial language has permeated diplomatic élites. From here, it is a small step to the International Political Economy research programme on the grip of dominant ideologies across élites, such as neoliberalism and the Washington consensus (Gill 1990).

Whereas traditionally, realists trained the maxims of a given successful diplomacy to the next generation of practitioners, the very understanding of the new diplomacy requires observers to engage with sociology and political economy, outside the world-view of the classical realist. The knowledge of the classical diplomatic codes no longer suffices. In the new diplomacy, as well as in present world politics, there is no way back to the former unity of diplomatic culture and the language of International Relations.

These attempts belie a longing for a less theoretical discipline. But there is no way back to the presumed golden age. In the old testament, Adam and Eve experienced sudden shame for their nakedness after their fall from paradise. Realism has been seen as naked for quite some time now. It cannot recover its original innocence. An empiricism of 'telling history as it was' can no longer appeal to the tacit consensus of the academic and political community. Consequently, it has to drape its virtues into arguments. This introduces an objectifying distance into International Relations. Once this distance is introduced, the role of the discipline turns from implicit socializing into explicit debate. Its now explicit interpretation is open to criticism and needs not only empirical but also theoretical and normative justification.

TRYING HARDER: A POST-WALTZIAN REALIST THEORY

Not only is there no way back to the unity of diplomatic culture and the language used within International Relations, but also the unity of realist assumptions and International Relations as a science is lost.

According to Waltz, the most faithful and thoughtful attempt so far to rescue the rich realist tradition out of neorealism is found in the *Logic of Anarchy* (Buzan, Jones and Little 1993). Their book is a response to two realist crises. It addresses the decline of realism as a unifying, indeed discipline-defining paradigm, and the resulting fragmentation of the discipline. But it also reacts against critics of the Waltzian solution to this decline. It is informed by the interdependence debate which triggered the fragmentation of the discipline, as well as the methodological turn in the aftermath of Waltz which found realism fragmented. The *Logic of Anarchy* is a realist response to the crisis both of realism and of neorealism.

Buzan, Jones and Little try to partly prove Kenneth Waltz wrong, so as to get realism right. They are not just starting from Waltz; they do, at least so I would claim, follow him in one very important sense, namely in the function of the enterprise. First, they want to defend the borders of International Relations as a discipline, when they assume that it is 'a legitimate and independent field of inquiry' (Buzan, Jones and Little 1993: 6). Second, on the basis of realist assumptions they want to provide 'a wide-ranging and integrative general theory of international relations' (Buzan, Jones and Little 1993: 65). The underlying purpose is to provide a redefinition of both International Relations and realism such as the traditional overlap, if not confusion, of the two can be upheld. Waltz did so by severely reducing the subject-matter of International Relations and realism accordingly. *The Logic of Anarchy* acknowledges the untenable narrow boundaries put up by Waltz, and then proposes to expand realism accordingly.

The following discussion of the *Logic of Anarchy* cannot address all the issues of this rich book. It is conducted with a view to assessing whether the book can save a wider post-Waltzian realism without jeopardizing Waltz's attempt to keep realism and the boundaries of the discipline united. This section tackles *The Logic of Anarchy*'s incisive amendments to Waltz's approach, particularly the offered definition of international politics – which Waltz interestingly lacked – the conceptual analysis of power, the understanding of change, and Waltz's meta-theory.

My argument is that, ultimately, *the Logic of Anarchy* is returning to a multi-causal framework of analysis very similar to that of the global 'web' (see Chapter 8), with some new added historical leverage, but also some meta-theoretical contradictions between the authors. It is meta-theoretically and conceptually informed classical realism. Moreover, the *Logic of Anarchy* symbolizes maybe more than any other book the unsuccessful attempt to articulate an encompassing version of realism which overlaps with the boundaries of International Relations, and which could provide at the same time scientific justification for realist assumptions: it is a co-authored but independently signed work which develops a theory and then adds meta-theoretical conditions of a theory which contradict this very approach. The unity of realist theory and International Relations as an independent field of inquiry is not in reach.

Getting a grip on politics and power

Already some earlier responses to the crisis of realism had indicated the very narrow – and implicit – definition of international politics (see Chapters 10 and 11). For Waltz, international politics referred to what states do, mainly war and diplomacy. Instead, the *Logic of Anarchy* proposes that the 'essence of [politics] concerns the shaping of human behaviour for the purpose of governing large groups of people' (Buzan *et al.* 1993: 35). Politics is understood as a question of governing. It explicitly comprises more than just inter-state relations (Buzan *et al.* 1993: 42).

Such a definition is very consequential for the entire theory which follows. It allows the differentiation of the international system in several sectors. This, in turn, is linked to the disaggregation of capabilities, that is power, which is used in the sense of resources. The reconceptualization of power proceeds by making two distinctions: between aggregated and disaggregated power, and between attributive and relative power.

Following the ground-breaking work of David Baldwin (as collected in 1989), the *Logic of Anarchy* does not see why power should be understood solely as a lump, as overall power. Barry Buzan writes, very correctly, that 'trying to think in terms of aggregated power has led, *inter alia*, to the over-ambitious and inconclusive debate about polarity and war' (Buzan *et al.* 1993: 61). Instead, he advocates the study of disaggregated polarity debates. Waltz has restrained from this move, because the consequences of disaggre-gating power would make a defence of systemic realism more problematic. And indeed, such a move not only undermines the causal quality of the balance of overall power, but also of all the disaggregated ones.

In a Waltzian view of overall power, this question would be resolved by the assumption that the overall power makes its will prevail in different sec-tors (or, and that is another circularity in power-based realism, *vice versa*: the states which prevail in different sectors have most overall power). There-fore, an aggregate concept is fundamental for systemic realists, even if diffi-cult to defend.

Buzan argues that such a concept is impossible. This claim derives from Baldwin's conceptual analyses. Since resources are not fungible across different sectors, we cannot easily aggregate them. It is not obvious what military capabilities, a convertible currency, a large internal market, and a widely shared language add up to. But for the same reason, that is, for the lacking measure for making power fungible across sectors, we do not have a theory of linkage. If we had a theory about how, let alone how much, the power of a shared language translates into strategic advantages, we would have a theory of linkage, and could, by the same token, construct a unified power index. In other words, if one asserts that there can be no aggregate concept for reasons of fungibility, which is certainly the concep-tually better position, then also a theory of linkages cannot just be assumed.

And this is most damaging for the way out proposed by Buzan, namely the analysis of disaggregated balances of power. Disaggregating power into, say, a political or economic sector, is meant to limit the comparison of similar resources, say military material, which, in turn, allows the analyst to establish sectorial polarities. But linkage means that the power structures of, say, international finance, sometimes also cultural predominance, have an effect on military polarity. But it is not evident exactly how this is so. If we knew we would not need to disaggregate power in the first place. Hence, the *Logic of Anarchy* leaves us not only with fragmented sectorial polarities, but with little explanatory power as long as we do not know how sectors interrelate. In a nutshell, the *Logic of Anarchy* comes back full circle to the same debates of power and interdependence in the 1970s, that have made Waltz insist on an aggregate concept – leaving them un-resolved.

Besides the distinction between aggregate and disaggregate capabilities, there is a second distinction between two types of power in the *Logic of Anarchy*, between relative and attributive power. Following Ruggie's ideas, attributive or absolute power is of major importance for the theoretical project to the extent it helps to define a new level of analysis in-between unit and structure (and an implicit theory of history) (Ruggie [1983] 1986).

Unfortunately, Buzan refers to relative power also as relational power. This misunderstanding sheds a very peculiar light on the project. Baldwin has introduced the idea from political theory that power is a relational concept. It is not the resource or property of an actor. Resources are just power bases. Power itself lies in the relation between actors. Baldwin's preferred example is a coercive attempt in which a person threatens another with a gun and shouts 'your money or your life'. The sanction of killing, and the visible means for realizing it, generally provide a powerful threat. Yet, if the threatened person is preparing to commit suicide, or does not value life so highly, the coercive capacity of the threat is reduced accordingly. Awareness of this relational aspect can also be consciously used as a defense against threats. President Harry Truman tried to impress Joseph Stalin at the Potsdam conference in 1945 by telling him that the United States had developed an atomic bomb. Stalin, however, by feigning indifference, reduced the impact of this possible bargaining chip. Thus, any power instrument becomes a potential power resource only if its control is valued by other actors in the interaction. Power comes out of this relation, not from the power holder alone (Baldwin 1985: 22; and Baldwin 1989: 207).

Buzan is perfectly aware of this when he refers to Morgenthau's conception of politics as psychological control. But the entire theory, and this is a central point elaborated later, goes on without any reference to the understanding of actors. Unfortunately, and despite realists' repeated attempts, power, as a relational concept, cannot work as the central concept in a systemic realist approach (Guzzini 1993, 1994b).

Understanding change: back to multiple unweighed determinacy

Undoubtedly the major contribution of *The Logic of Anarchy* is to have developed Ruggie's (1986 [1983]) conceptual grounds such as to reintegrate the study of change into a systemic realist theory of International Relations. Systemic change, strictly understood, is still available only as the somewhat unreal shift from anarchy to hierarchy, as in Waltz's first tier of the structure. Yet change within this system, and qualitatively important ones, are not reduced to the shifts in the (military) balance of power. They can stem from changes in the second (functional differentiation) and third tier (distribution of capabilities) of the international structure, as well as from a new level of analysis, in between structure and unit, called interaction capacity.

Already in the last section we started to open up the third tier of the structure. There is more than military relations to the international system. Having furthermore political, economic and societal sectors allows for shifts, and thus change, in their distribution of capabilities of, respectively, political stability, economic capabilities and ideology (Buzan *et al.* 1993: 63).

Much more far-reaching is the opening of the second tier of the structure, what Waltz called functional differentiation. The book contends that it is perfectly possible to conceive of anarchical systems which are not just including like-units, but comprise different types of units which do not share a common political system (Buzan *et al.* 1993: 146). Hence, the evolution of the nature of states, as for instance the shift from city-states to empires and nation-states (Buzan *et al.* 1993: 118), is a possible qualitative change which can perfectly happen under anarchy.

A completely new level is introduced with what they call interaction capacity, defined as:

> aspects of absolute capability that transcend the unit level, but which are not structural in the sense of having to do with the positional arrangement of the units. They are systemic not only because they represent capabilities that are deployed throughout the system, but also, and mainly, because they profoundly condition the significance of structure and the meaning of the term system itself.
>
> (Buzan *et al.* 1993: 72)

Interaction capacity is a condition for the very structural logic (Buzan *et al.* 1993: 73). This applies because interaction capacity is the necessary condition to distinguish different types of anarchical systems and their underlying properties. Where little interaction capacity exists, there might be no international system at all, and certainly the pressures for socialization and competition, that Waltz describes as the effect of anarchy, do not apply. Similarly, if interaction capacity passes over a certain threshold, the international system turns into an international society, and again the Waltzian features do not necessarily apply; functional differentiation can more easily happen. Consequently, the three levels, structure, interaction capacity and unit-level are not on the same causal footing: interaction capacity is logically prior to the others.

That neorealist theorists who want to understand change give a primordial although not exclusive place to technological change, which is said to be more important then societal capabilities (Buzan *et al.* 1993: 71), is not untypical: it is certainly nothing new from Keohane and Nye's (1977) 'economic process' as the starting model for understanding change, to be combined with the study of power distribution and norms (see Fig. 8.1, showing the global 'web'). Again, the solution to Waltz's problems bring us squarely back to the problems the global 'web' posed for realism. Having replaced Waltz's solution to the fragmentation of the discipline and the related crisis of realism, it is still a question, whether *the Logic of Anarchy* can succeed where his attempts – namely to keep realism alive as the centrepiece of International Relations as an independent discipline – fell short.

Whereas the attempt to maintain an independent field of inquiry will be dealt with in the next section, I would argue that it will be difficult for *The Logic of Anarchy* to get such a realist theory back to the centre of International Relations. As with Keohane and Nye (1977) and some of the realist writers in International Political Economy, the book does not represent a causal empirical theory. There is no clear-cut 'if–then' relationship established, but just a conceptual framework which indicates a host of causal variables whose exact weight is not made precise. It is a conceptually and meta-theoretically informed type of classical realism. That is certainly a perfectly legitimate position. It is exactly against such unscientific theories, however, which repeatedly prompted the discipline to develop more scientific ones. Waltz became successful for having suggested stringent and easy causal determinations. *The Logic of Anarchy* rightly debunks them. But since it does not replace them, as it should according to the present canons of a social science, the search for another scientific Waltz will go on. *The Logic of Anarchy* has taken the realist Waltz very seriously, when it was the presumed 'scientist' Waltz who was successful in the first place.

From Waltz through Carr to internal contradiction: resurrecting (or constructing) a non-positivist realist tradition

As initially stated, the *Logic of Anarchy* responds both to the crisis of realism and of neorealism. Turning here to the meta-theoretical level, it seems that the book takes even more of the criticisms on board, indeed, so much to make its position hardly distinguishable from their critics, including the dreaded poststructuralists.

Jones's starting point is an epistemological fudge in Waltz's meta-theory. On the one hand, the *Theory of International Politics* states that theories do not derive from empirical correlations, but that empirical knowledge derives from theories. In other words, theories are not the result of knowledge, but the condition for it. On the other hand, Waltz insists on the empirical testability of knowledge, of falsification as a methodological ideal, albeit remote in International Relations. Here knowledge is constructed, there it stems from value-neutral tests.

In order to resolve this contradiction, according to Jones, falsification has to go, and with it the 'evident positivist lie of scientific detachment and objectivity' (Buzan *et al.* 1993: 236). Meta-theoretical coherence is achieved by concentrating on the social construction of knowledge and of the central importance language plays therein. What follows is the resurrection of Carr's scepticism and materialist theory of knowledge (see Chapter 2) directed against Waltz.

As mentioned earlier, Carr assumed that truth claims are not just the neutral representation of an outside world, but part of it: they actively shape that world. Knowledge, in turn, is conditioned by the social setting in which it is generated. Remember Carr's biting riposte of the complacent British theorists who assumed a harmony of interests when it served the interests of the powerful of the day in keeping the *status quo*. The social scientist must hence assume that theory serves a purpose, to use the phrase of a Carr-inspired historical materialist scholar, Robert Cox ([1981] 1986), who coined this to criticize Waltz. Once the scholars become aware of theories being purposeful, so Cox maintains, they must turn critical and include a reflection on this purpose into their theorizing. If not, it is just blind problem-solving theory, or worse, unreflected ideology.

According to Jones, this leads Waltz to reverse Carr's unity of theory and practice. For Waltz, theory is used as a neutral ground for proposing realist practices. For Carr, practice, which is always normative, informs the development of theories. Hence, Waltz's attempt to be politically effective by carrying a scientific shield, appears to Jones as the ultimate ideological weapon (1993: 178–9), a critique which was already advanced by Ashley ([1984] 1986). By denying, as Waltz does, that thought and observation are participating in the observed world, the scholar severs himself from the (hermeneutic) link which is the condition of scientific understanding (1993: 231).

Consequently, Charles Jones sees the way forward in International Relations theory in the 'close empirical study of the diplomatic and foreign policy-making community, its practice and discourse', 'employing the techniques of analysis of the literary critic', to supply an account 'of the tensions that have formed around contested concepts, the strategies by which usages of key terms have been established and maintained, and the implications such established usages have had for social action' (Buzan *et al.* 1993: 235).

This is a neat description of main research programmes inspired by post-structuralism or constructivism, whether with regard to the analysis of foreign policy practice and discourse (Campbell 1992, 1993), or the analysis of central terms of International Relations theory, such as anarchy (Wendt 1992), power (Ashley 1989, Guzzini 1993, 1994b), or sovereignty (Walker 1993a; Bartelson 1995). It is less obvious, however, how this can fit realism, or, more problematically, the initial part of the book. When Jones criticizes Waltz for privileging structure over unit and hence also efficient cause over intention (Buzan *et al.* 1993: 187), it is difficult to see how this same criticism should not be applied against his co-authors. When he wants to bring back the analysis of interpretation, symbolism, persuasion, motive, and the unconscious (Buzan *et al.* 1993: 234), then alongside the materialist account of structures, there should have been an analysis of language, realist and structuralist language, at equal footing. Jones' hermeneutical meta-theory clashes with Buzan's theory whose continuity with Waltz's power-materialism is remarkable.

The redundancy of anarchy

The most paradoxical and consequential aspect of *The Logic of Anarchy* is that, by having skilfully redefined the parameters of the Waltzian structure, the authors end up making the assumption of anarchy redundant. This shatters the second purpose of Waltz's theory, namely to legitimately set International Relations apart from the study of domestic politics. The disciplinary divisions cannot be upheld.

The deep structure is defined by anarchy and by functional differentiation. Barry Buzan goes to some length to allow for functional differentiation without giving up the assumption of anarchy. Differentiation exists when the sovereignty of units is limited to a range of political functions (Buzan *et al*. 1993: 42). Buzan is aware that this opens the door to a conceptualization of the international system not as anarchic, but as hierarchical, albeit unlike a state. In anticipation of such a move, he writes:

> Some would like to push the idea of differentiation down this path by having it include role differentials such as great and small powers, neutrals, allies, hegemons, and such like. The temptation should be resisted. Differentiation of functions refers to function as a unit and only in that sense does it link to the essence of deep structure, which is about government. Differentiation of roles is best dealt with at the unit level.
>
> (Buzan *et al*. 1993: 46)

This is rather awkward. Waltz relies upon a system theory. Systems are defined by the totality of their relations, that is, all parts are linked up to a coherent whole. It does not make a difference here if one refers to a biological analogy or to the feedback loops of cybernetic systems. In all cases, different organs or subunits are responsible for different functions. And these functions cannot be defined with regard to the inner working of these subunits, but are, of course, defined with regard to the whole: a liver is functionally differentiated from a heart not because it has a different texture, as it were, but because it has a different task for the body. Similarly, it seems bizarre, as the quote suggests, to understand the function of a thermostat by dealing with the thermostat, and not with the heating system. Indeed, many functions within the international system make no sense whatsoever at the unit level. How can one understand the function of an international lender of last resort, without reference to an international monetary system? Waltz (1979: 197) correctly writes that 'units previously alike become functionally distinct as some of them take on system-wide tasks. This is the governmental solution'.

One reason why Buzan insists on this conceptual mistake might be that, despite functional differentiation, the theory infers the existence of anarchy from the fact that the same kind of structural effects of socialization and competition still apply. Hence, whatever differentiation there is, we would still populate an anarchical system, because its logic is still with us.

But do we? Jones can be taken as a witness against it. He reminds us, that the analogy on which the international structure is modelled, the market, exists in hierarchical political settings (Buzan *et al.* 1993: 194). Since also markets generate competition and socialization (imitation), then such effects are possible also in hierarchical systems, and not simply under anarchy. If the basic idea of neorealism and of *the Logic of Anarchy* alike, is the conditioning effects of international political structure (Buzan *et al.* 1993: 238), then this applies with the same force also to domestic political structures. Indeed, this is basic to any structure, so understood. In other words, the supposed logic of anarchy is simply the usual behaviourial constraint of structures as seen by structuralist theories.

As a result, the same structural effects cannot justify anarchy as opposed to hierarchy on the international level. Indeed, anarchy adds nothing significant or causal to the understanding of the deep structure, as compared to the second tier, functional differentiation. Little later writes, that 'the functional differentiation of political units is seen to dictate the character of the anarchic deep structure of the system' (Buzan *et al.* 1993: 88). Anarchy becomes a context posited 'out there', without causal relevance. Hence, Buzan's attempt to redefine the structural level, such as to allow the historical analysis of change, ends up depriving anarchy of any significance. The simple truth is that a concept like anarchy which can accommodate so many different international systems, indeed all historical systems known to us, is meaningless (for a similar argument, see also Rosenberg 1994: Part I).

The logical consequence of *The Logic of Anarchy* is that the level of anarchy is redundant. And the second tier, if correctly understood, shows features of role differentiation which imply a more vertical view of governing. By dropping the assumption of anarchy as the strict demarcation between domestic and international affairs, for its heuristic disadvantages (Milner 1991), we would have to understand the international system as a system of authority and rule (Onuf and Klink 1989) where the idea of like-units is at best a legal fiction, at worst a smoke-screen to hide structural power and responsibilities.

Whereas some realist theories in International Political Economy (see Chapter 11) have given up the divide between domestic and international affairs, the *Logic of Anarchy* remains squarely in the old divide. I would suggest that this is due to the authors' and Waltz's second purpose, namely to keep International Relations apart from other fields of inquiry. The new broader theory is meant to include more features, such as to make it unnecessary for International Relations to be swallowed from other disciplines or taken over by a broader International Political Economy. If such an undertaking has to rely on the void concept of anarchy, it will not be successful.

In this interpretation which covers, of course, only a part of the entire project, *The Logic of Anarchy* stands for the attempt to keep the boundaries of International Relations and realism overlapping (as with the general theory) and to reinstall realism as the leading school of thought in the discipline. This unity is not in reach. The authors wanted to build on Waltz's compromise of a restricted, but methodologically acceptable realism. Their own compromise is, however, likely to be unacceptable to both the discipline and realists. By reconceptualizing Waltz's concept of structure, the book leaves out Waltz's general causal theory, and proposes instead a wider framework of analysis with multiple unweighed causes. This will not be welcomed by that part of the discipline which sees in general causal theories the scientific legitimation of their doing. Waltz might have been wrong, but he stuck to, if not legitimated, that canon. It is likewise probable that realists who have been developing these more general frameworks of analysis will find *The Logic of Anarchy* much too narrow exactly because it does not leave Waltz's anarchy assumption. As realist International Political Economy testifies (see Chapter 11), there is much realist heritage to be safeguarded in such wider approaches, but it is not exactly the Waltzian neorealist approach. In other words, *The Logic of Anarchy* proposes a methodologically open systemic theory, which accommodates many of Waltz's theoretical shortcomings, but, at the end of the day, it cannot make a convincing point for its restricted realist theory.

JUST FORGET ABOUT REALISM: THE IMPOSSIBLE OPTION

Many realists after Morgenthau, with some exceptions like Gilpin, contend that their theory should not be derived from human nature. But then where is the origin of realist scepticism? Since Aron (see Chapter 3), realism can no longer presuppose the maximization of power as a general goal. But without this core assumption, it becomes very difficult to differentiate realism from other approaches. As many realists argue, from Wolfers to Buzan in *The Logic of Anarchy*, realism cannot even assume that there is only one logic of anarchy, or one single way to phrase the security dilemma. But then, is there any determinacy left? Finally, in reaction to the criticisms of the meta-theoretical debates in the eighties, realism can no longer rely on an empiricist methodology, as Jones (in Buzan, Jones and Little 1993) shows: the balance of power is not just 'out there', but a theoretical construct, and at times, an institution of the scientific community and the community of statesmen. It is neither natural nor innocent, nor unchangeable.

When all has been said and done, what is left of realism? For all those who believe in general causal theories, the straightforward answer is not much. Certainly there is not enough to keep it going (except as welcome strawman or null-hypothesis for the article industry). Yet despite all, realism is still around. Indeed, we cannot just get rid of realism by proclaiming it dead. The reason for its resiliency, however, is not that it is a generally shared common sense, 'which goes without saying', nor that it is a well-defended explanatory theory, although some of its assumptions can be fruitfully employed.

Realism is part of the collective memory and self-definition of international actors, academics or politicians alike, which order thought, suggest analogies and empower attitudes to political action. Hence, it is necessary to engage with realism, although this is emphatically not all what needs to be done in International Relations, theory and practice. Only by doing so we can move beyond our main tradition and school of thought. One cannot study world politics without understanding the main frame of thought within which it has been consciously conducted. Very often the world realism depicts is not out there, but realism is.

This does not mean that the critical thought developed in all these chapters can be forgotten. Indeed, the idea was to open realism up to discussion and to invite the practitioners to more self-criticism, so as to avoid the many possible self-fulfilling prophecies of realism. This chapter has argued that there is no way back to an empiricist realism. Similarly, there is little justified hope in realism as a causal explanatory theory. Its continuing existence points to the thesis which framed this book, that we have to understand realism as a historical practice, academic and political, rather than only as a theory. Realism does not passively reflect the world; it does something to it.

This line of thought has been proposed mainly by historical sociologists and materialists, as well as constructivist and poststructuralist theories. Realism as a practice has becomes a privileged object of study, not only for this book (George 1994). This section analyses some of the internal critiques, that is those which take realist concerns very seriously. Since we cannot just step out of our tradition, the critical emphasis comes from making realism visible as a practice, and from turning it against the many irresponsible claims committed in its name.

The main line of critique can be summarized as follows: realism does not take its central concepts seriously enough. To start with, its critiques claim that realism is a sceptical practice which however, stops short of problematizing the inherent theory of the state. It is, second, a practice which informs an international community. Third, international politics is not power politics because it resembles realist precepts, but because the international community which holds a realist world-view acts in such a way as to produce power politics: it is a social construction. Realist expectations might hold, not because they objectively correspond to something out there, but because agents make them the maxims that guide their actions. Finally, this can have very significant policy effects: even at the end of the Cold War which might have shattered realist world-views, realist practices could mobilize old codes, such as to belittle the potential historical break of the post-Berlin wall system. Realism still underlies major re-conceptualization of the present international system, from Huntington's geocultural reification to 'neo-medievalism' – and justifies the foreign policies which can be derived from them.

Taking scepticism seriously: the sceptical critique of the realist ontology of the state

Poststructuralism is a theoretical framework which combines a meta-theory of intersubjective interpretivism (see Chapter 13) with a moral theory of radical scepticism. As paradoxical as it might seem to some, poststructuralism in International Relations represents a sceptical critique of what is usually seen as the sceptical theory *par excellence*, namely realism (for the following, see Guzzini 1997b). More consequential for this discussion, the poststructuralist normative critique of realism implies a conceptual critique which makes the attempt of a scientific version of realism questionable from the start.

A common reference for both realism and poststructuralism is Max Weber (Walker 1988–1989: 12–13, 1993b: 148–53). What makes the reference to Weber so appealing for these theories, is his analysis of the success of Western civilization, understood as a process of rationalization, which Weber combines with a sense of lost spiritual unity, with disenchantment, as he calls it. Weber is the heir of Kant and of Nietzsche. In a world that has lost its God, there will be a clash of multiple gods (Weber 1988 [1919]). There is neither a divine nor a rational solution to the plurality of values. Hence, modernity is ambivalent. It frees individuals from arbitrary rule, and it has the potential to imprison them in the ever expanding grid of instrumental rationality, Weber's iron cage.

Within this context, a new self-comprehension of the individual, a new subjectivity, arises. It takes its origins in what Aron (1969: 287) calls the Promethean ambition of early modernity, that is, the ambition to become masters and owners of nature through the use of science and technology. In a world where rationality does not provide the final word for moral choices, such a subject is both the bearer of progress and the greatest danger to Enlightenment. The danger arises at two levels. On the individual level, there is the risk that the will to power is all what there can be to morality, a path often associated with Nietzsche and Carl Schmitt's 'decisionism'. Against this risk, realists usually follow Weber's solution of an 'ethics of responsibility'. This ethics should oppose decisionism and protect a sphere of moral reasonable choice form the inexorable advance of rationalization. But then, as Rob Walker asks: responsibility for whom?

And here again, realists seem to follow Weber at least in principle, when the addressee of ethics is the national community. There is an in-built tendency to *prima facie* legitimation of the will to power on the national level, called then 'power politics'. Such a derivation has been decried by (some) realists themselves (Aron 1967b) and not all policies pursued in its name will find the blessing of the realist. But, and here the poststructuralist critique of realism acquires a more radical sceptical tone, the way realist theory is constructed blends out alternative understandings of world politics where governing is not tied to the state. Put differently, for the poststructuralist, realism does not justify why its scepticism stops short of the state: realism reifies the state as a moral actor.

Taking power seriously: the tacit power of realist discourses

Both poststructuralists and constructivists argue that anarchy and sovereignty, the basic conceptual couple realism uses to set international relations aside from domestic politics, do not refer to a natural or necessary fact. Instead, these concepts make sense within the meaning world of an international community of statesmen. In turn, the academic community of neorealists erroneously takes this social practice for mind-independent objective reality. In other words, international politics is not determined by power-materialism, reducible to a mechanistic model. It is a social construction of historically evolving institutions in which power materialism plays a changing role. As such, international politics cannot derive from a rationally optimizable national interest, a position, as it were, which reduces political decisions to an efficiency calculus.

A social practice is made out of a community of actors. Hence, the preceding argument relies on the identification of a community within the international sphere. In a sociological move influenced by Pierre Bourdieu, Richard Ashley argues that such a community exists in the subjectivity and in the practices of realism itself, 'as a network of historically fabricated practical understandings, precedents, skills, and procedures that define competent international subjectivity and that occupy a precariously held social *space*' (Ashley 1987: 411). This is inherent in the romantic vision of realists, who see themselves in a two-front struggle. They are the defenders of the nation against the inherent violence of international relations, as well as the warning voices against the attempts to export domestic ideals, even democratic, into a realm where their application would lead to unnecessary war. The assumptions of realism legitimate a community located at the borders between domestic and international politics, and at the margins of the liberal discourse of the West. This community perceives itself as the heroic adjustment to a necessity. Making realism visible as a practice, opens it up to criticism, and questions its uncontested and naturalized quality.

Again, criticism proceeds by taking a central concept of realism, power, more seriously than realists themselves. It focuses on the question how this community could silence the constructed and historical character of its existence. Its scepticism cannot stop at the description of the international system as simple necessity. But it does also not believe in the conspiracy of the wicked realists who intentionally conceal their power. It sees this power socially reproduced by the practices of the international community of realists (Ashley 1989). It is a form of impersonal power (Guzzini 1993, 1994b). It lies in the routine practices of this community, in its taken-for-granted and self-evident understandings.

An intersubjective power analysis must tackle the meta-theoretical level which underlies realist analysis and its deliberate policies. 'The theory of knowledge is a dimension of political theory because the specific symbolic power to impose the principles of the construction of reality – in particular, social reality, is a major dimension of political power' (Bourdieu 1977: 165). Here the epistemological trend of the last decade is as much a sign of a discipline in crisis, as an attempt by some to lay bare the tacit epistemological power of neorealist discourse (Ashley 1986 [1984], 1988; Runyan and Peterson 1991: 75–6, 97–8).

Taking international society seriously: the social construction of power politics

Once the international community of this construction has been identified, once the power of discourses is accepted, it is possible to pursue an analysis of the shared understandings which lead to the impression of the necessity of power politics, and which make the enterprise of realism as a power-materialist scientific approach possible. National interest/security or power do not appear as something objectively given, but are socially constructed – and contestable.

If realism is a practice which constructs socially what we see as power politics (Wendt 1992a), then an important empirical research programme should focus on concepts. This study of concepts does not just try to clarify what they mean, but what we do by using them. Let me illustrate with two common concepts in International Relations, prominent in realism, namely security and power.

Security redefined

Ole Wæver's (1995) aim has been to shift away from the conceptual analysis which simply focuses on the different meanings of security. Instead, the analysis should apprehend what is done by calling something a security issue. For him, security stands for a particular pattern to understand events, which mobilizes specific policy dispositions.

The security discourse refers to a subject, a threat and a reference object of threat (say, military). It has mainly been used in the national military security environment. There, it singles out issues of high importance for which a state of high alert, and special fast-track decision-making are justified. Joseph Nye once nicely captured this essence of the security discourse by comparing security to oxygen. As long as you have it, you do not notice it. But when it seems lacking, all other issues become secondary.

Wæver's research starts when an issue is called a security issue. For him, this is not a neutral description first which asks for political action later. Securitization is politics itself. It is an act, often by authorized élites, which results in moving a particular problem into a principled level, where all necessary means could be legitimated. In this respect, security is the enemy of politics: it moves an issue out of the sphere of bargaining and compromise.

Understanding securitization as a practice which mobilizes certain dispositions, can help the analyst to gain new empirical insights. Ole Wæver used it for understanding what happened during détente. When the nuclear stalemate put all political initiatives on ice, the West used a form of desecuritizing strategy. The Kremlin has long resisted opening up economically and culturally, to accepting human rights and political dissent. It often invoked reasons of sovereignty or national security – claiming flexibility on any of these issues would weaken the communist struggle against international capitalism. Western détente policy persistently tried to get economic and cultural issues away from high politics, aiming to de-securitize. The result was the compromise of the Final Declaration of Helsinki in 1975, where the West gave up the territorial claims (first basket) it was anyway unable to achieve, in return for gaining improvements in the second and third baskets (economic and cultural relations, and human rights). With the hindsight of Charter 77, the rising dissidence movements, and the revolutions of 1989, the strategy was sound. Paradoxically as it may sound at first hand, European security was improved by desecuritizing several issues. Similarly, the recent Russian attempts to influence its 'near abroad' with reference to its Russian minorities, can be countered by a strategy which desecuritizes citizenship, as, for instance, in Latvia and Estonia (Schmelling 1995). Another fruitful empirical application of this approach to security is the analysis of the securitization of societal issues (Wæver 1993), when, for instance, the migrant is no longer seen as just a different, or an other, but, as a potential threat of a national security discourse (Huysmans 1995).

The construction of power

Hedley Bull (1977) writes that although we do, of course, know that there is no such a thing as a balance of power, it is a concept we cannot do without. He is right in a double sense. First, the balance of power is a concept that diplomats use to make their trade. Second, for the first reason and only this, the observer cannot do without it.

Power might not be fungible, but diplomats work on measures to give power a translatable meaning. Traditional compensation politics must rely on some measure across different power sectors. Before diplomats can count, they must decide what counts. Hence, the balance of power or any equilibrium idea of this kind is based upon a social construction, sometimes an agreement, of the diplomatic community. They share a common measure of power although they would be hard-pressed to define it exactly.

Hence, as with the security discourse, measurement of power is a political act. The diplomats who represent states endowed with one particular power resource will do their best to enhance the latter's value. The Soviet government's stress on military, and not economic, factors was a case in point. The rush for mass-destructive weapons is as much a concern of security as a question of power in the sense of acquiring a resource which is commonly considered to be at the top rank. The prestige, in turn, is traded for particular compensations or attentions. Sometimes, such agreements on measures and treatments, if generally shared, might diplomatically recreate something similar to the supposedly mechanical balance of power (Kivi 1996).

On the second level of observation, the existence of balance of power as a social construct means that we cannot simply forget about it because we found out that no mechanical balance exists. The concept does not refer to anything in the objective structures of the international system. It is a fallacy to think that since it is reproduced in the diplomatic culture, it must correspond to an objectified reality, a fallacy which has daunted much realist writings, both scientific and classical. But it is a device used by diplomats, and as such it exists, and is consequential for international politics.

In his inaugural lecture in Zürich, the Swiss scholar Daniel Frei (1969) urged his fellow political scientists to help practical policy with a neutral and measurable concept of power. He was perfectly aware both of the practical needs of such a concept and of its difficult scientific underpinning. This lucid text shows the political value of concepts which travel between the academic and the political community. Power is a device used by academics, and as such has effects on the production of knowledge and the reproduction of the traditional diplomatic culture.

The mobilization of collective memory at the end of the Cold War

Realism should be taken seriously for the way it informs our understanding of historical changes. Realism, as an implicit framework of analysis has much shaped the 'lessons of history' which influence our way of making sense of international politics. Versailles, Munich, Vietnam do not only stand for complex historical events, but for metaphors which guide our understanding. They are written into the collective memory of statesmen and academics (for these examples, this applies to the West, at least). They are the contested, but often commonly shared, understanding of what the lessons of the past should be.

The study of collective memory is part of the study of power in International Relations (for this entire section, see Guzzini 1994b). It applies to the two main practices of International Relations, to the level of the community of diplomats (in its widest understanding) and of academics. Realist lessons of the past are among the most powerful links between these two communities. They hold a powerful grip on individual decision-makers, as well as on the professional history tellers who write up the lessons for the future.

The way the US administration and the International Relations academia handled the second Gulf War is an empirical illustration of this form of intersubjective power. It can be shown that many historical analogies drawn from the Second World War influenced major US decision-makers (Lakoff 1991; Luke 1991). Historical analogies can, of course, be consciously used to influence outcomes. This is the usual task of propaganda. But historical analogies do more. They suggest patterns of understanding and consequently conduct which can elude the conscious control of the decision-maker. They can clarify events by letting the mind focus on particular data. This does, however, not imply to say that they determine behaviour, a step which would result in a kind of structural determinism. What can be said is that the capacity to have a particular event inscribed within a script of a historical analogy is a forceful device for legitimating that action which is thought to be the lesson of this historical event. When Saddam Hussein was likened to Hitler, his regime to a totalitarian regime which opposed the rules of the international system, when Iraq was said to be close to having its nuclear bomb, when, in other words, the second Gulf War was a remake of the Second World War, massive intervention was not only warranted, but required.

Similarly, the international community of International Relations experts reacted in a way much influenced by these lessons of the past. Lawrence Freedman (1991), in his characteristically succinct manner, summarized the two lessons that wars in the Third World, in particular the Vietnam War, have apparently taught the US: that an intervention either results in a quagmire or in escalation (or the worst, both). The discussion around the last Gulf War intervention was for long steeped within these two parameters before the Second World War analogy finally helped to overcome it.

The understanding of the second Gulf War as a remake of the Second World War also influenced the understanding of the end of the Cold War at large. Central issues are not social relations and domestic changes, or questions of legitimacy, but good old territorial politics and the threat of Third World nuclear powers. The threat is not internal disruption and the rise of nationalism, but nuclear proliferation. Not the fall of the Berlin wall, but the war around Kuwait became the paradigm for understanding future world politics.

Indeed, the recent discussion about the new type of international relations after the end of the Cold War provides perfect examples on how realist assumptions still persist, even when authors claim to have left them behind. Two recent interpretations of present world affairs, neomedievalism and the clash of civilization, might exemplify this move. Neomedievalism uses realist assumptions to understand the new referring to the time before the modern state system; the clash of civilization just returns to realist assumptions which were prominent before and during the Cold War.

Defining the present system as a form of neomedievalism takes realist politics of sovereign states as the norm and then must understand any development as a return, in new disguises, to the time before the modern state system. Historical epochs remain defined according to the realist canon.

The trouble is that the analogy is so abstract, indeed ahistorical, that it seems ill-suited to catch exactly those changes brought about by the social and economic changes over the last centuries, including the recent globalization of production and finance which asked for conceptual and theoretical innovation in the first place. As could be expected, the analogy is not new, but was already played out in earlier realist writings. Well before globalization, realists referred to it whenever they needed to conceptualize multiple or overlapping sovereignties (Wolfers 1962: 242 on the new medievalism; Bull 1977).

Similarly, the Cold War clash of power and ideologies is said to be replaced by a 'clash of civilization' (Huntington 1993), which turns out to be an updated culturalist version of geopolitics (see Mackinder 1944 [1919]). Whereas new medievalism reaches back to pre-modern international politics to apprehend the present system, the clash-of-civilization idea renews the pre-war geopolitical tradition in realism, which has always been cultural determinist. Seeing at Huntington's thesis from this perspective, the clash of civilizations is nothing new, but a preordained feature of international affairs which has been temporarily overlaid by the clash of ideologies. Moreover, Huntington revives the Cold War discourse. He divides the world into different civilizations (poles) which occupy different cultural areas (territories) at the borders of which (e.g. iron or bamboo curtains) friction is likely to occur. In particular, the Western world (democracy) will face the combined onslaught of civilizations which, by their self-definition, cannot compromise (totalitarianism). Huntington seems to be looking for a new enemy. In other words, it is not a new problem which spurs a Western response, but Western strategic solutions which are in search of a problem.

Consequently, taking realism seriously as a still widely shared device for constructing knowledge, helps in raising the awareness of the way in which often very contestable historical analogies influence our understanding, and can predispose to action. Such a conceptual analysis is hence not an idle thought, but a prerequisite to seeing a larger variety of policy options and to facing possible self-fulfilling prophecies.

CONCLUSION

This chapter made three arguments about the present development of realism in International Relations and International Political Economy. First, it showed that the unity between diplomatic discourse and the discipline of International Relations, so self-evident in the times of Morgenthau, can no longer be upheld. Both worlds of international politics and of diplomacy have changed.

Second, it showed a similar failure when realists tried to save the overlap of realism with the central explanatory theory of International Relations, that is, to save realism as the discipline's identity defining theory or paradigm. This was illustrated by a critique of the *Logic of Anarchy*, the most elaborate revision of Waltz's theory which aims at responding to the critics of realism and neorealism alike. This work can neither provide a meta-theoretically coherent realism, nor a version which would be acceptable to the present academic criteria of an empirical theory.

As a result of this double failure, realism is at a crossroads. Either it follows the scientific road, and then pursues its fragmentation within and outside the narrowed discipline. Or it goes back to its normative and historical roots but, then, it can no longer cover the research agenda of International Relations, nor claim the scientific core position that it has been used to taking since 1945. In the past, realists have resisted this dilemma. This resistance, played out in both ways, has given cadence to realism's evolution, and until now, also the evolution of International Relations as a discipline. This has been the double story of this book. As long as this resistance continues, the story will continue.

Third, this last chapter has argued that although the evolution of realism has been mainly a disappointment as a general causal theory, we have to deal with it. On the one hand, realist assumptions and insights are used and merged in nearly all frameworks of analysis offered in International Relations or International Political Economy. One of the book's purposes was to show realism as a varied and variably rich theory, so heterogeneous that it would be better to refer to it only in plural terms. On the other hand, to dispose of realism because some of its versions have been proven empirically wrong, ahistorical, or logically incoherent, does not necessarily touch its role in the shared understandings of observers and practitioners of international affairs. Realist theories have a persisting power for constructing our understanding of the present. Their assumptions, both as theoretical constructs, and as particular lessons of the past translated from one generation of decision-makers to another, help mobilizing certain understandings and dispositions to action. They also provide them with legitimacy.

Despite realism's several deaths as a general causal theory, it can still powerfully enframe action. It exists in the minds, and is hence reflected in the actions, of many practitioners. Whether or not the world realism depicts is out there, realism is. Realism is not a causal theory that explains International Relations, but, as long as realism continues to be a powerful mind-set, we need to understand realism to make sense of International Relations. In other words, realism is a still necessary hermeneutical bridge to the understanding of world politics. Getting rid of realism without having a deep understanding of it, not only risks unwarranted dismissal of some valuable theoretical insights that I have tried to gather in this book; it would also be futile. Indeed, it might be the best way to tacitly and uncritically reproduce it.

Bibliography

Abendroth, Wolfgang (1973) 'International Relations, Völkerrecht und Außenpolitik als Teildisziplinen der politischen Wissenschaft – ein Disput mit Ernst Otto Czempiel', in Ekkehart Krippendorff (ed.) *Internationale Beziehungen*, Köln: Kiepenheuer & Witsch, pp. 13–37.

Adorno, Theodor *et al.* (1969) *Der Positivismusstreit in der deutschen Soziologie*, Neuwied: Luchterhand.

Alemann, Ulrich v. and Erhard Forndran (1979) *Methodik der Politikwissenschaft. Eine Einführung in Arbeitstechnik und Forschungspraxis*, 2nd edn, Stuttgart: Kohlhammer.

Alker jr, Hayward R. and Thomas J. Biersteker (1984) 'The Dialectics of World Order: Notes for a Future Archeologist of International Savoir Faire', *International Studies Quarterly* 28, 2, pp. 121–42.

Alker jr, Hayward R. ([1986] 1996) 'The presumption of anarchy in world politics: on recovering the historicity of world society', in Hayward R. (ed.) *Rediscoveries and reformulations: humanistic methodologies for international studies*, Cambridge: Cambridge University Press, pp. 355–93.

Allison, Graham T. (1971) *Essence of Decision: Explaining the Cuban Missile Crisis*, Boston: Little Brown.

Allison, Graham T. and Morton Halperin (1972) 'Bureaucratic Politics: A Paradigm and Some Policy Implications', in Raymond Tanter and Richard Ullman (eds) *Theory and Policy in Intenational Relations*, Princeton: Princeton University Press.

Aron, Raymond (1984) *Les dernières années du siècle*, Paris: Julliard.

—— (1976) *Penser la guerre, Clausewitz. II: L'âge planétaire*, Paris: Gallimard.

—— (1969) *Les désillusions du progrès. Essai sur la dialectique de la modernité*, Paris: Calmann-Lévy.

—— (1967a) 'What is a Theory of International Relations?', *Journal of International Affairs* XXXI, pp. 185–206.

—— (1967b) 'Max Weber et la politique de puissance', in *Les étapes de la pensée sociologique*, Paris: Gallimard, pp. 642–56.

—— (1962) *Paix et guerre entre les nations*, Paris: Calmann-Lévy, 1984 (8th edn).

Ashley, Richard K. (1989) 'Imposing International Purpose: Notes on a Problematic of Governance', in Ernst-Otto Czempiel and James Rosenau (eds) *Global Changes and Theoretical Challenges: Approaches to World Politics for the 1990s*, Lexington, MA.: Lexington Books, pp. 251–90.

—— (1988) 'Untying the Sovereign State: A double reading of the Anarchy Problematique', *Millennium: Journal of International Studies* 17, 2 (Summer), pp. 227–62.

—— (1987) 'The Geopolitics of Geopolitical Space: Toward a Critical Social Theory of International Politics', *Alternatives* XII, 4, pp. 403–34.

—— (1986 [1984]) 'The Poverty of Neorealism', in Robert O. Keohane (ed.) *Neorealism and its Critics*, New York: Columbia University Press, pp. 255–300.

Axelrod, Robert and Robert Keohane (1986) 'Achieving cooperation under anarchy: strategies and institutions', in Kenneth Oye (ed.) *Cooperation under anarchy*, Princeton: Princeton University Press, pp. 226–54.

Baldwin, David A. (ed.) (1993a) *Neorealism and Neoliberalism: The Contemporary Debate*, New York: Columbia University Press.

—— (1993b) 'Neoliberalism, Neorealism, and World Politics', in David A. Baldwin (ed.) *Neorealism and Neoliberalism: The Contemporary Debate*, New York: Columbia University Press, pp. 3–25.

—— (1989) *Paradoxes of Power*, Oxford: Blackwell.

—— (1985) *Economic Statecraft*, Princeton: Princeton University Press.

Banks, Michael (1985) 'The Inter-Paradigm Debate', in Margot Light and A.J.R. Groom (eds) *International Relations: A Handbook of Current Theory*, London: Frances Pinter, pp. 7–26.

—— (1984) 'The Evolution of International Relations', in Michael Banks (ed.) *Conflict in World Society: A new perspective on International Relations*, Brighton: Harvester Press, pp. 3–21.

Banks, Michael and Martin Shaw (eds) (1991) *State and Society in International Relations*, London: Harvester/Wheatsheaf Press.

Barnes, Barry (1982) *T.S. Kuhn and Social Science*, London: Macmillan.

Barone, Charles A. (1985) *Marxist Thought on Imperialism: Survey and Critique*, London: Macmillan.

Bartelson, Jens (1996) 'Short circuits: society and tradition in international relations theory', *Review of International Studies* 22, 4 (October), pp. 339–60.

—— (1995) *A Genealogy of Sovereignty*, Cambridge: Cambridge University Press.

Beitz, Charles (1979) *Political Theory and International Relations*, Princeton: Princeton University Press.

Bendor, Jonathan and Thomas H. Hammond (1992) 'Rethinking Allison's models', *American Political Science Review* 86, 2 (June), pp. 301–22.

Berg-Schlosser, Dirk, Herbert Maier and Theo Stammen (1981) *Einführung in die Politikwissenschaft*, 3rd edn, München: Beck.

Berki, R.N. (1981) *On Political Realism*, London: Dent & Sons.

Bernstein, Richard (1983) *Beyond Objectivism and Relativism: Science, Hermeneutics, and Praxis*, Philadelphia: University of Pennsylvania Press.

Blaug, Marc (1975) 'Kuhn versus Lakatos, or paradigms versus research programmes in the history of economics', *History of Political Economy* 7, 4, pp. 399–433.

Bobbio, Norberto (1981) 'La teoria dello stato e del potere', in Pietro Rossi (ed.) *Max Weber e l'analisi del mondo*, Torino: Einaudi, pp. 215–46.

—— (1976) *Quale socialismo?* Torino: Einaudi.

Bourdieu, Pierre (1980) *Le sens pratique*, Paris: Éd. Minuit.

—— (1977) *Outline of a Theory of Practice*, transl. by Richard Nice, Cambridge *et al.*: Cambridge University Press.

Bracher, Karl-Dietrich (1982) *Zeit der Ideologien. Eine Geschichte politischen Denkens im 20. Jahrhundert*, Stuttgart: DVA.

Brecher, Michael (1993) *Crises in World Politics*, Oxford: Pergamon Press.

Brenner, Robert (1977) 'The origins of capitalist development: A critique of Neo-Smithian Marxism', *New Left Review* 104, pp. 25–92.

Brewer, Anthony (1990) *Marxist Theories of Imperialism*, 2nd edn, London, New York: Routledge.

Brown, Chris (1992) *International Relations Theory: New Normative Approaches*, New York *et al.*: Harvester Wheatsheaf.

Bull, Hedley (1984) 'The revolt against the West', in Hedley Bull and Adam Watson (eds) *The Expansion of International Society*, Oxford, New York: Oxford University Press, pp. 217–28.

—— (1979) 'The state's positive role in world affairs', *Dædalus* 108, 4, pp. 111–23.

—— (1977) *The Anarchical Society: A Study of Order in World Politics*, London: Macmillan.

—— (1969) 'International Theory: The Case for a Classical Approach', in Klaus Knorr and James Rosenau (eds) *Contending Approaches to International Politics*, Princeton: Princeton University Press, pp. 20–38.

—— (1966a) 'Society and Anarchy in International Relations', in Herbert Butterfield and Martin Wight (eds) *Diplomatic Investigations: Essays in the Theory of International Relations*, Cambridge, UK: Cambridge University Press, pp. 35–50.

—— (1966b) 'The Grotian Conception of International Society', in Herbert Butterfield and Martin Wight (eds) *Diplomatic Investigations: Essays in the Theory of International Relations*, Cambridge, UK: Cambridge University Press, pp. 51–73.

—— and Adam Watson (eds) (1984) *The Expansion of International Society*, Oxford, New York: Oxford University Press.

Burton, John W. (1986) *Global Conflict: The Domestic Sources of International Crisis*, 2nd edn, Brighton: Harvester Press.

Buzan, Barry (1991a) 'New patterns of global security in the twenty-first century', *International Affairs* (London) 67, 3, pp. 431–51.

—— (1991b) *People, States and Fear: An Agenda for International Security Studies in the Post-Cold War Era*, 2nd edn, New York et al.: Harvester Wheatsheaf.

—— (1984) 'Economic structure and international security: the limits of the liberal case', *International Organization* 38, 4 (Autumn), pp. 597–624.

Buzan, Barry, Charles Jones and Richard Little (1993) *The Logic of Anarchy: Neorealism to Structural Realism*, New York: Columbia University Press.

Calleo, David and Susan Strange (1984) 'Money and World Politics', in Susan Strange (ed.) *Paths to International Political Economy*, London: George Allen and Unwin, pp. 91–125.

Campbell, David (1993) *Power Without Principles: Sovereignty, Ethics, and the Narratives of the Gulf War*, Boulder and London: Lynne Rienner Publishers.

—— (1992) *Writing Security: United States Foreign Policy and the Politics of Identity*, Minneapolis: University of Minnesota Press.

Caporaso, James A. (1978) 'Introduction to the special issue on dependence and dependency in the global system' (and) 'Dependence, dependency, and power in the global system: a structural and behavioral analysis', *International Organization* 32, 1 (Winter), pp. 2–43.

Caporaso, James and W. Ladd Hollist (1985) 'International Political Economy research: What is it and where do we turn for concepts?', in W. Ladd Hollist and Lamond Tullis (eds) *The International Political Economy*, Boulder, Colo.: Westview Press, pp. 27–49.

Cardoso, Fernando Henrique (1977) 'The consumption of dependency theory in the United States', *Latin American Research Review* 12, pp. 7–24.

—— (1973) 'Associated-Dependent Development: Theoretical and Practical Implications', in Alfred Stepan (ed.) *Authoritarian Brazil: Origins, Policies and Future*, New Haven, London: Yale University Press, pp. 142–76.

Carlsnaes, Walter (1992) 'The Agency-Structure Problem in Foreign Policy Analysis', *International Studies Quarterly* 36, 3 (September), pp. 245–70.

Carr, Edward Hellet (1961) *What is history?*, 2nd edn. (1987) edited by R. W. Davies, London: Penguin.

—— (1946) *The Twenty Years' Crisis: An Introduction to the Study of International Relations*, 2nd edn, London: Macmillan.

Carrère d'Encausse, Hélène (1984) *1956, La déstalinisation commence*, Bruxelles: Éditions Complexe.

Choucri, Nazli (1980) 'International Political Economy: A Theoretical Perspective', in Ole R. Holsti, Randolph M. Siverson and Alexander L. George (eds) *Change in the International System*, Boulder, Colo.: Westview Press, pp. 103–129.

Claude, Inis L. (1962) *Power and International Relations*, New York: Random House.

—— (1989) 'The Balance of Power Revisited', *Review of International Studies* 15, 2 (April), pp. 77–85.

Cohen, Benjamin J. (1973) *The Question of Imperialism: The Political Economy of Dominance and Dependence*, London: Macmillan.

Collier, David (ed.) (1979) *The New Authoritarianism in Latin America*, Princeton: Princeton University Press.

Connolly, William (1991) *Identity/Difference: Democratic Negotiations of Political Paradox*, Ithaca: Cornell University Press.

Cox, Robert W. ([1981] 1986) 'Social Forces, States and World Orders: Beyond International Relations Theory (and Postscript 1985)' in Robert O. Keohane (ed.) *Neorealism and its Critics*, New York: Columbia University Press, pp. 204–54.

—— (1983) 'Gramsci, Hegemony and International Relations: An Essay in Method', *Millennium: Journal of International Studies* 12, 2 (Summer), pp. 162–75.

Czempiel, Ernst-Otto (1981) *Internationale Politik. Ein Konfliktmodell*, Paderborn: Schöningh.

Dahl, Robert A. (1958) 'A Critique of the Ruling Elite Model', *American Political Science Review* 52, pp. 463–9.

Denemark, Robert A. and Kenneth P. Thomas (1988) 'The Brenner-Wallerstein Debate', *International Studies Quarterly* 32, 1 (March), pp. 47–65.

Der Derian, James and Shapiro, Michael (eds) (1989) *International/Intertextual Relations: Postmodern Readings in World Politics*, Lexington, MA: Lexington Books.

Dessler, David (1989) 'What's at stake in the agent-structure debate?', *International Organization* 43, 3 (Summer), pp. 441–73.

Deutsch, Karl W. (1966) *The Nerves of Government: Models of Political Communication and Control*, 2nd rev. edn, New York: The Free Press.

—— et al. (1957) *Political Community in the North Atlantic Area: International Organization in the light of Historical Experience*, Princeton: Princeton University Press.

Deutsch, Karl W. and J. David Singer (1964) 'Multipolar Power Systems and International Stability', *World Politics* XVI, 3, pp. 390–406.

Dos Santos, Teodonio (1970) 'The Structure of Dependence', *American Economic Review* LX (May), pp. 231–6.

Dowding, Keith M. (1991) *Rational Choice and Political Power*, Hants: Edward Elgar.

Durkheim, Émile (1937) *Les règles de la méthode sociologique*, Paris: Presses Universitaires de France.

Elshtain, Jean Bethke (1987) *Women and War*, Brighton: The Harvester Press.

Elster, Jon (1989) *Nuts and Bolts for the Social Sciences*, Cambridge: Cambridge University Press.

Enloe, Cynthia (1989) *Bananas, Beaches and Bases: Making Feminist Sense of International Relations*, London: Pandora.

Esping-Andersen, Gøsta (1990) *The Three Worlds of Welfare Capitalism*, Cambridge: Polity Press.

Evans, Peter (1995) *Embedded Autonomy: State and Industrial Transformation*, Princeton: Princeton University Press.

—— (1979) *Dependent Development: The Alliance of Multinational, State and Local Capital in Brazil*, Princeton: Princeton University Press.

Evans, Peter, Dietrich Rueschemeyer and Theda Skočpol (eds) (1985) *Bringing the State Back in*, Cambridge, Mass.: Cambridge University Press.

Ferguson, Yale H. and Richard W. Mansbach (1988) *The Elusive Quest: Theory and International Politics*, Columbia. S.C.: University of South Carolina Press.

Feyerabend, Paul (1970) 'Consolations for the specialist', in Imre Lakatos and Alan Musgrave (eds) *Criticism and the Growth of Knowledge*, Cambridge: Cambridge University Press, pp. 197–230.

Fontaine, André (1965) *Histoire de la Guerre Froide. Tome I: De la Révolution d'octobre à la guerre de Corée, 1917–1950*, Paris: Fayard.

Foster-Carter, Aidan (1978) 'The modes of production controversy', *New Left Review* 107 (January–February), pp. 47–77.

Frank, André Gunter (1966) 'The Development of Underdevelopment', *Monthly Review* 18, 4, pp. 17–31.

Freedman, Lawrence (1991) 'Escalators and quagmires: expectations and the use of force', *International Affairs* (London) 67, 1 (January), pp. 15–31.

—— (1989) *The Evolution of Nuclear Strategy*, 2nd rev. edn, London: Macmillan.

Frei, Daniel (1969) 'Vom Mass der Macht', *Schweizer Monatshefte* 49, 7, pp. 642–54.

Gaddis, John Lewis (1982) *Strategies of Containment: A Critical Appraisal of Postwar American National Security Policy*, Oxford: Oxford University Press.

—— (1978) 'The Strategy of Containment', in Thomas H. Etzold and John Lewis Gaddis (eds) *Containment: Documents on American Policy and Strategy, 1945–1950*, New York: Columbia University Press, pp. 25–37.

—— (1972) *The United States and the Origins of the Cold War 1941–1947*, New York: Columbia University Press.

Geertz, Clifford ([1973] 1993) 'Thick Description: Toward an Interpretive Theory of Culture', in *The Interpretation of Cultures*, London: Fontana Press, pp. 3–30.

George, Alexander (1979) 'The Causal Nexus between Cognitive Beliefs and Decision-Making Behavior: The "Operational Code" Belief System', in Laurence Falkowski (ed.) *Psychological Models in International Relations*, Boulder, Colo.: Westview Press, pp. 95–124.

George, Jim (1994) *Discourses of global politics: A critical (re)introduction to international relations*, Boulder, Colo.: Lynne Rienner.

—— (1993) 'Of Incarceration and Closure: Neo-Realism and the New/Old World Order', *Millennium: Journal of International Studies* 22, 2 (Summer), pp. 197–234.

Giddens, Anthony (1985) *The Nation-State and Violence*, Cambridge: Polity Press.

Giesen, Klaus-Gerd (1992) *L'éthique des relations internationales. Les théories anglo-américaines contemporaines*, Bruxelles: Bruylant.

Gill, Stephen (1990) *American Hegemony and the Trilateral Commission*, Cambridge: Cambridge University Press.

Gill, Stephen and David Law (1989) 'Global Hegemony and the Structural Power of Capital', *International Studies Quarterly* 33, 4 (December), pp. 475–99.

—— (1988) *The Global Political Economy*, Brighton: Harvester Wheatsheaf.

Gilpin, Robert with the assistance of Jean Gilpin (1987) *The Political Economy of International Relations*, Princeton: Princeton University Press.

Gilpin, Robert ([1984] 1986) 'The Richness of the Realist Tradition', In Robert O. Keohane (ed.) *Neorealism and its Critics*, New York: Columbia University Press, pp. 301–21.

—— (1981) *War and Change in World Politics*, New York: Cambridge University Press.

—— (1977) 'Economic Interdependence and National Security in Historical Perspective', in Klaus Knorr and Frank N. Trager (eds) *Economic Issues and National Security*, Kansas: Regents Press, pp. 19–66.

—— (1975) 'Three Models of the Future', *International Organization* 29, 1 (Winter), pp. 37–60.

—— (1971) 'The Politics of Transnational Economic Relations', in Robert O. Keohane and Joseph S. Nye, jr. (eds) *Transnational Relations and World Politics*, Cambridge, Mass and London: Harvard University Press, pp. 48–69.

Gombrich, E.H. (1959) *Art and Illusion: A Study in the Psychology of Pictoral Representation*, London: Phaidon Press.

Granowetter, Mark (1985) 'Economic Structure and Social Structure: The Problem of Embeddedness', *American Journal of Sociology* 91 (November), pp. 481–510.

Grieco, Joseph (1993) 'Understanding the Problem of International Cooperation: The Limits of Neoliberal Institutionalism and the Future of Realist Theory', in David Baldwin (ed.) *Neorealism and Neoliberalism*, New York: Columbia University Press, pp. 301–38.

—— (1988) 'Anarchy and the Limits of Cooperation: A Realist Critique of the Newest Liberal Institutionalism', *International Organization* 42, 4 (Autumn), pp. 485–507.

Griffiths, Martin (1992) *Realism, Idealism and International Politics: A Reinterpretation*, London and New York: Routledge.

Grosser, Alfred (1956) 'L'Etude des Relations Internationales: Specialité Américaine?', *Revue Française de Science Politique* III, pp. 634–51.

Gutting, Gary (1980), 'Introduction', in Gary Gutting (ed.) *Paradigms and Revolutions: Appraisals and Applications of Thomas Kuhn's Philosophy of Science*, Notre Dame: University of Notre Dame Press, pp. 1–21.

Guzzini, Stefano (1997a) 'Robert Gilpin: The realist quest for the dynamics of power', in Iver B. Neumann and Ole Wæver (eds) *The Future of International Theory: Masters in the Making?*, London and New York: Routledge, pp. 121–44.

—— (1997b) 'Maintenir les dilemmes de la modernité en suspens: analyse et éthique poststructuralistes en Relations Internationales', in Klaus-Gerd Giesen (ed.) *L'éthique de l'espace politique mondial: métissages interdisciplinaires*, Bruxelles: Bruylant, pp. 247–85.

—— (1995) 'The "Long Night of the First Republic": years of clientelistic implosion in Italy', *Review of International Political Economy* 2, 1 (Winter), pp. 27–61.

—— (1994a) 'La longue nuit de la Premiére République. L'implosion clientéliste en Italie', *Revue Française de Science Politique* 44, 6 (décembre), pp. 979–1013.

—— (1994b) *Power Analysis as a Critique of Power Politics: Understanding Power and Governance in the Second Gulf War*, Florence: European University Institute, PhD thesis.

—— (1993) 'Structural power: the limits of neorealist power analysis', *International Organization* 47, 3 (Summer), pp. 443–78.

—— (1988) *T.S. Kuhn and International Relations: International Political Economy and the Inter-Paradigm Debate*, London School of Economics and Political Science, MSc(Econ) Thesis.

Guzzini, Stefano, Anna Leander, Jochen Lorentzen and Roger Morgan (1993) 'New Ideas for a Strange World: Mélanges for Susan', in Roger Morgan, Jochen Lorentzen, Anna Leander, and Stefano Guzzini (eds) *New Diplomacy in the Post-Cold War World: Essays for Susan Strange*, London: Macmillan, pp. 3–23.

Haas, Ernst (1953) 'The Balance of Power: Prescription, Concept or Propaganda?', *World Politics* V (July), pp. 442–77.

Habermas, Jürgen (1985) 'Die Krise des Wohlfahrtsstaates und die Erschöpfung utopischer Energien', in *Die Neue Unübersichtlichkeit*, Frankfurt am Main: Suhrkamp, pp. 141–63.

—— (1976) *Rekonstruktion des Historischen Materialismus*, Frankfurt am Main: Suhrkamp.

Haftendorn, Helga (1980) 'Theorie der Internationalen Beziehungen', in Wichard Woyke (ed.) *Handwörterbuch Internationale Politik*, 2nd edn, Opladen: Leske und Budrich.

Halliday, Fred (1990) '"The sixth great power": on the study of revolutions and international relations', *Review of International Studies* 16, 3 (July), pp. 207–21.

—— (1987) 'State and Society in International Relations: A second agenda', *Millennium: Journal of International Studies* 16, 2 (Summer), pp. 215–29.

—— (1986) *The Making of the 2nd Cold War*, 2nd edn, London: Verso.

Hassner, Pierre (1995) *La paix et la violence. De la bombe atomique au nettoyage éthnique*, Paris: Éditions Esprit.

—— (1972) *Europe in the Age of Negotiation*, The Washington Papers No. 8, Beverly Hills: Sage.

—— (1968a) 'Change and Security in Europe. Part I: The Background', *Adelphi Papers* 45 (February).

—— (1968b) 'Change and Security in Europe. Part II: In Search of a System', *Adelphi Papers* 49 (July).

Hempel, Carl G. (1965) *Aspects of Scientific Explanation and other Essays in the Philosophy of Science*, London: The Free Press.

Herring jr., George C. (1973) *Aid to Russia, 1941–1946: Strategy, Diplomacy, the Origins of the Cold War*, New York: Columbia University Press.

Herrmann, C.F. (ed.) (1972) *International Crisis: Insights from Behavioural Research*, London: Collier-Macmillan and New York: Free Press.

Herz, John (1950) 'Idealist Internationalism and the Security Dilemma', *World Politics* II, pp. 157–80.

Hodgson, Geoffrey M. (1988) *Economics and Institutions: A Manifesto for a Modern Institutional Economics*, Cambridge: Polity Press.

Hoffman, Mark (1991) 'Restructuring, Reconstruction, Reinscription, Rearticulation: Four Voices in Critical International Theory', *Millennium: Journal of International Studies* 20, 2, pp. 169–85.

—— (1988) 'States, Cosmopolitanism and Normative International Theory', *Paradigms* 2, 1 (June), pp. 60–75.

—— (1987) 'Critical theory and the inter-paradigm debate', *Millennium: Journal of International Studies* 16, 2 (Summer), pp. 231–49.

Hoffmann, Stanley (1981) *Duties beyond Borders: On the Limits and Possibilities of Ethical International Politics*, Syracuse, NY: Syracuse University Press.

—— (1978) *Primacy or World Order: American Foreign Policy since the Cold War*, New York, McGraw Hill.

—— (1977) 'An American Social Science: International Relations', *Dædalus* CVI, Summer, pp. 41–60.

—— (1965) *The State of War*, New York: Praeger Publishers.

Hollis, Martin (1994) *The philosophy of social science: an introduction*, Cambridge: Cambridge University Press.

Hollis, Martin and Steve Smith (1992) 'Structure and Action: Further Comment', *Review of International Studies* 18, 2 (April), pp. 187–8.

—— (1991) 'Beware of gurus: structure and action in international relations', *Review of International Studies* 17, 4 (October), pp. 399–403.

—— (1990) *Explaining and Understanding International Relations*, Oxford: Clarendon Press.

Holsti, K.J. (1985) *The Dividing Discipline: Hegemony and Diversity in International Theory*, Boston: Allen & Unwin.

Holsti, Ole R. (1976) 'Foreign Policy Formation Viewed Cognitively', in Robert Axelrod (ed.) *Structure of Decision*, Princeton: Princeton University Press, pp. 18–54.

Huntington, Samuel P. (1993) 'The Clash of Civilizations?', *Foreign Affairs* 72, 3, pp. 22–42.

—— (1968) *Political Order in Changing Societies*, New Haven: Yale University Press.

Huysmans, Jef (1995) 'Migrants as a security problem: dangers of securitising societal issues', in Robert Miles and D. Thränhardt (eds) *Migration and European Integration: The Dynamics of Inclusion and Exclusion*, London: Pinter, pp. 53–72.

—— (1992) 'Discourse–Knowledge–Practice: Reinterpreting the Polarity–Stability Debate', paper presented at the Inaugural Pan-European Conference of International Relations, Heidelberg, 16–20 September 1992.

Jervis, Robert (1976) *Perception and Misperception in International Politics*, Princeton: Princeton University Press.

Jessop, Bob (1990) 'Regulation theories in retrospect and prospect', *Economy and Society* 19, pp. 153–216.

Jouvenel, Bertrand de (1972 [1945]) *Du pouvoir. Histoire naturelle de sa croissance*, Paris: Hachette.

Jones, J.R. Barry (1982) 'International Political Economy: Perspectives and Projects. Part II', *Review of International Studies* 8, 1, pp. 39–52.

—— (1981) 'International Political Economy: Problems and Issues. Part I', *Review of International Studies* 7, pp. 245–60.

Kaiser, Karl (1971) 'Transnational Relations as a Threat to the Democratic Process', in Robert O. Keohane and Joseph S. Nye, jr. (eds) *Transnational Relations and World Politics*, Cambridge, Mass and London: Harvard University Press, pp. 356–70.

—— (1969) 'Transnationale Politik. Zu einer Theorie der multinationalen Politik', in Ernst-Otto Czempiel (ed.) *Die anachronistische Souveränität*, PVS Sonderheft No.1, Köln: Westdeutscher Verlag, pp. 80–109.

Kaplan, Morton A. (1969), 'Variants on Six Models of the International System', in James Rosenau (ed.) *International Politics and Foreign Policy: A Reader in Research and Theory*, New York: Free Press, pp. 291–303.

Katzenstein, Peter J. (1985) *Small States in World Markets: Industrial Policy in Europe*, Ithaca: Cornell University Press.

Kennan, George F. (1985–6) 'Morality and Foreign Policy', *Foreign Affairs* 64, pp. 205–18.

—— (1967) *Memoirs, 1925–1950*, Boston: Little, Brown.

—— (1958) *Russia, the Atom and the West: The BBC Reith Lectures 1957*, Oxford: Oxford University Press.

—— (1951) *American Diplomacy 1900–1950*, Chicago: The University of Chicago Press.

Keohane, Robert O. (1993) 'Institutional Theory and the Realist Challenge after the Cold War', in David Baldwin (ed.) *Neorealism and Neoliberalism*, New York: Columbia University Press, pp. 269–300.

—— (1989 [1988]) 'International Institutions: Two Approaches', in Robert Keohane, *International Institutions and State Power: Essays in International Relations Theory*, Boulder, Colo.: Westview Press, pp. 158–79.

—— (1984) *After Hegemony: Cooperation and Discord in the World Political Economy*, Princeton: Princeton University Press.

—— (1986 [1983]) 'Theory of World Politics: Structural Realism and Beyond', in Robert O. Keohane (ed.) *Neorealism and its Critics*, New York: Columbia University Press, pp. 158–203.

—— (1980) 'The Theory of Hegemonic Stability and changes in international economic regimes, 1967–1977', in Ole R. Holsti, Randolph M. Siverson and Alexander L. George (eds) *Change in the International System*, Boulder, Colo.: Westview Press, pp. 131–62.

Keohane, Robert O. and Nye jr., Joseph S. (1987) '*Power and Interdependence Revisited*', *International Organization* 41, 4 (Fall), pp. 725–53.
—— (1977) *Power and Interdependence: World Politics in Transition*, Boston: Little, Brown.
—— (eds) (1972) *Transnational Relations and World Politics*, Cambridge, MA and London: Harvard University Press.
Kindermann, Gottfried-Karl (ed.) (1986) *Grundelemente der Weltpolitik*, 3rd edn, München: Piper Verlag.
Kindleberger, Charles P. (1986a) 'Hierarchy versus inertial cooperation', *International Organization* 40, 4 (Fall), pp. 841–7.
—— (1986b) 'International Public Goods without International Government', *The American Economic Review* 76, 1 (March), pp. 1–12.
—— (1981) 'Dominance and Leadership in the International Economy: Exploitation, Public Goods and Free Riders', *International Studies Quarterly* 25, 2 (June), pp. 242–53.
—— (1976) 'Systems of International Economic Organization'', in David Calleo (ed.) *Money and the Coming World Order*, New York: New York University Press for the Lehrmann Institute, pp. 15–39.
—— (1986) *The World in Depression, 1929–1939*, 2nd edn, Berkeley: University of California Press.
Kissinger, Henry A. (1983) *The Years of Upheaval*, Boston: Little Brown.
—— (1979) *The White House Years*, Boston: Little Brown.
—— (1969) *American Foreign Policy*, New York: Norton.
—— (1957) *A World Restored*, Boston: Houghton Mifflin.
Kivi, Risto (1996) *The Balance of Power: An Imaginary Equilibrium*, Budapest: The Central European University, MA Thesis.
Knorr, Klaus (1973) *Power and Wealth: The Political Economy of International Power*, London: Macmillan.
Kohler-Koch, Beate (1989) 'Zur Empirie und Theorie internationaler Regime', in Beate Kohler-Koch (ed.) *Regime in den internationalen Beziehungen*, Baden-Baden: Nomos, pp. 17–88.
Koslowski, Roy and Friedrich V. Kratochwil (1994) 'Understanding change in international politics: the Soviet empire's demise and the international system', *International Organization* 48, 2 (Spring 1994), pp. 215–47.
Krasner, Stephen D. (1985) *Structural Conflict: The Third World Against Global Liberalism*, Berkeley: University of California Press.
—— (1982a) 'Structural Causes and Regime consequences: Regimes as Intervening Variables', *International Organization* 36, 2 (Spring), pp. 185–205.
—— (1982b) 'Regimes and the Limits of Realism: Regimes as Autonomous Variables', *International Organization* 36, 2 (Spring), pp. 497–510.
Kratochwil, Friedrich (1993) 'The embarassment of changes: neo-realism and the science of Realpolitik without politics', *Review of International Studies* 19, 1 (January 1993), pp. 63–80.
—— and Yosef Lapid (eds) (1996) *The return of culture and identity in International Relations theory*, Boulder, Colo.: Lynne Rienner.
—— and John Gerard Ruggie (1986) 'International organization: a state of the art on an art of the state', *International Organization*, 40, 4 (Autumn), pp. 753–75.
Krause, Keith and Michael Williams (eds) (1997) *Critical security studies: concepts and cases*, Minneapolis: University of Minnesota Press.
Krippendorff, Ekkehart (1988) '*Wie die Großen mit den Menschen spielen.' Goethes Politik*, Frankfurt am Main: Suhrkamp.
—— (1985) *Staat und Krieg. Die historische Logik politischer Unvernunft*, Frankfurt am Main: Suhrkamp.

—— (1977) *Internationale Beziehungen als Wissenschaft. Einführung 2*, Frankfurt am Main: Campus Verlag.

—— (1963) 'Ist Außenpolitik *Außen*politik? Ein Beitrag zur Theorie und der Versuch, eine unhaltbare Unterscheidung aufzuheben', in Ekkehart Krippendorff (ed.), *Internationale Beziehungen*, Köln: Kiepenheuer and Witsch, 1972, pp. 189–213.

Kuhn, Thomas (1970a) *The Structure of Scientific Revolutions*, 2nd edn, Chicago: University of Chicago Press.

—— (1970b) 'Reflections on my critics', in Imre Lakatos and Alan Musgrave (eds) *Criticism and the Growth of Knowledge*, Cambridge: Cambridge University Press, pp. 231–78.

Laclau, Ernesto (1979) *Politics and Ideology in Marxist Theory: Capitalism, Fascism, Populism*, London: Verso Ed.

LaFeber, Walter (1993) *America, Russia and the Cold War, 1945–1992*, 7th edn, New York: McGraw Hill.

Lakoff, George (1991) 'Metaphor and War: The Metaphor System Used to Justify War in the Gulf', *Peace Research* 23, 2 and 3 (May), pp. 25–32.

Lall, Sanjaya (1975) 'Is "Dependence" a useful concept in analysing underdevelopment?', *World Development* 3, 6 (November–December), pp. 799–810.

Lapid, Yosef (1989a) 'The Third Debate: On the Prospects of International Theory in a Post-Positivist Era', *International Studies Quarterly* 33, 3 (September), pp. 235–54.

—— (1989b) '*Quo vadis* International Relations? Further Reflections on the "Next Stage" of International Theory', *Millennium: Journal of International Studies* 18, pp. 77–88.

Leander, Anna (1997) *From Leadership to Cooperation: The Role of the Turkish State in Bargaining with Foreign Investors in the 1980s*, Florence: European University Institute, PhD thesis.

Lebow, Richard Ned (1994) 'The long peace, the end of the cold war, and the failure of realism', *International Organization* 48, 2 (Spring 1994), pp. 249–77.

Leffler, Melvyn P. (1992) *The Preponderance of Power: National Security, the Truman Administration, and the Cold War*, Stanford: Stanford University Press.

Lehmbruch, Gerhard (1969) 'Konkordanzdemokratien im internationalen System. Ein Paradigma für die Analyse von internen und externen Bedingungen politischer Systeme', in Ernst-Otto Czempiel (ed.) *Die anachronistische Souveränität*, Opladen: Westdeutscher Verlag, pp. 139–63.

Levy, Jack S. (1989) 'The Causes of War: A Review of Theories and Evidence', in Philip E. Tetlock, Jo L. Husbands, Robert Jervis, Paul C. Stern and Charles Tilly (eds) *Behavior, Society and Nuclear War Vol. 1*, New York: Oxford University Press, pp. 209–333.

Light, Margot (1988) *The Soviet theory of international relations*, Brighton: Harvester Wheatsheaf.

Linklater, Andrew (1990) *Beyond Realism and Marxism: critical theory and international relations*, London: Macmillan.

—— (1982) *Men and Citizens in the Theory of International Relations*, London: Macmillan, 1982.

Little, Richard and Steve Smith (eds) (1988) *Belief Systems and International Relations*, Oxford: Basil Blackwell.

Loth, Wilfried (1983) *Die Teilung der Welt. Geschichte des Kalten Krieges 1941–1955*, 4th edn, München: Deutscher Taschenbuch Verlag.

Lowry, S. Todd (1979) 'Bargain and Contract Theory in Law and Economics', in Samuels J. Warren (ed.), *The Economy as a System of Power: Papers form the*

Journal of Economic Issues, Vol. I: Corporate Systems, New Brunswick, N.J.: Transaction Books, pp. 261–82.

Luke, Timothy W. (1991) 'The Discipline of Security Studies and the Codes of Containment', *Alternatives* 16, pp. 315–44.

Luxemburg, Rosa (1985 [1921]), 'Die Akkumulation des Kapitals oder Was die Epigonen aus der Marxschen Theorie gemacht haben. Eine Antikritik', in *Gesammelte Werke. Band 5: Ökonomische Schriften*, Berlin: Dietz Verlag, pp. 413–523.

—— (1985 [1913]), 'Die Akkumulation des Kapitals. Ein Beitrag zur ökonomischen Erklärung des Imperialismus', in *Gesammelte Werke. Band 5: Ökonomische Schriften*, Berlin: Dietz Verlag, pp. 5–411.

Lynch, Allen (1989) *The Soviet study of international relations*, Cambridge, Mass., Cambridge University Press.

Mackinder, Halford John (1944 [1919]) *Democratic Ideals and Reality*, Harmondsworth: Penguin.

MacLean, John (1988) 'Marxism and International Relations: A Strange Case of Mutual Neglect', *Millennium: Journal of International Studies*, vol. 17, pp. 295–319.

—— (1981) 'Marxist Epistemology, Explanations of "Change" and the Study of International Relations', in Barry Buzan and R.J. Barry Jones, eds, *Change in the Study of International Relations*, London: Frances Pinter, pp. 46–67.

Maghroori, Ray and Bennett Ramberg (eds) (1983) *Globalism versus Realism*, Boulder, Colo.: Westview Press.

Mann, Michael (1986) *The Sources of Social Power, vol. I*, Cambridge: Cambridge University Press.

Mansbach, Richard W. and John A. Vasquez (1981) *In search for theory: A new paradigm for global politics*, New York: Columbia University Press.

Marx, Karl (1987 [1859]) *Zur Kritik der Politischen Ökonomie. Erstes Heft*, 11th edn, Berlin: Dietz Verlag.

Mastanduno, Michael, David A. Lake and G. John Ikenberry (1989) 'Toward a Realist Theory of State Action', *International Studies Quarterly* 33, 4 (December), pp. 457–74.

Mastermann, Margaret (1970) 'The Nature of a Paradigm', in Imre Lakatos and Alan Musgrave (eds) *Criticism and the Growth of Knowledge*, Cambridge: Cambridge University Press, pp. 59–89.

McKinlay, R.D. and Richard Little (1986) *Global Problems and World Order*, Maddison, WI: University of Wisconsin Press.

Mearsheimer, John (1990) 'Back to the Future: Instability in Europe after the Cold War', *International Security* 15, 1 (Summer), pp. 5–56.

Meinecke, Friedrich (1965 [1924]) *Machiavellism: the doctrine of raison d'état and its place in modern history*, New York: Praeger.

Merle, Marcel (1982) *Sociologie des Relations Internationales*, 3rd edn, Paris: Dalloz.

Meyers, Reinhard (1994) 'Virtuelle Scheingefechte im ontologischen Cyberspace? Nachfragen zum Duktus und zum Gehalt einer Theoriedebatte', *Zeitschrift für Internationale Beziehungen* 1, 1 (Juni), pp. 127–37.

—— (1990) 'Metatheoretische und methodologische Betrachtungen zur Theorie der internationalen Beziehungen', in Volker Rittberger (ed.) *Theorien der Internationalen Beziehungen: Bestandsaufnahme und Forschungsperspektiven*, Köln: Westdeutscher Verlag, pp. 48–68.

—— (1984) 'Historische Soziologie', in Andreas Boeckh (ed.) *Pipers Wörterbuch zur Politik. Band 5: Internationale Beziehungen. Theorien-Organisationen-Konflikte*, München: Piper, pp. 188–91.

—— (1979) *Weltpolitik in Grundbegriffen. Band 1: Ein lehr- und ideengeschichtlicher Grundriß*, Düsseldorf: Droste Verlag.

Milner, Helen (1992) 'International theories of cooperation among nations: strengths and weaknesses', *World Politics* 44, 3 (April), pp. 466–96.
—— (1991) 'The assumption of anarchy in international relations theory: a critique', *Review of International Studies* 17, 1 (January), pp. 67–85.
Morgenthau, Hans J. (1970) 'The Intellectual and Political Functions of Theory', in *Truth and Power: Essays of a Decade 1960-70*, London: Pall Mall Press, pp. 248–61.
—— (1965) *Vietnam and the United States*, Washington, D.C.: Public Affairs Press.
—— (1960) *Politics among Nations: The Struggle for Power and Peace*, 3rd edn, New York: Knopf.
—— (1948) *Politics among Nations: The Struggle for Power and Peace*, New York: Knopf.
—— (1946) *Power Politics versus Scientific Man*, Chicago: University of Chicago Press.
—— (1936) 'Positivisme mal compris et théorie réaliste du Droit international' (tirada aparte de la 'Colección de Estudios históricos, jurídicos, pedagógicos y literarios'. Homenaje a D. Rafael Altamira).
—— (1933) *La notion du 'politique' et la théorie des différends internationaux*, Paris: Sirey.
Mouritzen, Hans (1997) 'Kenneth Waltz: a critical rationalist between international politics and foreign policy', in Iver B. Neumann and Ole Wæver (eds) *The Future of International Theory: Masters in the Making?*, London and New York: Routledge, pp. 66–89.
Musgrave, Alan E. (1980) 'Kuhn's Second Thoughts', in Gary Gutting (ed.) *Paradigms and Revolutions: Appraisals and Applications of Thomas Kuhn's Philosophy of Science*, Notre Dame, London: University of Notre Dame Press, pp. 39–53.
Nardin, Terry (1983) *Law, Morality and the Relation of States*, Princeton: Princeton University Press.
Navari, Cornelia (ed.) (1991) *The condition of states: a study in international political theory*, Milton Keynes: Open University Press.
—— (1982) 'Hobbes and the "Hobbesian tradition" in international thought', in *Millennium: Journal of International Studies* 11, 3 (Summer), pp. 203–22.
Neufeld, Mark (1993) 'Interpretation and the "Science" of International Relations', *Review of International Studies* 19, 1 (January), pp. 39–61.
Niebuhr, Reinhold (1941) *The Nature and Destiny of Man: A Christian Interpretation. Volume I: Human Nature*, New York, C. Scribner & Sons.
North, Douglass C. (1990) *Institutions, Institutional Change, and Economic Performance*, Cambridge: Cambridge University Press.
Nye, Jr., Joseph S. (1990) 'Soft Power', *Foreign Policy* 80 (Fall), pp. 153–171.
—— (1988) 'Neorealism and Neoliberalism', *World Politics* 40, 2, pp. 235–51.
O'Connor, James (1970) 'The Meaning of Economic Imperialism', in Robert I. Rhodes (ed.) *Imperialism and Underdevelopment: A Reader*, New York: Monthly Review Press, pp. 101–49.
Odell, John S. (1988) 'From London to Bretton Woods: Sources of Change in Bargaining Strategies and Outcomes', *Journal of Public Policy* (special double issue: 'International Monetary Cooperation, Domestic Politics, and Policy Ideas', edited by John S. Odell and Thomas D. Willett) 8, 3/4 (July–December), pp. 287–315.
O'Donnell, Guillermo (1978) 'Reflections of the Patterns of Change in the Bureaucratic-Authoritarian State', *Latin American Research Review* 13, 1, pp. 3–38.
—— (1973) *Modernization and Bureaucratic-Authoritarianism: Studies in South American Politics*, Berkeley: Institute of International Studies, University of California.

Olson, Mancur (1965) *The Logic of Collective Action: Public Goods and the Theory of Groups*, Cambridge: Harvard University Press.

Onuf, Nicholas (1989) *World of our making: rules and rule in social theory and international relations*, Columbia, S.C.: University of South Carolina Press.

—— and Frank F. Klink (1989) 'Anarchy, Authority, Rule', *International Studies Quartely* 33, 2 (June), pp. 149–73.

Oye, Kenneth (ed.) (1985) *Cooperation under Anarchy*, Princeton: Princeton University Press.

Palan, Ronen P. (1992) 'The Second Structuralist Theories of International Relations', *International Studies Notes* 17, 3 (Fall), pp. 22–9.

—— (1989) *Non-governmental Interactions among Social Formations as the Bridge between the Structuralist Theory of the State and the Study of International Relations*, London: London School of Economics and Political Science, PhD thesis.

—— and Brook M. Blair (1993) 'On the idealist origins of the realist theory of international relations', *Review of International Studies* 19, 4 (October), pp. 385–99.

Palma, Gabriel (1980) 'Dependency and Development: A Critical Overview', in Dudley Seers (ed.) *Dependency Theory: A Critical Reassessment*, London: Frances Pinter, pp. 20–73.

Patomäki, Heikki (1996) 'How to tell better stories about world politics', *European Journal of International Relations*, 2, 1 (March), pp. 105–33.

—— (1995) 'How to open up world political spaces: the possibility of Republican politics', in Heikki Patomäki (ed.) *Peaceful Changes in World Politics*, Tampere: TAPRI Research Report, no. 71, pp. 28–80.

—— (1992) 'From normative utopias to political dialectics: beyond a deconstruction of the Brown–Hoffman debate', *Millennium: Journal of International Studies* 21, 1 (Spring), pp. 53–71.

Peterson, V. Spike (1992) 'Security and sovereign states: what is at stake in taking feminism seriously?', in V. Spike Peterson (ed.) *Gendered States: Feminist (Re)visions of International Relations*, Boulder and London: Westview, pp. 31–64.

Pocock, J.G.A. (1973) 'Languages and Their Implications: The Transformation of the Study of Political Thought', in his *Politics, Language and Time: Essays on Political Thought and History*, New York: Atheneum.

Pogge, Thomas W. (1994) 'An Egalitarian Law of Peoples', *Philosophy and Public Affairs* 23, 3 (Summer), pp. 195–224.

Polanyi, Karl (1957) *The Great Transformation: the political and economical origins of our time*, Beacon Hill: Beacon Press.

Popper, Karl (1970) 'Normal science and its dangers', in Imre Lakatos and Alan Musgrave (eds) *Criticism and the Growth of Knowledge*, Cambridge: Cambridge University Press, pp. 51–8.

Ragin, Charles C. (1987) *The comparative method: moving beyond qualitative and quantitative strategies*, Berkeley: University of California Press.

Reynolds, Charles (1973) *Theory and Explanation in International Politics*, London: Martin Robertson.

Reynolds, Philip A. (1980) *An Introduction to International Relations*, London, New York: Longman.

Rittberger, Volker and Hummel, Hartwig (1990) 'Die Disziplin "Internationale Beziehungen" im deutschsprachigen Raum auf der Suche nach ihrer Identität: Entwicklung und Perspektiven', in Volker Rittberger (ed.) *Theorien der Internationalen Beziehungen. Bestandsaufnahme und Forschungsperspektiven*, Opladen: Westdeutscher Verlag, pp. 17–47.

Rosecrance, Richard (1977 [1963]) *Action and Reaction In World Politics: International Systems in Perspective*, Boston: Little Brown, 2nd edn.

—— (1966), 'Bipolarity , Multipolarity and the Future', *Journal of Conflict Resolution* 10, 3, pp. 314–27.

Rosenberg, Justin (1994) *The Empire of Civil Society: a Critique of the Realist Theory of International Relations*, London, New York: Verso.

Ruggie, John Gerard (1993) 'Territoriality and beyond: problematizing modernity in International Relations', *International Organization* 47, 1 (Winter), pp. 139–74.

—— (1986 [1983]) 'Continuity and Transformation in the World Polity: Toward a Neorealist Synthesis', In Robert O. Keohane (ed.) *Neorealism and its Critics*, New York: Columbia University Press, pp. 131–57.

—— (1982) 'International Regimes, Transactions, and Change: Embedded Liberalism in the Postwar Economic Order', *International Organization* 36, 2 (Spring), pp. 379–415.

Runyan, Anne Sisson and V. Spike Peterson (1991) 'The radical future of realism: feminist subversions of International Relations theory', *Alternatives* 16 (Winter), pp. 67–106.

Russett, Bruce (1985) 'The mysterious case of vanishing hegemony: or is Mark Twain really dead?', *International Organization* 39, 2 (Spring), pp. 207–31.

Schmelling, Erik (1995) *The securitization of citizenship issues: a case study of Estonia and Latvia*, Budapest: The Central European University, MA Thesis.

Senghaas, Dieter (1988) *Konfliktformationen im internationalen System*, Frankfurt am Main: Suhrkamp.

—— (1982) 'Autozentrierte Entwicklung', in Dieter Nohlen and Franz Nuscheler (eds) *Handbuch der Dritten Welt 1. Unterentwicklung und Entwicklung: Theorien – Strategien – Indikatoren*, 2nd rev. edn, Hamburg: Hoffmann und Campe, pp. 359–79.

Singer, J. David (1961) 'The Level-of-Analysis Problem in International Relations', in Klaus Knorr and Sidney Verba (eds) *The International System: Theoretical Essays*, Princeton: Princeton University Press, pp. 77–92.

Skocpol, Theda (1979) *States and Social Revolutions: A comparative analysis of France, Russia and China*, Cambridge, Mass.: Cambridge University Press.

—— (1977) 'Wallerstein's World Capitalist System: A Theoretical and Historical Critique', *American Journal of Sociology* 82, pp. 1075–90.

Smith, Michael Joseph (1986) *Realist Thought from Weber to Kissinger*, Baton Rouge: Lousiana State University Press.

Smith, Steve (1995) 'The self-images of a discipline: a genealogy of International Relations Theory', in Ken Booth and Steve Smith (eds) *International Relations Theory Today*, Oxford: Polity Press, pp. 1–37.

—— (1987) 'The Development of International Relations as a Social Science', *Millennium: Journal of International Studies* 16, Summer, pp. 189–206.

—— (1980) 'Allison and the Cuban Missile Crisis: A Review of the Bureaucratic Politics Model of Foreign Policy Decision-Making', *Millennium: Journal of International Studies* 9, 1 (Spring), pp. 21–40.

Smouts, Marie-Claude (1993) 'Some thoughts on international organizations and theories of regulation', *International Social Science Journal* XLV, November, pp. 443–51.

Snidal, Duncan (1985) 'The Limits of Hegemonic Stability Theory', *International Organization* 39, 4 (Autumn), pp. 579–614.

Spanier, John (1980) *American Foreign Policy since World War II*, New York: Holt, Rinehart and Winston.

Sparti, Davide (1992) *Se un leone potesse parlare. Indagini sul comprendere e lo spiegare*, Firenze: Sansoni.

Spegele, Roger D. (1996) *Political Realism in International Theory*, Cambridge: Cambridge University Press.

Staniland, Martin (1985) *What is Political Economy?*, New Haven and London: Yale University Press.

Steinbruner jr, John D. (1974) *The Cybernetic Theory of Decision*, Princeton: Princeton University Press.

Stopford, John and Strange, Susan with John S. Henley (1991) *Rival States, Rival Firms: Competition for World Market Shares*, Cambridge: Cambridge University Press.

Strange, Susan (1990a) 'The Name of the Game', in N. Rizopoulos (ed.) *Sea-Changes: American Foreign Policy in a World Transformed*, New York: Council on Foreign Relations Press, pp. 238–74.

—— (1990b) 'Finance, Information, and Power', *Review of International Studies* 16, 3 (July), pp. 259–74.

—— (1989) 'Toward a Theory of Transnational Empire', in Ernst-Otto Czempiel and James Rosenau (eds) *Global Changes and Theoretical Challenges: Approaches to World Politics for the 1990s*, Lexington, MA: D.C. Heath and Co., pp. 161–77.

—— (1988a) *States and Markets: An Introduction to International Political Economy*, New York: Basil Blackwell.

—— (1988b) 'The Future of the American Empire', *Journal of International Affairs* 42, 1, pp. 1–19.

—— (1987) 'The Persistent Myth of Lost Hegemony', *International Organization* 41, 4 (Autumn), pp. 551–74.

—— (1986a) 'Supranationals and the State', in John Hall (ed.) *States in History*, Oxford: Oxford University Press, pp. 289–306.

—— (1986b) *Casino Capitalism*, London: Basil Blackwell.

—— (1985) 'Interpretations of a decade', in Loukas Tsoukalis (ed.) *The policial economy of international money: in search of a new order*, London: Sage, pp. 1–44.

—— (1984) 'What about International Relations?', in Susan Strange (ed.) *Paths to International Political Economy*, London: Frances Pinter, pp. 183–98.

—— (1982a) 'Cave! Hic Dragones: A Critique of Regime Analysis', *International Organization* 36, 2 (Spring), pp. 479–96.

—— (1982b) 'The Politics of Economics: A Sectoral Analysis', in Wilfried H. Hanrieder (ed.) *Economic Issues in the Atlantic Community*, New York: Praeger Publishers, pp. 15–26.

—— (1976) 'International Monetary Relations', in Andrew Shonfield (ed.) *International Economic Relations in the Western World, 1959–1971*, vol. 2, Oxford: Oxford University Press.

—— (1971) *Sterling and British Policy*, London: Oxford University Press.

—— (1970) 'International Economics and International Relations: A Case of Mutual Neglect', *International Affairs* 46, pp. 304–15.

Suganami, Hidemi (1996) *On the causes of war*, Oxford: Clarendon Press.

Tickner J. Ann (1992) *Gender in International Relations: Feminist Perspectives on Achieving Global Security*, New York: Columbia University Press.

Tooze, Roger (1988) 'The Unwritten Preface: "International Political Economy" and Epistemology', *Millennium: Journal of International Studies*, vol. 17, pp. 285–93.

Tucker, Robert W. and David C. Hendrickson (1992) *The Imperial Temptation: The New World Order and America's Purpose*, New York: Council of Foreign Relations Press.

Ulam, Adam B. (1968) *Expansion and Coexistence: The History of Soviet Foreign Policy, 1917–1967*, New York: Praeger.

van der Pijl, Kees (1984) *The Making of an Atlantic Ruling Class*, London: Verso.

van Kersbergen, Kees (1995) *Social Capitalism: A study of Christian Democracy and the Welfare State*, London, New York: Routledge.

Vasquez, John (1987) 'The steps to war: toward a scientific explanation of correlates of war findings', *World Politics* 40 (October), pp. 108–45.
—— (1983) *The Power of Power Politics: A Critique*, London: Frances Pinter.
Verbeek, Bertjan (1992) *Anglo-American Relations 1945–56: A comparison of neo-realist and cognitive approaches to the study of international relations*, Firenze: European University Institute, PhD thesis.
Vincent, John (1986) *Human Rights and International Relations*, Cambridge: Cambridge University Press.
—— (1981) 'The Hobbesian Tradition in Twentieth-Century International Thought', *Millennium: Journal of International Studies* 10, 2 (Summer), pp. 91–101.
—— (1974) *Nonintervention and international order*, Princeton: Princeton University Press.
Wæver, Ole (1996) 'The rise and fall of the Inter-Paradigm Debate', in Steve Smith, Ken Booth, and Marysia Zalewski (eds) *International theory: positivism and beyond*, Cambridge: Cambridge University Press, pp. 149–85.
—— (1995) 'Securitization and desecuritization', in Ronnie Lipschutz (ed.) *On Security*, Columbia: Columbia University Press, pp. 46–86.
—— (1993) 'Societal security: the concept', in Ole Wæver, Barry Buzan, Morten Kelstrup and Pierre Lemaitre, *Identity, Migration and the New Security Agenda in Europe*, London: Pinter, pp. 17–40.
—— (1992) 'International society – theoretical promises unfulfilled?', *Cooperation and Conflict* 27, 1, pp. 97–128.
—— (1990) 'Three Competing Europes: German, French, Russian', *International Affairs* (London) 66, 3 (July), pp. 477–94.
—— (1989) 'Beyond the "Beyond" of Critical International Theory', Working Paper 1/1989, Copenhagen: Centre for Peace and Conflict Research.
Wæver, Ole, Barry Buzan, Morten Kelstrup and Pierre Lemaitre (1993) *Identity, Migration and the New Security Agenda in Europe*, London: Pinter.
Wallerstein, Immanuel (1984) *The Politics of the World-Economy: The States, the Movements and the Civilizations*, Cambridge: Cambridge University Press and Paris: Editions de la Maison des Sciences de l'Homme.
—— (1979 [1974]) 'The Rise and Future Demise of the World-Capitalist System: Concepts for Comparative Analysis', in his *The Capitalist World Economy*, Cambridge: Cambridge University Press and Paris: Editions de la Maison des Sciences de l'Homme, pp. 387–415.
Walker, R.B.J. (1993a) *Inside/Outside: International Relations as Political Theory*, Cambridge: Cambridge University Press.
—— (1993b) 'Violence, modernity, silence: from Max Weber to international relations', in David Campbell and Michael Dillon (eds) *The Political Subject of Violence*, Manchester: Manchester University Press, pp. 137–60.
—— (1991) 'State Sovereignty and the Articulation of Political Space/Time', *Millennium: Journal of International Studies* 20, 3, pp. 445–61.
—— (1990) 'Security, Sovereignty, and the Challenge of World Politics', *Alternatives* XV, 1, pp. 3–27.
—— (1989) 'History and Structure in the Theory of International Relations', *Millennium: Journal of International Studies* 18, 2 (Summer), pp. 163–183.
—— (1988–1989) 'Ethics, Modernity and the Theory of International Relations', Princeton: Center of International Studies, Princeton University, unpubl. manuscript.
—— (1987) 'Realism, Change, and International Political Theory', *International Studies Quarterly* 31, 1 (March), pp. 65–86.
—— (1980) *Political Theory and the Transformation of World Politics*, Princeton University, World Order Studies Program, Occasional Papers No. 8.

Walt, Stephen M. (1991) 'The renaissance of security studies', *International Studies Quarterly* 35, 2 (June), pp. 211–39.

—— (1987) *The Origins of Alliances*, Ithaca: Cornell University Press.

Walter, Andrew (1993) *World Power and World Money: The Role of Hegemony and International Monetary Order*, rev. edn, New York: Harvester Wheatsheaf.

Waltz, Kenneth (1993) 'The Emerging Structure of International Politics', *International Security* 18, 2, pp. 44–79.

—— (1986) 'Response to my critics', in Robert O. Keohane (ed.) *Neorealism and its Critics*, New York: Columbia University Press, pp. 322–45.

—— (1979) *Theory of International Politics*, Reading: Addison-Wesley.

—— (1970) 'The Myth of National Interdependence', in Charles Kindleberger (ed.) *The International Corporation*, Cambridge, MA.: MIT Press, pp. 205–23.

—— (1969 [1967]) 'International Structure, National Force and the Balance of World Power', reprinted in James A. Rosenau (ed.), *International Politics and Foreign Policy: A Reader in Research and Theory*, New York: Free Press, pp. 304–14.

—— (1964) 'The Stability of a Bipolar World', *Dædalus* 43, 3, pp. 881–901.

—— (1959) *Man, the State, and War*, New York: Columbia University Press.

Warren, Bill (1980) *Imperialism: Pioneer of Capitalism*, London: New Left Books.

Wassmund, Hans (1982) *Grundzüge der Weltpolitik. Daten und Tendenzen von 1945 bis zur Gegenwart*, München: Beck.

Webb, Michael and Stephen D. Krasner (1989) 'Hegemonic Stability Theory: An empirical assessment', in *Review of International Studies* 15, 2 (April), pp. 56–76.

Weber, Max (1977 [1917]) *Politik als Beruf*, Berlin: Duncker & Humblot.

—— (1988 [1921]) 'Wissenschaft als Beruf', in *Gesammelte Aufsätze zur Wissenschaftslehre*, Tübingen: J.C.B. Mohr (Paul Siebeck), pp. 582–613.

Wendt, Alexander (1992) 'Anarchy is what states make of it: the social construction of power politics', *International Organization* 46, 2 (Spring), pp. 391–425.

—— (1992b) 'Levels of Analysis v. Agents and Structures: Part III', *Review of International Studies* 18, 2 (April), pp. 181–5.

—— (1991) 'Bridging the theory/meta-theory gap in international relations', *Review of International Studies* 17, 4 (October), pp. 389–92.

—— (1987) 'The agent-structure problem in international relations', *International Organization* 41, 3 (Summer), pp. 337–70.

Wendt, Alexander and Raymond Duvall (1989) 'Institutions and International Order', in Ernst-Otto Czempiel and James Rosenau (eds) *Global Changes and Theoretical Challenges. Approaches to World Politics for the 1990s*, Lexington, MA.: Lexington Books, pp. 51–74.

Wight, Martin (1991) *International theory: the three traditions*, Leicester: Leicester University Press.

—— (1966) 'Why is there no international theory?' in Herbert Butterfield and Martin Wight (eds) *Diplomatic Investigations: essays in the theory of International Relations*, Cambridge, UK: Cambridge University Press.

—— (1979 [1946]) *Power Politics*, edited by Hedley Bull and Carsten Holbraadt, Harmondsworth: Penguin.

Williams, Phil (1976) *Crisis Management*, London, Martin Robertson and New York: Halsted Press.

Williamson, Oliver E. (1985) *Economic Organization: Firms, Markets, and Policy Control*, Brighton: Wheatsheaf.

Wohlforth, William C. (1994/1995) 'Realism and the End of the Cold War', *International Security* 19, 3 (Winter), pp. 91–129.

Wolfers, Arnold (1962) *Discord and Collaboration. Essays on International Politics*, Baltimore and London: The Johns Hopkins University Press.

Wright, Georg Henrik von (1971) *Explanation and Understanding*, Ithaca: Cornell University Press.
Wright, C. Ben (1976) 'Mr X and Containment', *Slavic Review* 35, pp. 1–32.
Yergin, Daniel (1978) *Shattered Peace: The Origins of the Cold War and the National Security State*, Boston: Houghton Mifflin.

Index

agent-structure debate 196–7
alliance politics 104
  anarchy: in hegemonic stability
  theory 160; in Morgenthau 27; its
  qualification 40–4, 96; its redundancy
  224–6; and market analogy 225; in
  Waltz's definition of structure 127
Aron, R. 41, 46–8, 64n2, 77, 78, 113,
  132n1, 134

balance-of-power (concept/theory): and
  correlation of forces 88; definitions
  and meanings 45–6; as homeostatic
  or market equilibrium 37, 128;
  multidimensionality 100; Waltz's
  theory 127, 134
behaviouralism 36–7, 109, 133n2
Bretton Woods 147–153 , 178
Bull, H. 42–4, 214, 215
bureaucratic politics 76

Carr, E.H. 19–24, 30–1, 145, 158, 177,
  223
Clausewitz: the Clausewitz-Lenin
  debate 174; formula 64; formula
  reversed 19
complex interdependence 113
constructivism: epistemological 117,
  205 ; constructivist research 223,
  231–2
containment: its application 57–61; the
  conception by Kennan 54–7; and
  détente 100; and peaceful coexistence
  89–90
correlation of forces 87–9; compared
  with balance of power 88
crisis management 65
Cuban missile crisis 64–76

cybernetics 37, 70
Cyprus crisis (1974) 104

decision-making: Allison's models
  66–74; and cognitive processes 74
dependency theories: and hegemonic
  stability theory 158–9; intellectual
  roots 162–4; schools 164–6
détente policy 95, 98–107
diplomacy: concert 17, 96–7, changed
  nature of 182–3, 215–17; secret 17
discipline of International Relations:
  academic community 121–2;
  boundaries 27, 121, 157, 177, 180,
  225–6; collective memory of xii, 212,
  227; identity crisis 7–11, 32, 80,
  108–9; self-understanding xi, 7, 120,
  188
domestic analogy 11, 24, 139, 141,
  154–5

empiricism: definition of 33; and fact/
  value distinction 120–1,
English School of International
  Relations 42, 48, 134, 153–4, 200
epistemology: Weberian 65, 78, 133n1

falsificationism 33–4, 128, 130 (*see also*
  epistemology, methodology)
feminism: and the public-private divide
  139
first debate of International Relations
  16, 31, 109, 179, 186

Gilpin, R. 118, 144–5, 168–76

hegemonic stability theory: definition
  142–4; decline thesis 144, 150–3;